CW01667916

This book belongs to

Age

Favourite Goalkeeper

Favourite Defender

Favourite Midfielder

Favourite Striker

Favourite Match

Written by twocan
Contributors: Rob Mason & Ben Price

A TWOCAN PUBLICATION

©2015. Published by twocan under licence from Brighton & Hove Albion FC.

Every effort has been made to ensure the accuracy of information within this publication but the publishers cannot be held responsible for any errors or omissions. Views expressed are those of the author and do not necessarily represent those of the publishers or the football club.

All rights reserved.

ISBN 978-1-909872-45-5

PICTURE CREDITS
Brighton and Hove Albion Football Club, Action Images and Press Association

£8

AMERICAN EXPRE
COMMUNITY STADIUN
Heineken
Heineken
Heineken
HARVEYS
Brewers
L&S PRINTING
mexmast

CHANDLERS
www.chandlers-bmw.co.uk
Reflex
Tomorrow's nutrition today

CONTENTS

TRAIN TO WIN

Footballers are getting fitter and fitter. In football each generation of players are faster, fitter and stronger than before.

Clubs have more and more support staff, to provide everything a player will need to help them become the supreme athlete. These days, teams have fitness & conditioning coaches and nutritionists, who make sure every player is in the best physical shape they can be.

In pre-season, clubs carry out all kinds of tests on their players to monitor their progress and ensure each individual reaches and maintains peak fitness. A lot of work is done in the gym with weights, designed to make sure players have the strength not to be easily knocked off the ball and that they also possess the stamina to get through 90 minutes and not fade in the game's latter stages.

Of course, while fitness is essential, ultimately it is their ability that matters. Footballers like to train with the ball and work hard on their skills. A lot of drills are undertaken to develop and maintain each player's ability on the ball. Coaching staff also work on team play, formations and developing understandings on the pitch.

A large proportion of goals come from set-pieces, so teams work on not just taking them, but defending free-kicks, corners and throw ins. Every team has a specialist dead-ball expert who they rely on for these important moments in games. Some teams prefer man-for-man marking and some use the zonal approach. In man-for-man marking, every player has a responsibility to mark a particular opponent, while zonal marking means every player has an area of the pitch that they have to defend.

Whichever system is used, it is important that players work hard in training so that they are a fully fit and well organised unit, and can perform together, successfully as a team.

SQUAD 2015/16

NIKI MAENPAA 01

Position: Goalkeeper **Nationality:** Finnish **DOB:** 23.01.85
Height: 6'3" (190cm) **Weight:** 13st 5lbs (85kg)

Maenpaa signed with Brighton this summer following his release from Dutch side, VVV-Venlo. He is the current first-choice Finnish national goalkeeper and has won 24 full caps for his country.

BRUNO SALTOR 02

Position: Defender **Nationality:** Spanish **DOB:** 01.10.80
Height: 5'10" (179cm) **Weight:** 11st 11lbs (75kg)

Since joining the Seagulls from Valencia in 2012, Bruno has been a regular in the first team. He brings experience to the field, and all being well, should pass the 100-game mark by the end of the 2015/16 season!

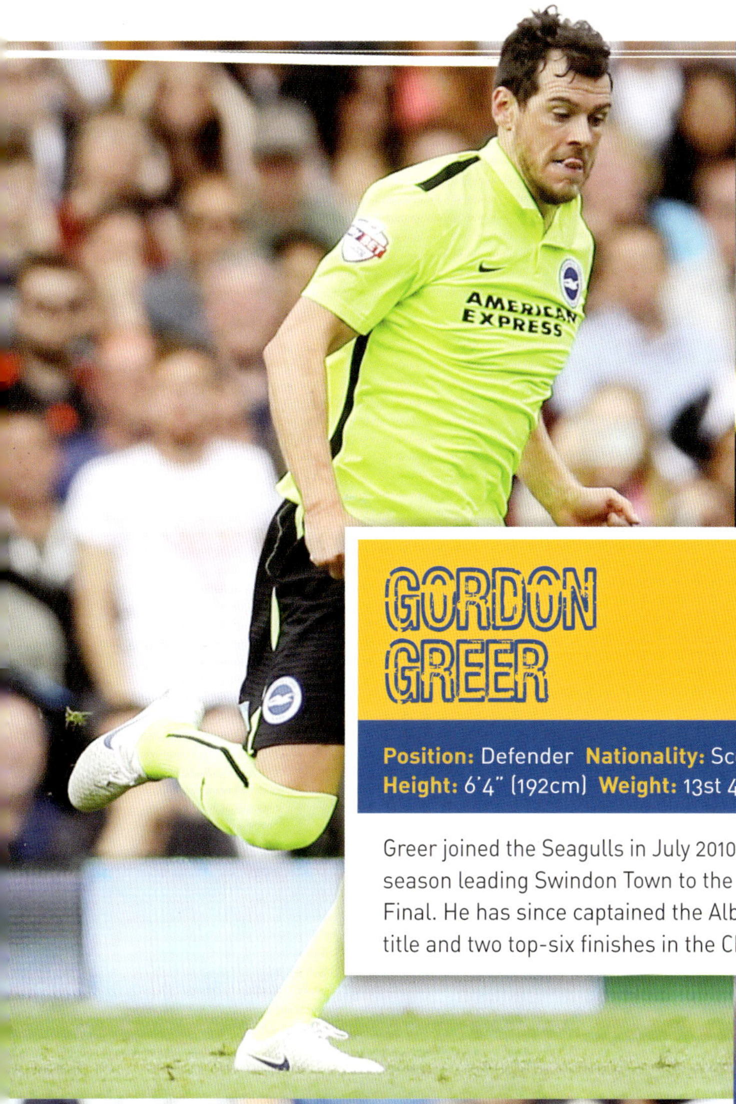

GORDON GREER 03

Position: Defender **Nationality:** Scottish **DOB:** 14.12.80
Height: 6'4" (192cm) **Weight:** 13st 4lbs (84.5kg)

Greer joined the Seagulls in July 2010 following a successful season leading Swindon Town to the League One Play-Off Final. He has since captained the Albion to the League One title and two top-six finishes in the Championship.

LEWIS DUNK 05

Position: Defender **Nationality:** English **DOB:** 21.11.91
Height: 6'4" (192cm) **Weight:** 13st 11lbs (87.6kg)

Dunk is a graduate of Albion's centre of excellence. He re-established himself as first-choice centre back last season, finished the season as top scorer and was runner-up to Calderon for Player of the Season!

UWE HUENEMEIER 04

Position: Defender **Nationality:** German **DOB:** 09.01.86
Height: 6'1" (185cm) **Weight:** 12st 6lbs (79kg)

Huenemeier signed for the Seagulls from SC Paderborn this summer. He rose through the ranks at Borussia Dortmund's youth academy and made his first-team debut for the German giants against Bayern Munich in December 2005.

DALE STEPHENS 06

Position: Midfielder **Nationality:** English **DOB:** 12.12.89
Height: 6'1" (185cm) **Weight:** 11st 3lbs (71kg)

Stephens returned from long-term injury in February 2015 and re-established himself in the first team, making 16 appearances and scoring two goals during the 2014/15 run in, helping the side secure Championship safety.

BERAM KAYAL 07

Position: Midfielder **Nationality:** Israeli **DOB:** 02.05.88
Height: 5'10" (178cm) **Weight:** 11st 9lbs (74kg)

Kayal made his debut for Albion in the 3-2 defeat to Nottingham Forest in February 2015, coming off the bench to score Albion's second. He became a fans' favourite and has become a regular starter.

ANDREW CROFTS 08

Position: Midfielder **Nationality:** Welsh **DOB:** 29.05.84
Height: 5'9" (175.2cm) **Weight:** 11st 7lbs (73kg)

A combative midfielder and Welsh international, Crofts has been unlucky with injuries over recent seasons. He suffered another ACL injury in October 2014 but returned to full training this summer.

SAM BALDOCK 09

Position: Striker **Nationality:** English **DOB:** 15.03.89
Height: 5'7" (170cm) **Weight:** 10st 8lbs (67kg)

Baldock arrived at Brighton in August 2014 from Bristol City. He found the net four times during his first season with the Seagulls, including a fine finish against Ipswich, before a knee injury ended his season early.

TOMER HEMED 10

Position: Striker **Nationality:** Israeli **DOB:** 02.05.87
Height: 6'0" (183cm) **Weight:** 12st 4lbs (78kg)

Israeli-born Hemed has enjoyed a decade-long playing career to date, playing football in his native Israel and in Spain. The 6ft tall frontman has also enjoyed success on the international stage.

CHRIS O'GRADY 11

Position: Striker **Nationality:** English **DOB:** 25.01.86
Height: 6'3" (190.5cm) **Weight:** 12st 4lbs (78kg)

O'Grady signed for the Seagulls in July 2014 and scored his first goal in January 2015 in an FA Cup win against Brentford. On 1 September, he joined Nottingham Forest on loan for the remainder of the season.

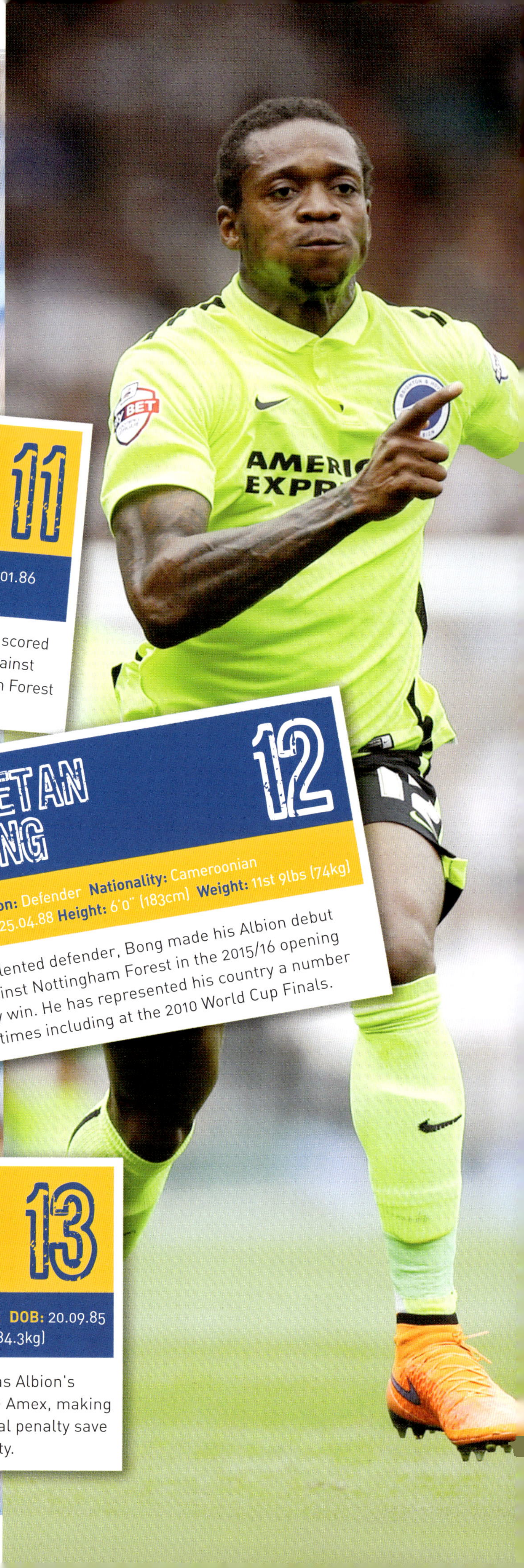

GAETAN BONG 12

Position: Defender **Nationality:** Cameroonian **Weight:** 11st 9lbs (74kg)
DOB: 25.04.88 **Height:** 6'0" (183cm)

A talented defender, Bong made his Albion debut against Nottingham Forest in the 2015/16 opening day win. He has represented his country a number of times including at the 2010 World Cup Finals.

DAVID STOCKDALE 13

Position: Goalkeeper **Nationality:** English **DOB:** 20.09.85
Height: 6'3" (190.5cm) **Weight:** 13st 4lbs (84.3kg)

Stockdale quickly established himself as Albion's number one last season, his first at the Amex, making numerous vital stops, including a crucial penalty save during the 4-3 win over Birmingham City.

INIGO CALDERON 14

Position: Defender **Nationality:** Spanish **DOB:** 04.01.82
Height: 5'11" (180cm) **Weight:** 13st 0lbs (82.5kg)

Calderon has enjoyed success with the Seagulls, making over 200 appearances for the club. In 2014/15, fans voted him Player of the Season and his display's earned him a one-year contract extension.

JAMIE MURPHY 15

Position: Striker **Nationality:** Scottish **DOB:** 28.08.89
Height: 5'9" (175cm) **Weight:** 10st 1lbs (64kg)

Murphy joined Brighton from Sheffield Utd this summer, who he helped to the League One Play-Offs last season. He has represented Scotland at U21 level and has over 60 career goals and over 200 appearances to his name.

CASPER ANKERGREN 16

Position: Goalkeeper **Nationality:** Danish **DOB:** 09.11.79
Height: 6'3" (190cm) **Weight:** 15st 2lbs (96kg)

Ankergren has played over 70 games for the Seagulls in his four years with the club and he signed a contract extension in the summer of 2015. He has also started work on gaining his coaching badges.

CONNOR GOLDSON 17

Position: Defender **Nationality:** English **DOB:** 18.12.92
Height: 6'3" (191cm) **Weight:** 13st 5lbs (85kg)

Goldson signed for Brighton from Shrewsbury Town this summer. He was named in the PFA League Two Team of the Year and also scooped Shrewsbury's Players' Player award and Player of the Year for the 2014/15 campaign.

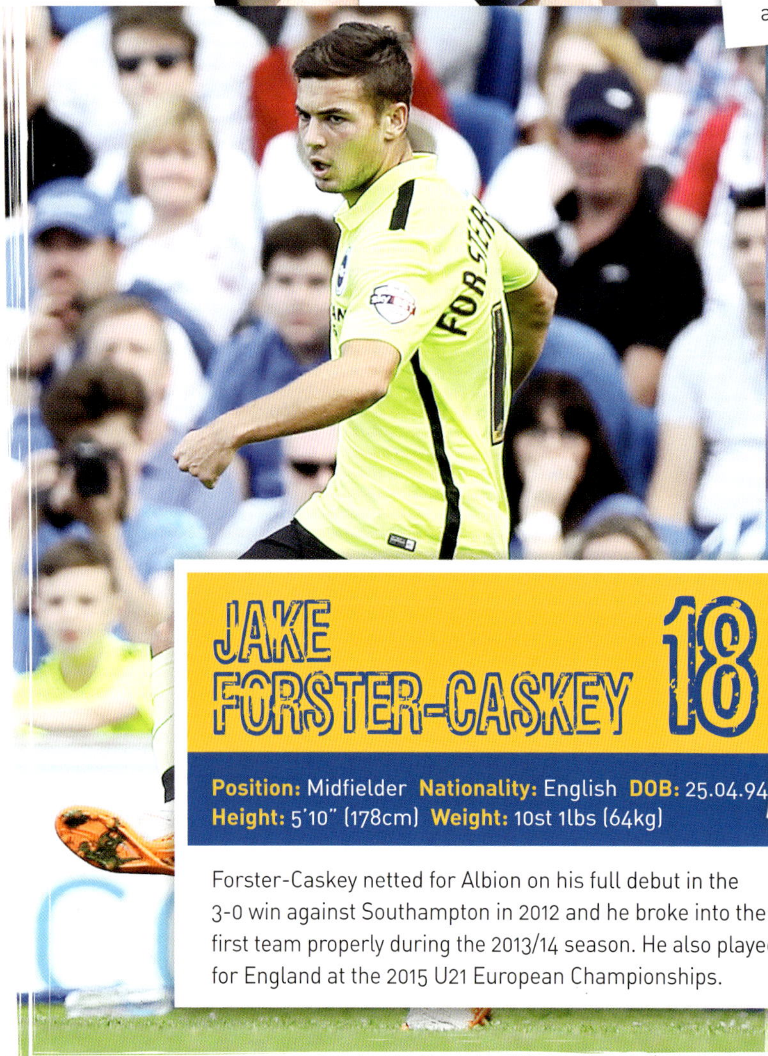

JAKE FORSTER-CASKEY 18

Position: Midfielder **Nationality:** English **DOB:** 25.04.94
Height: 5'10" (178cm) **Weight:** 10st 1lbs (64kg)

Forster-Caskey netted for Albion on his full debut in the 3-0 win against Southampton in 2012 and he broke into the first team properly during the 2013/14 season. He also played for England at the 2015 U21 European Championships.

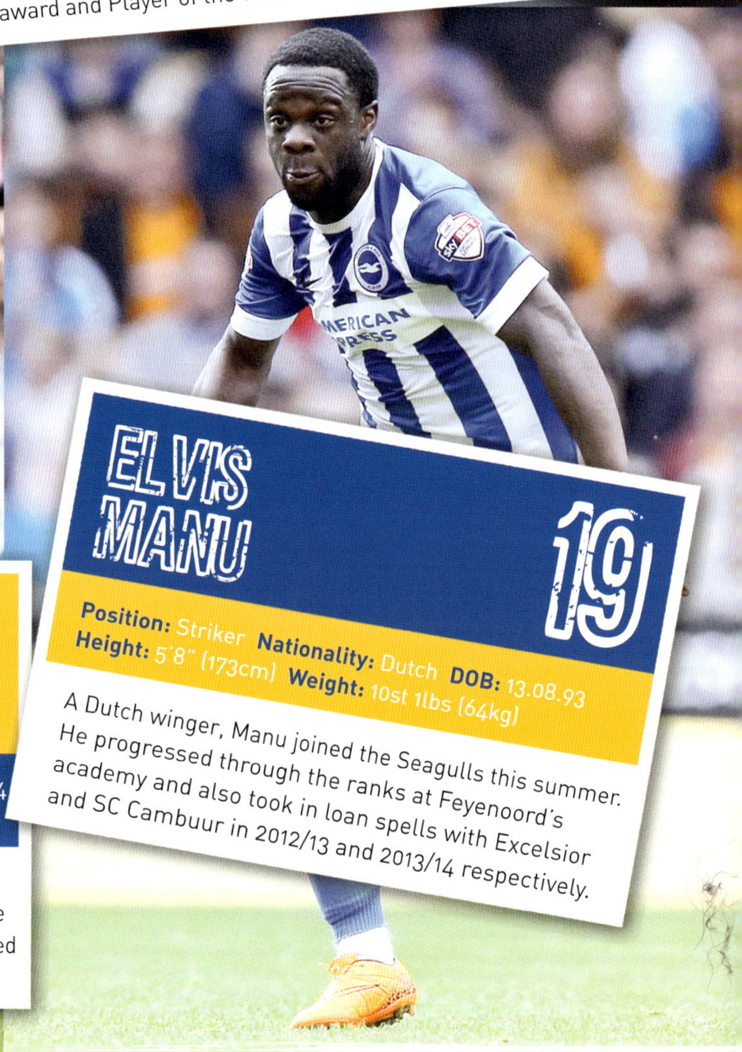

ELVIS MANU 19

Position: Striker **Nationality:** Dutch **DOB:** 13.08.93
Height: 5'8" (173cm) **Weight:** 10st 1lbs (64kg)

A Dutch winger, Manu joined the Seagulls this summer. He progressed through the ranks at Feyenoord's academy and also took in loan spells with Excelsior and SC Cambuur in 2012/13 and 2013/14 respectively.

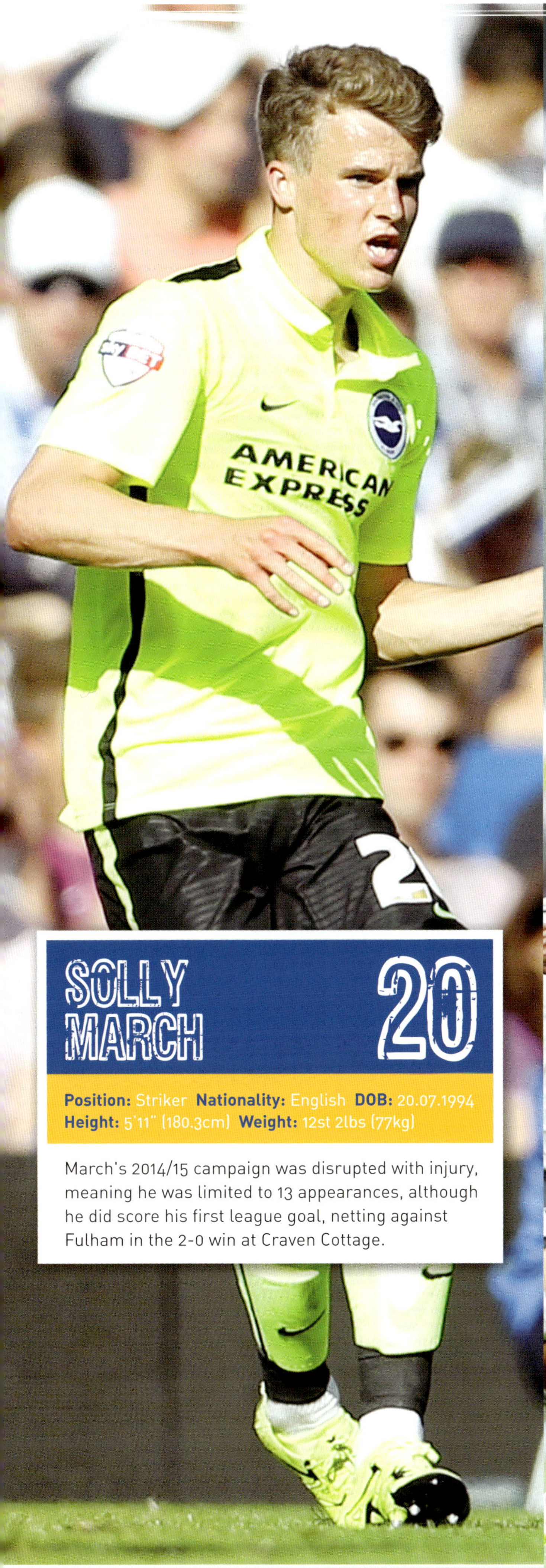

SOLLY MARCH 20

Position: Striker **Nationality:** English **DOB:** 20.07.1994
Height: 5'11" (180.3cm) **Weight:** 12st 2lbs (77kg)

March's 2014/15 campaign was disrupted with injury, meaning he was limited to 13 appearances, although he did score his first league goal, netting against Fulham in the 2-0 win at Craven Cottage.

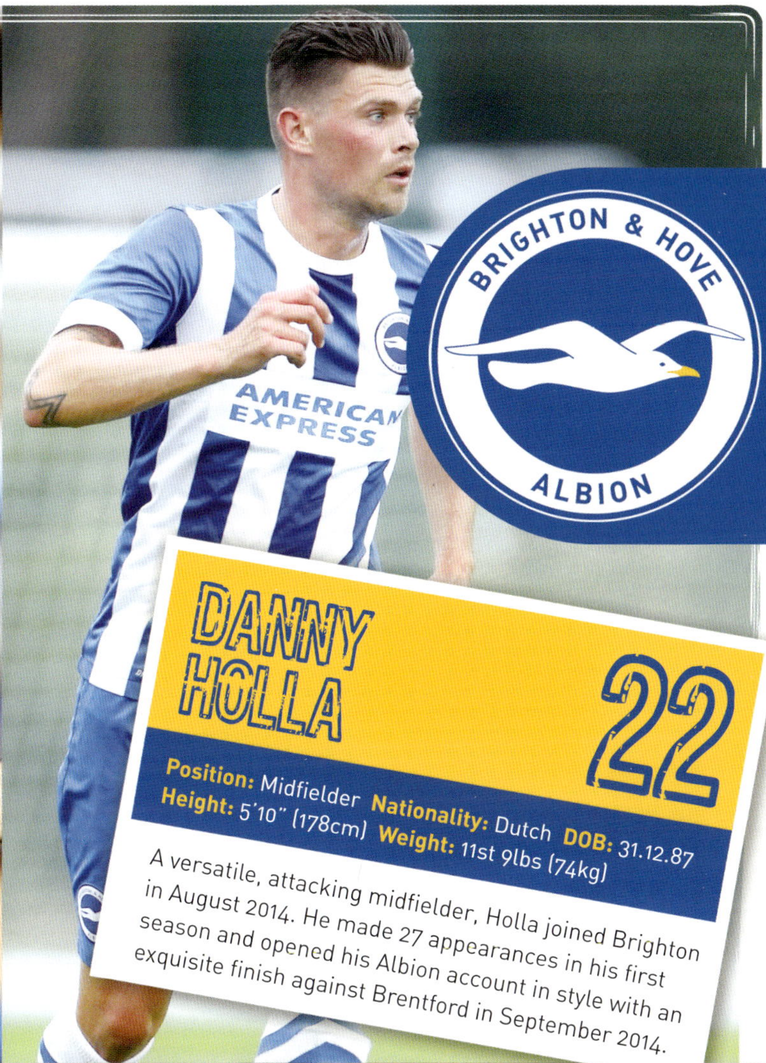

DANNY HOLLA 22

Position: Midfielder **Nationality:** Dutch **DOB:** 31.12.87
Height: 5'10" (178cm) **Weight:** 11st 9lbs (74kg)

A versatile, attacking midfielder, Holla joined Brighton in August 2014. He made 27 appearances in his first season and opened his Albion account in style with an exquisite finish against Brentford in September 2014.

LIAM ROSENIOR 23

Position: Defender **Nationality:** English **DOB:** 09.07.84
Height: 5'10" (178cm) **Weight:** 12st 0lbs (76kg)

Rosenior signed for Brighton in June 2015 following his release from Hull City. He has won international honours; playing for England at U20 and U21 level, playing in the 2007 European U21 Championships.

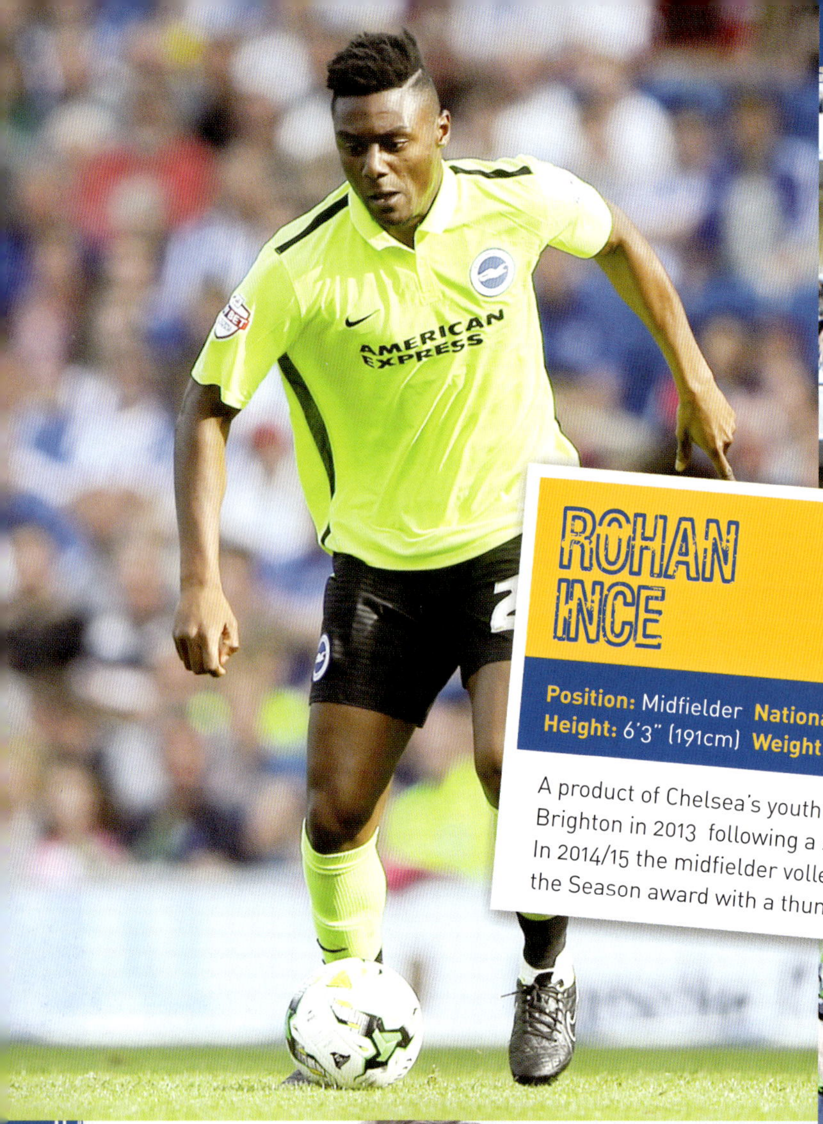

ROHAN INCE 24

Position: Midfielder **Nationality:** English **DOB:** 08.11.92
Height: 6'3" (191cm) **Weight:** 12st 8lbs (80kg)

A product of Chelsea's youth ranks, Ince signed with Brighton in 2013 following a successful trial period. In 2014/15 the midfielder volleyed his way to the Goal of the Season award with a thunderous finish at Swindon.

BOBBY ZAMORA 25

Position: Striker **Nationality:** English **DOB:** 16.01.81
Height: 6'0" (182.8cm) **Weight:** 11st 8lbs (73.4kg)

Zamora signed for Brighton for a third time in August 2015 - following a goal-laden three-year spell between August 2000 and July 2003. After he re-signed, LuaLua gave him his legendary number 25 shirt back!

GLEN REA 26

Position: Defender **Nationality:** English **DOB:** 03.09.94
Height: 6'1" (184cm) **Weight:** 11st 5lbs (73kg)

Rea has risen through the ranks at Albion and has established himself as a regular in the U21 squad and made the step up to the first-team in pre-season 2014. He is on loan at Southend United until January 2016.

PEREZ ADRIAN COLUNGA 27

Position: Striker **Nationality:** Spanish **DOB:** 17.11.84
Height: 5'8" (172cm) **Weight:** 11st 0lbs (70kg)

Colunga joined Albion from Getafe in August 2014. In his first season at the Amex he hit four goals, including a penalty against Fulham in Albion's 2-0 win, before joining La Liga's Granada on loan until the end of the season.

ADAM CHICKSEN 28

Position: Defender **Nationality:** English **DOB:** 27.09.91
Height: 5'8" (173cm) **Weight:** 11st 9lbs (74kg)

A versatile full-back, who can play either side of the defence and in midfield, Chicksen signed for Albion in July 2013. He spent time out on loan with Gillingham and Fleetwood during the 2014/15 season.

KAZENGA LUALUA 30

Position: Midfielder **Nationality:** Congolese **DOB:** 10.12.90
Height: 5'11" (180.3cm) **Weight:** 12st 0lbs (76.2kg)

An exciting winger with bags of pace, LuaLua enjoyed two loan spells with the Seagulls before signing permanently from Newcastle United in 2011. He is known for his trademark backflip celebration.

BRIGHTON & HOVE ALBION WOMEN'S FOOTBALL CLUB

The 2014/15 season was a thrilling one for the Albion which saw cup glory with the women securing a 2-0 victory over Chichester City in the final of the Sussex Women's Challenge Cup thanks to goals from Jay Blackie and Amy Taylor.

A memorable league campaign saw lots of exciting action on the pitch, and some brilliant victories, including a 3-0 win over West Ham, doing the double 3-2 and 5-2 home and away against Tottenham Hotspur and 5 goal demolitions over the likes of Plymouth Argyle, Charlton Athletic and Cardiff City. Despite these wins, the Albion narrowly finished as runners up in the FA Women's Premier League behind a strong Portsmouth FC Ladies team by an agonising 3 points.

The 2015/16 season sees the Albion women up for the challenge of going again and securing the league title in what promises to be another exciting season!

Brighton & Hove Albion Women's Football Club are founder members of the Football Association (FA) Women's Premier League and remain the highest-placed league team in Sussex.

Matches are usually played at the Culver Road ground in Lancing on Sundays with a 2pm kick-off time. Entry on the turnstile is priced at £3 for adults and is free for under-16s and Albion season-ticket holders.

Check out www.seagulls.co.uk for a full fixture list and come along and show your support to the Women soon, in their quest for Premier League glory!

CAN YOU MATCH EACH OF THESE MANAGERS TO THE YEARS THEY MANAGED BHAFC?

THE BIG MATCH

GUS POYET · RUSSELL SLADE · DEAN WILKINS
PETER J TAYLOR · BILLY LANE · MIKE BAILEY
STEVE COPPELL · STEVE GRITT · ALAN MULLERY
BRIAN HORTON

1976-1981 · 1951-1961 · 1998-1999 · 2009
1996-1998 · 2002-2003 · 1981-1982
2001-2002 · 2009-2013 · 2006-2008

1. MANAGER: YEARS:

2. MANAGER: YEARS:

3. MANAGER: YEARS:

4. MANAGER: YEARS:

5. MANAGER: YEARS:

6. MANAGER: YEARS:

7. MANAGER: YEARS:

8. MANAGER: YEARS:

9. MANAGER: YEARS:

10. MANAGER: YEARS:

ANSWERS ON PAGE 62

BRIGHTON & HOVE
ALBION
9
SAM
BALDOCK

LIAM ROSENIOR

First pair of football boots you owned?
I got a pair of HI-Tecs for Christmas when I was six.

Who was the first big influence on your career?
My Dad because he was a footballer as well and it was something that I always wanted to do.

Which club first spotted you?
Bristol Rovers. I went to their centre of excellence and then I went to Bristol City afterwards.

Best advice you've been given?
Enjoy and love what you do because it's the only way you can achieve what you want.

If you could play any sportsperson at their own game, who would it be?
I love basketball, so I would love to go one-on-one with Lebron James. I don't know if it would go well for me, but I would love to do that!

If you could have one superpower what it would be?
To be able to rewind certain things and then go back to do it again the right way.

If you could be best friends with anyone in the world, who would it be?
I don't really want to be best friends with anyone, as long as I can stay best friends with my kids then I'll be happy!

Something interesting we might not know about you?
I love reading about history. My favourite topics are World War II, the Ancient Greeks, Romans and Egyptians.

DALE STEPHENS

First pair of boots you owned? Reeboks

Who was the first big influence on your career?
Probably the Sunday League manager I had just before I signed for Bury, his name is Tommy Toole and he enabled me to have the opportunity to trial at Bury. Then my youth team manager Chris Beech at Bury, who really developed me as a player.

What pro club first spotted you?
Bury.

Best moment of my life? My daughter being born.

Best sportsperson in the world?
I would say Cristiano Ronaldo because he has all the qualities that a footballer needs.

If you could play any sportsperson at their own game, who would it be?
I would have a round with Rory McIlroy. I'm not saying that I'm any good, but it would be good to see him play.

If you could have one superpower what it would be?
I'd like to have Bernard's watch, so basically the ability to stop time!

If you could be best friends with anyone in the world, who would it be?
David Beckham.

Something interesting we might not know about you?
I can plaster or I could. I was definitely getting better at it!

BRUNO

Which club first spotted you?

RCD Espanyol. I joined in the under-18 age group and was there for four or five years and two years later I was a professional.

Best advice you've been given?

I've been given a lot of good advice over the years, especially from my Dad. We could speak more about football and he always told me to be honest and work, which is the same in life overall. It's something which I have followed throughout my career.

Best sportsperson in the world?

Right now I would have to say Lionel Messi. Of course you can have an argument inside football as to whether it's Cristiano or not, but I think football is the hardest sport and Messi is the best sportsperson. He can do amazing things, he can score, he can assist and always sees the next pass.

Best moment of your life?

Football is really important to me and I've had some great moments, but the best moments for me are having my children and meeting my wife.

If you could have one superpower what it would be?

The power to convince people, so I would win every argument. I would able to change a lot of things.

If you could be best friends with anyone in the world, who would it be?

The Pope. I would like to have a chat with him, because he knows a lot about the world and is a good person.

GLEN REA

First pair of boots you owned?

Probably either a pair of World Cups or Puma Kings. My Dad always advised to go for how they feel rather than how they look and they were the most comfortable pairs.

Best advice you've been given?

Just to enjoy every moment you play football no matter how far you get. Work hard. Simon Rusk [under-21 coach] once told me that hard work beats talent, unless talent works hard. That's a great bit of advice.

Best sportsperson in the world?

I would say Roger Federer for everything he's done in the game and he seems to be such a nice guy as well. I think he's the all-round sports person and has been brilliant for the last ten years.

Best moment of your life?

There are a few really. One was signing my first professional contract with Brighton and the other would be signing my most recent deal. The first time I was involved with Ireland as well.

If you could have one superpower what it would be?

I would like to fly because you could go anywhere, but I would want to fly fast rather than just hover. It would be like Will Smith in the film 'Hancock'!

Something interesting we might not know about you?

I'm a Brighton fan who used to have a season ticket at the Withdean and went to a lot of away games. I used to stick all the tickets on my bedroom wall!

BRIGHTON & HOVE
ALBION
GORDON
GREER
3

There are too many balls in these action shots!

Can you figure out which balls are real?

WHAT BALL?

Time to get to grips with the teams the Seagulls will be facing this season!

MEET YOUR RIVALS

Birmingham City

GROUND: St Andrew's **CAPACITY:** 30,016

MANAGER: Gary Rowett **NICKNAME:** Blues

DID YOU KNOW: Founded as Small Heath, they played in the Football Alliance before becoming founder members and first ever champions of the Football League Second Division.

Blackburn Rovers

GROUND: Ewood Park **CAPACITY:** 31,367

MANAGER: Gary Bowyer

NICKNAMES: Rovers, Blue and Whites

DID YOU KNOW: Blackburn Rovers' Latin motto is 'Arte et labore', the Club's translation of which is 'By Skill and Hard Work'.

Bolton Wanderers

GROUND: Macron Stadium **CAPACITY:** 28,723

MANAGER: Neil Lennon

NICKNAMES: The Trotters, The Whites, The White Men, The Men in White

DID YOU KNOW: Bolton have won the FA Cup four times - in 1923, 1926, 1929 and 1958.

Brentford

GROUND: Griffin Park **CAPACITY:** 12,300

HEAD COACH: Marinus Dijkhuizen

NICKNAME: The Bees

DID YOU KNOW: Brentford's most successful spell came during the 1930s, when they achieved consecutive top six finishes in the First Division.

Bristol City

GROUND: Ashton Gate Stadium

CAPACITY: Upgrading to 27,000 (by 2016)

MANAGER: Steve Cotterill **NICKNAME:** The Robins

DID YOU KNOW:
Bristol City won the Welsh Cup - despite being an English club - in 1934.

Burnley

GROUND: Turf Moor **CAPACITY:** 21,401

MANAGER: Sean Dyche **NICKNAME:** The Clarets

DID YOU KNOW:
Burnley's club colours of claret and blue were adopted in 1910 in tribute to the best club in English football at the time, Aston Villa.

Cardiff City

GROUND: Cardiff City Stadium **CAPACITY:** 33,280

MANAGER: Russell Slade

NICKNAME: The Bluebirds

DID YOU KNOW: Cardiff City is the only club from outside England to have won the FA Cup, which they won in 1927.

Charlton Athletic

GROUND: The Valley **CAPACITY:** 27,111

MANAGER: Guy Luzon

NICKNAME: The Addicks

DID YOU KNOW: Charlton were rare among football clubs, they reserved a seat on their directors' board for a supporter! (until 2008, when legal issues stopped them)

Derby County

GROUND: The iPro Stadium **CAPACITY:** 33,500

HEAD COACH: Paul Clement

NICKNAME: The Rams

DID YOU KNOW: Derby County's rival clubs are Nottingham Forest, Leicester City and Leeds United. Two of which they face this season!

Fulham

GROUND: Craven Cottage **CAPACITY:** 25,700

MANAGER: Kit Symons

NICKNAMES: The Cottagers, The Whites

DID YOU KNOW: Fulham has produced many English greats including Johnny Haynes, George Cohen, Bobby Robson, Rodney Marsh & Alan Mullery.

Huddersfield Town

GROUND: John Smith's Stadium

CAPACITY: 24,500 **MANAGER:** Chris Powell

NICKNAME: The Terriers

DID YOU KNOW: In 1926, Huddersfield became the first English team to win three successive league titles - no team has beaten this record!

My Albion Moments

In the summer of 2015, Albion supporters were asked to submit their favourite "Albion moments" from our long and storied club history.

The response was fantastic with 100s of fans' most memorable moments submitted to the club. From Seagulls both young and young at heart, the club received stories of classic goals and unlikely heroes, plus a mixture of the funnier Albion moments along with tales of hardships and the battle for our magnificent new stadium. 23 were selected and for the start of the 2015/16 season were put up, proudly sitting outside of the west stand - in the area affectionately nick-named by supporters "Legends alley".

Anyone can visit "Legends Alley" at the stadium at any time as it is on the outside of the stadium and completely free of charge - and if you visit www.seagulls.co.uk for the latest club museum opening times you could visit both in one day - they are well worth a visit! We have included a selection of "Albion Moments" here to give you a taste!

GAETAN
BONG
12

BRIGHTON & HOVE
ALBION
AMERICAN EXPRESS
SWORD

STAND OUT FROM THE CROWD

There are five British actors hidden in the crowd... can you find them all?

ANSWERS ON PAGE 62

BRIGHTON & HOVE ALBION

How much do you know the Seagull's last year?

Take our test and find out!

01

Who was the Seagulls' top goal scorer last season and how many did he score?

02

Who scored Brighton's final goal of the 2014/15 season?

03

Which former QPR, Fulham, West Ham, Spurs and Albion player re-signed for the Seagulls this summer on a free transfer?

04

Brighton beat FC Meyrin a whopping 6-1 in a pre-season friendly this year. But which country are they from?

05

Striker Tomer Hemed is now a permanent member of the BHAFC squad since he switched from Almería in the summer.

Which international team has he represented?

06

Who was the Seagulls' top appearance maker last season and how many appearances did he make in total?

07

Who was crowned Player of the Season for 2014/15?

TEST YOURSELF ON 2015

08

Chris Hughton joined the Brighton fold last season. Which was the last team he had managed?

09

This summer Brighton signed a Cameroonian defender who started his career with French club, Metz.

Who is he?

10

Which player spent some time on loan at Bury at the start of the 2015/16 season?

11

Who are the Seagulls playing in their last game of 2015?

12

Against whom was Brighton's first League win of the calendar year?

13

Who scored the first goal for Brighton this season?

14

Gordon Greer is holding onto the captain's reins for another season. How many League appearances did he make last season?

15

Rohan Ince received the Goal of the Season award last season, but against whom were Brighton playing when he made his winning strike?

ANSWERS ON PAGE 62

BRIGHTON & HOVE ALBION
7 BERAM KAYAL

CAN YOU MATCH EACH OF THESE FEATURES TO THE SEAGULLS PLAYER THEY BELONG TO?

THE BIG MATCH

ADAM CHICKSEN · LIAM ROSENIOR
BOBBY ZAMORA · TOMER HEMED
SAM BALDOCK · INIGO CALDERON
GLEN REA · CHRIS O'GRADY
NIKI MAENPAA · GAETAN BONG

1. PLAYER:

2. PLAYER:

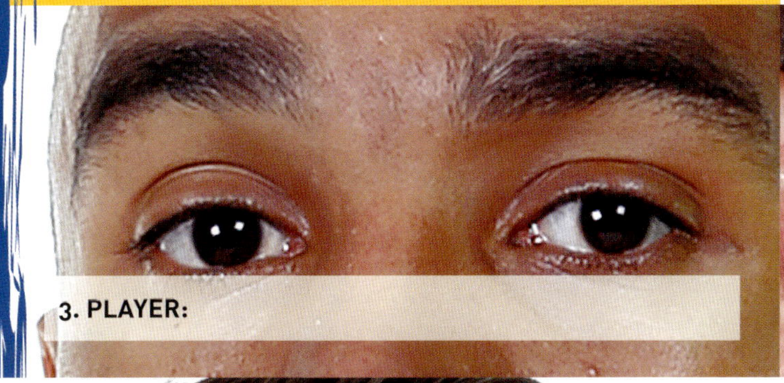

3. PLAYER:

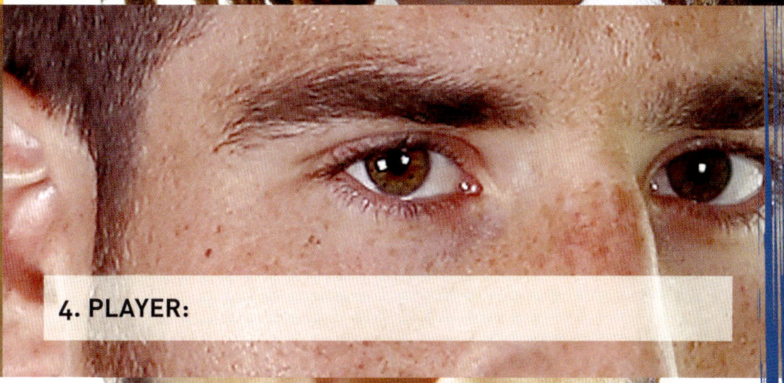

4. PLAYER:

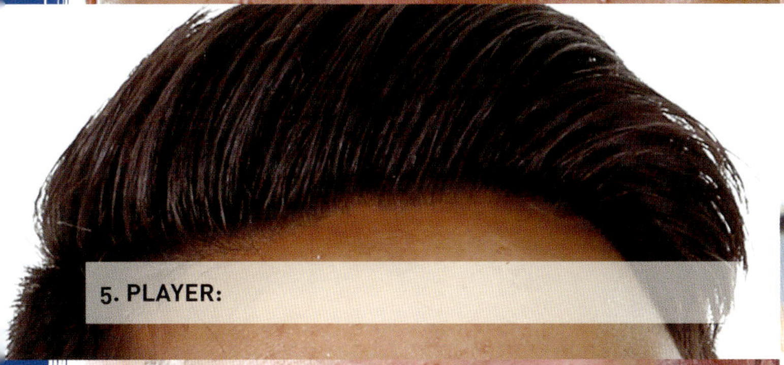

5. PLAYER:

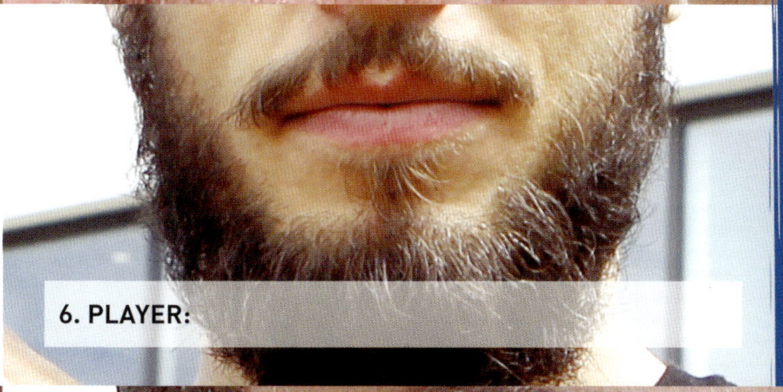

6. PLAYER:

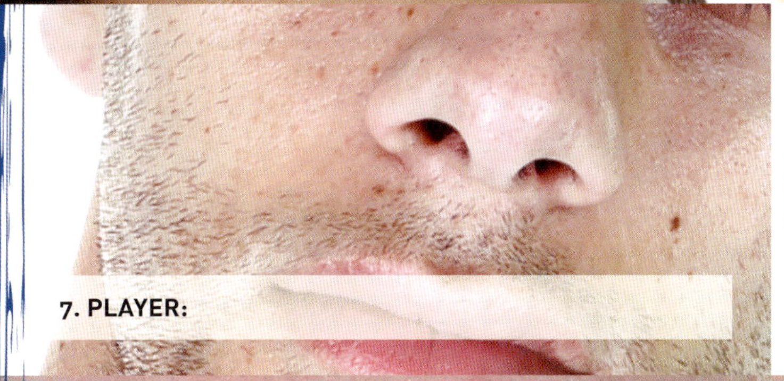

7. PLAYER:

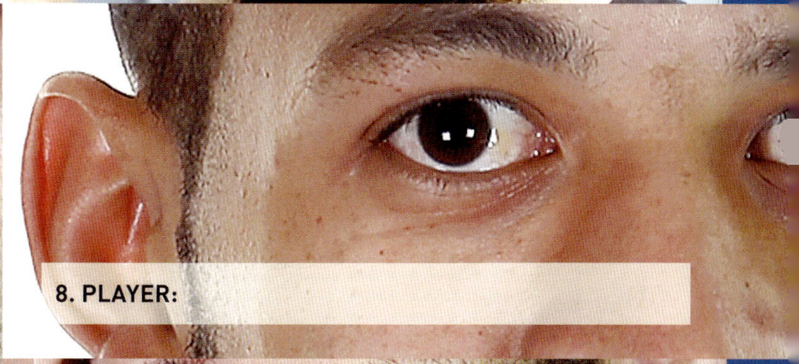

8. PLAYER:

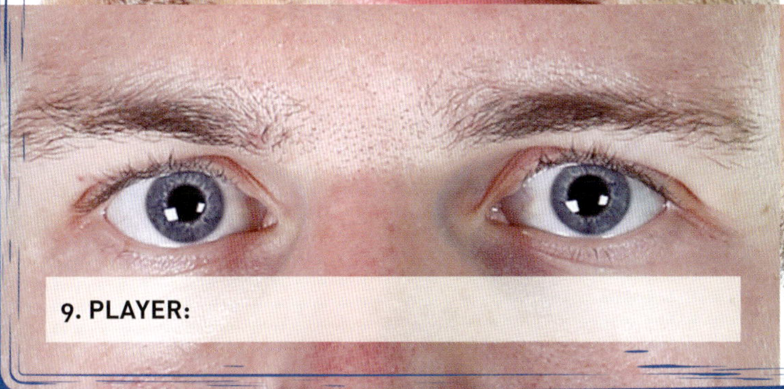

9. PLAYER:

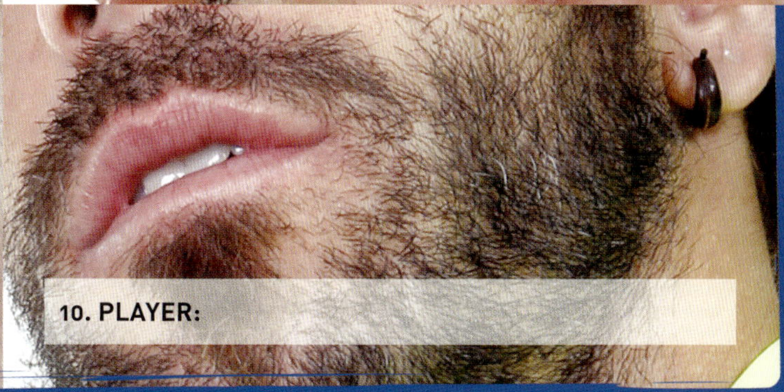

10. PLAYER:

ANSWERS ON PAGE 62

TEAM TALK

NIKI MAENPAA

Who was the first big influence on your career?
It was my older brother Asser who used to play football as well. I always followed him and I think he was the first big influence.

Which club first spotted you? It was FC Kasiysi.

Best advice you've been given?
To never give up and to believe in yourself, which applies to both life and football.

Best sportsperson in the world?
If I had to say the best sportsperson ever, I would have to say Michael Jordan. He was a great example as a sportsperson.

Best moment of your life?
That's a very hard question! The best moment of my sporting career would be making my professional debut as a footballer.

If you could play any sportsperson at their own game, who would it would be?
I would say Iker Casillas. I've been a big fan of him for some time and he's a great keeper.

If you could be best friends with anyone in the world, who would it be? My girlfriend. She is already and may be reading my answers!

Something interesting we might not know about you?
I like to play the guitar but I'm not very good at it, but I find it very relaxing.

JAMIE MURPHY

First pair of boots you owned? I remember having a pair of red Uhlsport boots, if you can remember them!

Who was the first big influence on your career? My Dad. He would go to every single game and still tries to get to every game now. He's followed me throughout my career.

Which pro club first spotted you?
Motherwell. I was 12 years old playing for Clyde Boys club and I got picked up and stayed there for 10 or 12 years.

Best advice you've been given?
Just to enjoy what you're doing and football is always better when you're relaxed and having fun.

Best sportsperson in the world?
I'll go for Lionel Messi because as a footballer, he's the one player that you look up to.

Best moment of your life?
The birth of my little girl, who is now seven months old.

If you could play any sportsperson at their own game, who would it would be? I'd play golf with Tiger Woods and I'd probably beat him at the moment!

If you could have one superpower what it would be?
To fly, I'm not very good on planes!

Something interesting we might not know about you?
I never played football on a grass pitch until the age of nine. In Glasgow the surfaces are all red ash. That really helped me develop my technique.

BOBBY ZAMORA

First pair of boots you owned?
I think they were a pair of Hi-Tecs, I don't know how old I was but that rings a bell.

Who was the first big influence on your career?
Probably Diego Maradona. I used to watch him as a kid on TV, especially at the World Cup. I used to watch Roberto Baggio as well. Those two stick out.

Which pro club first spotted you?
Charlton Athletic asked me to train with them and then I went on to West Ham after that, the club I supported.

Best advice you've been given?
Just to hit the target. It's corny but is probably the best advice you can get as a striker. You can't score if you don't get the target.

Best sportsperson in the world?
Probably Floyd Mayweather. He's been at the top of his game for a while now and I'm not sure if he'll ever be beaten. He creates a big buzz, he talks a lot, but backs it up with what he does in the ring.

If you could have one superpower what it would be?
To fly, you wouldn't have to wait around for aeroplanes!

If you could be best friends with anyone in the world, who would it be? I'm a big fan of Denzel Washington. I love all of his films as well.

Something interesting we might not know about you?
I love going fishing.

GAETAN BONG

First pair of boots you owned? Red Lottos

Which pro club first spotted you?
FC Metz when I was 13 and I stayed there until the age of 20.

Best advice you've been given?
Always keep working hard because we can be number one, but cannot get there without hard work.

Best sportsperson in the world?
For me it is Muhammad Ali.
He was the best sportsperson ever.

Best moment of your life?
The birth of my daughter, it's a feeling you can't explain.

If you could have one superpower what it would be?
I would like to be very fast like Flash!

If you could play any sportsperson at their own game, who would it be?
I would like to play with Michael Jordan because I think he's a great player and I like basketball. I would also take on Floyd Mayweather at boxing. I may get hit a few times, but why not!

If you could be best friends with anyone in the world, who would it be?
I would like to keep my current best friend, Rudy Gestede, who plays for Aston Villa.

Something interesting we might not know about you?
I am involved in a clothing brand called Thomas Demess.

My Albion Moments

Leaving home is always emotional
but Elliott Bennett's thunderbolt at Walsall
saw to it that the last action at Withdean
against Huddersfield Town would be to
see us crowned champions
and memories like that don't come around too often!

MY ALBION MOMENT
by Ady Packman

Albion 2 Huddersfield Town 3
Withdean, 30 April 2011

It all happened so fast...
Smith is in! he's going to score...
We're going to beat United...
We're going to win the FA Cup...

MY ALBION MOMENT
by Paul William Arnold

Albion 2 Manchester United 2
Wembley Stadium, 21 May 1983

Kit Napier scoring from a corner
at the Goldstone.
Magic!

MY ALBION MOMENT
by Keith Tester

Albion 2 Bury 0
Goldstone Ground, 27 December 1969

MANHUNT

Brighton's most recent Players of the Year are hidden in the grid, except for one... can you work out who?

A	T	P	O	R	N	U	N	B	S	W	A	D	M	H
P	S	T	F	O	R	C	R	G	I	D	B	J	H	A
R	G	O	G	C	U	Y	P	S	X	A	U	Q	F	R
C	H	A	P	M	A	N	U	H	L	R	T	Y	Z	T
G	N	S	D	I	G	W	E	E	D	E	T	F	T	E
D	M	S	E	K	A	N	B	O	J	W	E	E	M	V
K	C	I	H	P	L	E	T	W	L	C	R	U	I	A
E	T	H	D	J	L	B	M	F	D	A	S	R	N	P
F	P	W	C	N	F	R	Y	A	V	R	G	O	T	K
O	X	H	R	P	E	I	A	S	D	O	L	G	O	N
S	M	I	T	H	L	D	N	O	M	M	A	H	N	I
T	S	N	Z	Q	I	C	J	U	K	A	I	B	S	L
E	T	G	H	K	V	U	B	L	O	Z	H	T	D	T
R	C	N	L	A	R	T	E	N	A	H	S	C	M	W
D	F	W	S	M	C	T	E	A	C	U	L	L	I	P

Perry **Digweed**	Ian **Chapman**	Guy **Butters**	Andrew **Whing**
Mark **Gall**	Jeff **Minton**	Adam **Virgo**	Andrew **Crofts**
Steve **Foster**	Gary **Hart**	Paul **McShane**	Adam **El-Abd**
Kurt **Nogan**	Bobby **Zamora**	Dean **Hammond**	Liam **Bridcutt**
Peter **Smith**	Danny **Cullip**	Tommy **Elphick**	Matthew **Upson**

ANSWERS ON PAGE 62

BRIGHTON & HOVE ALBION
AMERICAN EXPRESS
32
BRUNO
SALTOR

PUZZLE IT OUT

CAREER WATCH

Work out the missing teams in David Stockdale's career.

2003 - 2006	York City
2006 - 2008	ANSWER
2008 - 2014	ANSWER
2014 - present	Brighton & Hove Albion

Who are yer?

Three Seagulls players are mixed up in this picture!

DERBY DAY

Can you match each team to their rival?

1
2
3
4

HOMELANDS

Match the player to their home country

Netherlands

Bruno

Beram Kayal

Finland

Israel

Niki Maenpaa

Sam Baldock

Cameroon

England

Gaetan Bong

Danny Holla

Spain

ANSWERS ON PAGE 62

Hull City

GROUND: KC Stadium **CAPACITY:** 25,450

MANAGER: Steve Bruce **NICKNAME:** The Tigers

DID YOU KNOW:
Hull changed their club badge in June 2014, becoming one of few English league teams without the club name on their crest.

Ipswich Town

GROUND: Portman Road **CAPACITY:** 30,311

MANAGER: Mick McCarthy

NICKNAMES: The Blues, The Tractor Boys

DID YOU KNOW: Ipswich last appeared in the Premier League in 2001/02, making them the Championship's longest-serving Club.

Leeds United

GROUND: Elland Road **CAPACITY:** 37,890

HEAD COACH: Uwe Rösler

NICKNAMES: The Whites, The Peacocks

DID YOU KNOW:
Leeds United fans have a salute which is known as the 'Leeds Salute'.

Middlesbrough

GROUND: Riverside Stadium **CAPACITY:** 34,742

HEAD COACH: Aitor Karanka

NICKNAMES: Boro, the Smoggies

DID YOU KNOW:
Middlesbrough won the League Cup in 2004, the club's first and only major trophy.

MK Dons

GROUND: *Stadium*mk **CAPACITY:** 30,500

MANAGER: Karl Robinson **NICKNAME:** The Dons

DID YOU KNOW:
The South stand of *Stadium*mk is known as the Cowshed by Dons' fans, as Milton Keynes is known for its Concrete Cows.

Nottingham Forest

GROUND: The City Ground **CAPACITY:** 30,576

MANAGER: Dougie Freedman

NICKNAME: The Reds

DID YOU KNOW:
Forest's most successful period was under manager Brian Clough, between 1975 and 1993.

Preston North End

GROUND: Deepdale **CAPACITY:** 23,404

MANAGER: Simon Grayson

NICKNAMES: PNE, The Whites, The Invincibles

DID YOU KNOW: Preston were promoted to the Championship last season via the play-offs.

QPR

GROUND: Loftus Road **CAPACITY:** 18,489

MANAGER: Chris Ramsey **NICKNAME:** The Hoops

DID YOU KNOW:
QPR's main rivals are Chelsea, Fulham and Brentford, with whom they contest what are known as West London Derbies.

Reading

GROUND: Madejski Stadium **CAPACITY:** 24,161

MANAGER: Steve Clarke

NICKNAME: The Royals

DID YOU KNOW:
Established in 1871, Reading is one of the oldest teams in England.

Rotherham United

GROUND: AESSEAL New York Stadium

CAPACITY: 12,021 **MANAGER:** Steve Evans

NICKNAME: The Millers

DID YOU KNOW:
The Chuckle Brothers are honorary presidents of Rotherham United!

Sheffield Wednesday

GROUND: Hillsborough Stadium **CAPACITY:** 39,732

MANAGER: Carlos Carvalhal

NICKNAMES: The Owls, Wednesday

DID YOU KNOW: Sheffield Wednesday were one of the founding members of the Premier League in 1992.

Wolves

GROUND: Molineux **CAPACITY:** 31,700

HEAD COACH: Kenny Jackett

NICKNAME: Wolves

DID YOU KNOW:
Wolves have won the FA Cup four times - in 1893, 1908, 1949 and 1960!

Every team have players who can hurt you. Take a look at the Championship's Danger Men

DANGER MEN

BLACKBURN ROVERS
JORDAN RHODES

Goal machine Jordan grew up with inside knowledge about how to beat goalkeepers. His dad, Andy was a former goalkeeper and was goalkeeping coach at Ipswich Town, where Jordan developed as a youngster. Following a trio of loans, he came to life at Huddersfield with 73 goals in 124 games and since becoming Blackburn's record signing has more than matched that tally.

BRENTFORD
JOTA

The Spanish midfielder won Brentford's 'Outstanding Moment of the Season' award, for his winner in the derby with Fulham and was nominated for the Bees' 2014 Mitre Goal of the Year award for his strike against Cardiff City. Technically gifted, Jota played for Real Madrid's 'B' team three years ago.

BIRMINGHAM CITY
DEMARAI GRAY

The teenager, who scored Blues' Goal of the Season against Wolves, when he ran from his own half, also bagged a hat-trick against Reading. Birmingham-born winger Demarai has the kind of pace and dribbling ability that scares defenders and has already been capped at U20 level by England.

BOLTON WANDERERS
EMILE HESKEY

Emile Heskey won't score too many goals this season, but whenever a side face the Trotters, the talk in the dressing room will be about how to detect Emile. The veteran England striker is as good a target man as there is. Big and strong Heskey holds the ball up brilliantly and has the experience of over 60 games for England and seven major trophies won with Leicester and Liverpool.

BRISTOL CITY
JONATHAN KODJIA

Last season's French Ligue 2 Player of the Year arrived at Ashton Gate in the summer. The pacey Ivorian striker scored 15 goals in 29 games last season, firing Angers to promotion to the top flight in France. Kodjia wasted no time in showing he had not left his goal touch across the channel, marking his home debut with a goal against Brentford and bagging another against Burnley before the end of August.

BURNLEY

ANDRE GRAY

Burnley smashed their transfer record to buy Andre Gray from Brentford, for a reported £9m fee. After bagging 18 goals for the Bees last season, Gray scored in the first two matches of this season, including one against newly promoted Bristol City, who had wanted to sign him. But Burnley stepped in to snap him up and will look to the former Luton Town man to fire them straight back into the top flight.

CHARLTON ATHLETIC

SIMON MAKIENOK

You can not miss Makienok, standing 6'7" with his blond ponytail! He has a real physical presence. Not only do his knock-downs put the ball in the danger-area for the Addicks attackers, but he is more than useful in his own box too, defending set-pieces.The Dane is a vital player for the men from the Valley.

FULHAM

ROSS McCORMACK

Scotland international McCormack, cost the Whites £11m in July 2014, an astonishing fee for a newly-relegated club. He proved his worth by netting 19 goals in 50 appearances. An impressive stat, given that he does not always play as an out-and-out striker. His all-round play often means that he is employed in a deeper role, where he is more involved in the game. If Fulham are to do well, McCormack will be a main man.

CARDIFF CITY

KENWYNE JONES

The spectacular sight of a Kenwyne Jones celebration somersault is something all Bluebirds fans love to see. The tall Trinidadian was once described as the most dangerous player in the game in the air by John Terry and certainly, on his day, no one can keep up with Kenwyne.

DERBY COUNTY

TOM INCE

Eleven goals in 18 games on loan last season persuaded the Rams to pay Hull City a reported £4.75m for the son of former England midfielder Paul. Tom is fast, two-footed, tricky and draws people to the ball, before releasing it at just the right moment. He could be the man to take Derby County to the top.

HUDDERSFIELD TOWN

NAHKI WELLS

Bermuda international Nahki Wells, became the Terriers record signing when he moved from Bradford City. He smashed 25 goals for City in 2012/13, which included strikes in the Play-off final and the Capital One Cup semi-final against Villa. Nahki notched 14 goals last season in his first full campaign with Huddersfield and with his pace and persistence, he will always spell danger for the opposition.

HULL CITY

MOSES ODUBAJO

Looking to bounce straight back to the top flight, the Tigers invested a reported £3.5m to capture England U20 Moses Odubajo from Brentford. He missed just one game last season as the Bees just missed out on promotion, losing in the Play-off semi final. A right-winger or right-back, Moses spent four years with Leyton Orient winning the O's Goal of the Season in 2011/12 and voted their Young Player of the Year, the following season.

LEEDS UNITED

MIRCO ANTENUCCI

The veteran Italian striker has represented nine clubs in his own country, including Torino, with whom he won promotion to Serie 'A' in 2011/12. Muscular and mobile, Mirco hit double figures for Leeds last season and scored a stunner against Burnley to start the current campaign with a bang.

MK DONS

DIEGO POYET

The 20-year-old son of Gus Poyet, England U20 international midfielder Diego made five Europa League appearances for West Ham this season, before joining MK Dons. His passing ability and footballing philosophy fits snugly into the Dons renowned possession game. Poyet was Charlton's Young Player of the Year, the season before last, despite not debuting until January of that campaign.

IPSWICH TOWN

DARYL MURPHY

Daryl did so well last season, he was not so much a Tractor Boy but a combine harvester, the way he scythed through defences, scoring 27 goals. The Republic of Ireland international hit the form of his life, confidently scoring all kinds of goals for the Portman Road outfit.

MIDDLESBROUGH

STEWART DOWNING

Boro splashed the cash, paying a reported £7m to bring Stewart Downing back to his first club, after a stellar season for West Ham. Starting out as a sizzling winger, Downing has developed into a player whose vision lets him create chances from a more central position, as well as always posing a threat himself.

NOTTINGHAM FOREST

BRITT ASSOMBALONGA

Britt Assombalonga will not be fit until the second half of the season, but he could be the man to fire Forest to promotion, if they can keep themselves in the running until then. Britt had scored 15 times before his injury in February, a tally that gives him over 50 in the last three years.

PRESTON NORTH END

DANIEL JOHNSON

Daniel's eight goals in the second half of last season, after joining in January, helped North End to promotion. Having earlier scored three times on loan to Oldham, Jamaican-born Johnson was in double figures for the season and after getting off to a good start with the first home goal at Deepdale this season, will hope to reach that target again.

READING

OLA JOHN

John signed for the Royals on a season-long loan in the summer from Benfica. He is a very talented forward with power, pace, the ability to beat his man, deliver quality balls into the box and also has an eye for goal himself. With all these attributes, Ola should help ensure Reading are a potent offensive force this campaign.

SHEFFIELD WEDNESDAY

MARCO MATIAS

Matias' early-season goal at Leeds marked him out as a special player. The way he lobbed the ball over Liam Cooper before applying the most spectacular finish was pure quality. Last season he scored 17 goals in 33 games in the Portuguese top flight for CD Nacional, while home fans saw his first goal at Hillsborough come against Middlesbrough in August.

QUEENS PARK RANGERS

CHARLIE AUSTIN

Barclays Premier League Player of the Month for December 2014, Charlie was called up by England, although he still awaits his first cap. QPR fans were relieved he did not move on in the transfer window, as many clubs were understandably keen on signing a player who has scored well over 100 goals for QPR, Burnley and Swindon after making his name in non-league football.

ROTHERHAM UNITED

JORDAN BOWERY

Bowery impressed so much as a youngster at Chesterfield, that Aston Villa spent £500,000 on him when he was only 21. Jordan is an impact player, with 28 of his 36 appearances last term coming off the bench, but a clue to his quality was that two of his five goals came against teams subsequently promoted to the Barclays Premier League.

WOLVERHAMPTON WANDERERS

BENIK AFOBE

Goals, goals, goals are what Afobe is all about. He struck three times in the first four games of this season after scoring 32 last term, 13 of them after his move to Molineux from MK Dons. The 22-year-old came through the ranks at Arsenal and the England U21 international was reportedly the subject of a £12m bid from Norwich City in August.

Can you identify these Seagulls stars?

ANSWERS ON PAGE 62

DAVID STOCKDALE

First pair of boots you owned?

They were Nike Tiempo. I wanted to wear them so badly that I walked on the concrete with them and my Dad told me off, because I messed the studs up!

Who was the first big influence on your career?

My Mum and Dad for their time and effort they put into my career and when I got released, my Dad wrote to every club in Yorkshire that he could get to physically and got me trials.

Which pro club first spotted you?

Huddersfield Town.

Best advice you've been given?

Stop the ball! It's been expanded in various ways over the years, but that has always been the basic message!

Best sportsperson in the world?

Usain Bolt just dominates everything and it's to his credit as well because he seems like such a nice guy. But I also think Jordan Spieth is amazing for what he's achieved, so those two stick out for me.

If you could play any sportsperson at their own game, who would it be?

I've got a good friend who plays golf, Ross Fisher and I beat him the first time I played him, so I'll go with him!

Best moment of your life?

The birth of my kids.

If you could have one superpower what it would be?

46 clean sheets!

If you could be best friends with anyone in the world, who would it be?

My best mate Niall O'Brien back home in Leeds.

Something interesting we might not know about you?

I can speak a little bit of Spanish. I listen to the Spanish lads here when they're talking to each other. I try to speak it when I'm away on holiday!

CASPER ANKERGREN

First pair of boots you owned? A pair of Lotto boots with this luminous green sign on the side.

Who was the first big influence on your career?
I had this coach in Koge before I went to Brondby and he turned things around for me. He played at a high level and was quite strict with me, which was good because I learned what it takes to be a professional footballer.

Which club first spotted you?
Brondby bought me in 2000.

Best advice you've been given?
That hard work pays off. Some of the keepers I played with as a youngster don't even play the game anymore, so that's one thing which sticks out.

Best sportsperson in the world?
Probably Lionel Messi. He performs time after time, does his job and scores his goals.

Best moment of your life?
Definitely when my daughter was born.

If you could have one superpower what it would be?
I would like to be able to fly.

If you could be best friends with anyone in the world, who would it be? I would like to meet Ricky Gervais and Karl Pilkington, but out of the two I would say Ricky Gervais.

Something interesting we might not know about you?
I used to deliver pizzas on a scooter when I was younger. I also worked in the kitchen at a restaurant.

SOLLY MARCH

First pair of boots you owned?
Some Adidas Copa Mundials.

Who was the first big influence on your career?
Probably my Dad. He supported me and took me to all my games.

Which pro club first spotted you? Crystal Palace.

Best advice you've been given?
Enjoy your football and work hard, then you'll get the best results.

Best sportsperson in the world?
Roger Federer. Just for the amazing career he's had and seems to be a really nice guy.

If you could play any sportsperson at their own game, who would it be?
Probably Rory McIlroy at golf

Best moment of your life?
Every time I step out onto the pitch at the Amex.

If you could have one superpower what it would be?
I'd just be Superman.

If you could be best friends with anyone in the world, who would it be?
Andrea Pirlo, because he's a superb player.

Something interesting we might not know about you?
I am someone who wants to buy lots of different properties.

My Albion Moments

For me it happened in slow motion.
A ballet of goalmouth action before my eyes.
Stooorrreeerrrrrrr!

MY ALBION MOMENT
by John Weir

Albion 1 Doncaster Rovers 0
Goldstone Ground, 26 April 1997

William Buckley.
90+7 mins on the clock.
Turned the Amex into absolute hysteria.
Amazing memories!

MY ALBION MOMENT
by David Stappleton

Albion 2 Doncaster Rovers 1
Amex, 6 August 2011

Just five years after that almost calamitous day at Hereford
and we celebrated our second successive promotion
at Withdean with a goalless draw against Swindon Town.
Bobby Zamora scored a total of 63 goals
in 2000/01 and 2001/02 which was a key reason
for our success at that time.

MY ALBION MOMENT
by Mark Sillience

Albion 0 Swindon Town 0
Withdean, 13 April 2002

AROUND THE CHAMPIONSHIP: There are a mixture of traditional and modern badges in the rest of the Championship and here we look at a selection of them.

IPSWICH TOWN: Ipswich's current badge came from a competition. The Tractor Boys' badge though doesn't include a tractor! Instead it shows a Suffolk 'Punch' horse, Suffolk being the county Ipswich is in.

The look of a turret above the horse is to indicate the historic buildings within Ipswich (these were moved to the top when the badge was slightly amended in 1995) while the wavy lines at the bottom are intended to show that Ipswich is near to the sea.

DERBY COUNTY: Being The Rams, Derby's badge is as you would expect, dominated by a Ram. A ram's head had been part of Derby's badge since they first used a badge in the mid-twenties. Since 1971 the badge has shown the whole animal.

WOLVERHAMPTON WANDERERS: **Obviously a wolf was inevitably going to become the dominant object on this badge! It started to prowl in the 1970s and for a while there were three wolves on Wolves' badge but since the early 1980s it has been the head of a single wolf on the club's badge.**

MIDDLESBROUGH: Middlesbrough's modern badge went back to he beginning by replacing the date 1986 with 1876. This was to re-introduce the date of the club's original formation rather than the date it was reformed following a financial disaster that saw it go into liquidation in 1986.

The badge shows a red lion in a shield headed by the name of the town with the words football club joining the date at the foot of the emblem.

NOTTINGHAM FOREST: Like a lot of clubs, Forest's initial badge was based on the coat of arms of their city. The modern day Forest badge is the work of graphic artist David Lewis who came up with the badge in 1973. It signalled a new start and came at the right time as Forest soon entered the most glorious part of their history. The wavy lines on their badge indicate the River Trent, rather than being near to the sea as on Ipswich's badge. The tree that makes up most of the badge indicates the famous Sherwood Forest.

SHEFFIELD WEDNESDAY: Animals often become emblems with which clubs become associated. In the case of Sheffield Wednesday their owl comes from the fact that the club has long been based in the suburb of Owlerton, although a century ago Owlerton was incorporated into Hillsborough which of course is now the name of The Owls' home ground.

Nowadays the badge has a simple drawing of an owl within a shield, together with the year of foundation, 1867, showing the Owls' wisdom comes from being one of the oldest clubs in the country.

BRIGHTON & HOVE
ALBION
AMERICAN EXPRESS
KAZENGA
LUALUA
30

CAN YOU MATCH EACH OF THESE PLAYERS TO THE SEASON THEY WON THE PLAYER OF THE YEAR AWARD?

THE BIG MATCH

MARK LAWRENSON · IAN CHAPMAN
BRIAN HORTON · DANNY CULLIP · ADAM EL-ABD
GARY STEVENS · MATTHEW UPSON
PETER SMITH · TERRY CONNOR · PERRY DIGWEED

1995/96 · 2010/11 · 1978/79 · 1982/83 · 1999/00
1976/77 · 1994/95 · 1986/87 · 2013/14 · 1990/91

1. PLAYER: SEASON:

2. PLAYER: SEASON:

3. PLAYER: SEASON:

4. PLAYER: SEASON:

5. PLAYER: SEASON:

6. PLAYER: SEASON:

7. PLAYER: SEASON:

8. PLAYER: SEASON:

9. PLAYER: SEASON:

10. PLAYER: SEASON:

ANSWERS ON PAGE 62

We have set you a huge challenge for the new year!

Every month there are two new tasks to complete.

Have you got what it takes?!

2016 CHALLENGE

JANUARY

- Do 25 keepy-uppies
- Come up with a new BHAFC chant!

FEBRUARY

- Take a selfie at a Championship Stadium
- Learn a new trick - around the world!

MARCH

- Nutmeg someone!
- Get an autograph from a Seagulls star

APRIL

- Take a selfie with a Seagulls player
- Do 50 keepy-uppies

MAY

- Work on your fitness - run 1 mile!
- Lob the keeper

JUNE

- Learn a new trick - catch the ball on your neck
- Set up a sponsored event with your mates and do your bit for charity!

JULY

- Work on your fitness - run 3 miles!
- Learn a new trick - keepy-uppies with a tennis ball

AUGUST

- Take a selfie with a Seagulls legend
- Do 75 keepy-uppies

SEPTEMBER

- Try out for your school footie team
- Do 10 keepy-uppies on your head

OCTOBER

- Pat Gully the Seagull on the back
- Take a selfie with Chris Hughton

NOVEMBER

- Work on your fitness - run 5 miles!
- Score from the penalty spot by hitting the underside of the crossbar

DECEMBER

- Do 100 keepy-uppies
- Start a chant at the match

ANSWERS

PAGE 20 · THE BIG MATCH

1. Brian Horton 1998-1999, 2. Dean Wilkins 2006-2008, 3. Steve Coppell 2002-2003, 4. Billy Lane 1951-1961, 5. Alan Mullery 1976-1981, 6. Gus Poyet 2009-2013, 7. Steve Gritt 1996-1998, 8. Mike Bailey 1981-1982, 9. Russell Slade 2009, 10. Peter J. Taylor 2001-2002

PAGE 25 · WHAT BALL?

Picture A - Ball 3, Picture B - Ball 4

PAGE 30 · STAND OUT FROM THE CROWD

Idris Elba, Benedict Cumberbatch, Emma Watson, Keira Knightley and Andrew Lincoln

PAGE 32 · TEST YOURSELF ON 2015

1. Lewis Dunk with 7 goals, 2. Dale Stephens, 3. Bobby Zamora, 4. Switzerland, 5. Israel, 6. David Stockdale, 46 appearances, 7. Inigo Calderon, 8. Norwich City, 9. Gaëtan Bong, 10. Christian Walton, 11. Ipswich Town, 12. Brentford, 13. Kazenga LuaLua, 14. 37, 15. Swindon Town

PAGE 35 · THE BIG MATCH

1. Bobby Zamora, 2. Gaetan Bong, 3. Chris O'Grady, 4. Tomer Hemed, 5. Adam Chicksen, 6. Niki Maenpaa, 7. Sam Baldock, 8. Liam Rosenior, 9. Glen Rea, 10. Inigo Calderon

PAGE 39 · MANH

Matthew Upson

PAGE 41 · PUZZLE IT OUT

Career Watch

2006-2008: Darlington, 2008-2014: Fulham

Who are yer?

Jake Forster-Caskey, Gordon Greer and Liam Rosenior

Derby Day

1. Derby County - Nottingham Forest, 2. Brighton & Hove Albion - Crystal Palace, 3.Ipswich Town - Norwich City, 4. Wolverhampton Wanderers - West Bromwich Albion

Homelands

Bruno - Spain, Beram Kayal - Israel, Niki Mäenpää - Finland, Sam Baldock - England, Gaëtan Bong - Cameroon, Danny Holla - Netherlands

PAGE 48 · MEGA PIXELS

1. Perez Adrian Colunga, 2. Tomer Hemed, 3. Gaetan Bong, 4. Inigo Calderon, 5. Beram-Kayal, 6. Jake Forster-Caskey, 7. Niki Maenpaa, 8. Bruno Saltor, 9. Lewis Dunk

PAGE 59 · THE BIG MATCH

1. Danny Cullip 1999/00, 2. Mark Lawrenson 1978/79, 3. Terry Connor 1986/87, 4. Adam El-Abd 2010/11, 5. Matthew Upson 2013/14, 6. Brian Horton 1976/77, 7. Perry Digweed 1990/91, 8. Ian Chapman 1995/96, 9. Peter Smith 1994/95, 10. Gary Stevens 1982/83

96.01.22.
SCOTTISH
NATIONAL GALLERY
OF MODERN ART
LIBRARY
H. Ger. x

Staatliche Kunsthalle Karlsruhe

Impuls Südwest

Kunst der 60er Jahre in Baden-Württemberg

Cantz

Leihgeber

Galerie Suzanne Fischer, Baden-Baden
Frau Suzanne Fischer

Ruhr Universität, Bochum, Sammlung Schulze-Vellinghausen
Frau Direktorin Prof. Dr. Monika Steinhauser,
Herr Dr. Kai-Uwe Hemken

Friedrich Ebert-Stiftung, Bonn
Herr Dr. Jürgen Burckhardt, Herr Dr. Dieter Dowe

Neues Museum Weserburg, Bremen,
und Stiftung Ludwig Roselius, Bremen
Herr Direktor Dr. Thomas Deecke

Galerie der Stadt Esslingen, Esslingen am Neckar
Frau Direktorin Dr. Renate Damsch-Wiehager

Galerie Neuendorf AG, Frankfurt am Main
Herr Hans Neuendorf

Galerie Bernd Slutzky, Frankfurt am Main
Herr Bernd Slutzky

Städtische Galerie im Städelschen Kunstinstitut,
Frankfurt am Main
Herr Direktor Prof. Dr. Herbert Beck,
Frau Dr. Ursula Grechca-Mohr

Galerie Schlichtenmaier, Grafenau
Herr Dr. Kuno Schlichtenmaier

Hamburger Kunsthalle, Hamburg
Herr Direktor Prof. Dr. Uwe M. Schneede,
Herr Dr. Helmut R. Leppien

Städtische Galerie im Prinz-Max-Palais, Karlsruhe
Frau Direktorin Dr. Erika Diruf-Rödiger

Wilhelm Loth-Stiftung, Karlsruhe
Herr Hans Dietrich Sauer, Vorsitzender des Vorstands
der L-Bank Baden-Württemberg

Sammlung Essl, Klosterneuburg
Frau Dr. Gabriele Bösch

Galerie Wilbrand, Köln
Herr Dieter Wilbrand

Städtische Kunsthalle Mannheim
Herr Direktor Prof. Dr. Manfred Fath,
Herr Dr. Jochen Kronjäger

Galerie der Stadt Rastatt
Herr Wolfgang Reiß, Stadtarchiv

Galerie der Stadt Stuttgart
Herr Direktor Dr. Johann-Karl Schmidt, Frau Dr. Ursula Zeller

manus-presse, Stuttgart
Herr Dr. Gerriet K. Friese

Sammlung Daimler-Benz, Stuttgart
Herr Direktor Hans J. Baumgart

Sammlung Rolf Deyhle, Stuttgart

Staatsgalerie Stuttgart
Herr Direktor Prof. Dr. Christian von Holst,
Frau Dr. Karin Frank von Maur

Ulmer Museum, Ulm
Frau Dr. Brigitte Reinhardt

Ferner danken wir den privaten Leihgebern,
die nicht genannt werden möchten.

Vorwort

1846 öffnete die Kunsthalle Karlsruhe ihre Tore. Zwar ist sie mit ihrem fürstlichen Grundstock drei Jahrhunderte und als öffentliche Akademiesammlung vier Jahrzehnte älter, doch erst seit der Eröffnung des von Heinrich Hübsch errichteten ersten Flügels trägt sie den Namen Kunsthalle. Als Einheit von Gemälde- und Skulpturengalerie und dem Kupferstichkabinett sammelt, bewahrt, erforscht und zeigt sie seither Kunst vom Spätmittelalter bis zur Gegenwart.

Das 150jährige Jubiläum ist willkommener Anlaß zu einer Ausstellungsfolge, in der sich die historische Vielfalt der Sammlung widerspiegelt. Weil die Kunsthalle das Schaffen der eigenen Zeit in ihren bedeutendsten Phasen immer besonders gepflegt hat, bildet bewußt eine Ausstellung des stürmischen Aufbruchs nach 1960 den Auftakt. Der eigenen Region besondere Beachtung zu schenken, ist hier gute Tradition. Die Ausstellung erhebt jedoch einen weitergehenden Anspruch: Sie bezieht mit herausragenden Beispielen auch den württembergischen Bereich ein; entscheidender aber ist, daß überregionale, wenn nicht internationale Maßstäbe den Ausschlag bei der Auswahl gaben. Es geht weniger um die Breite hiesigen Kunstgeschehens als um Werke von besonderem Rang und ihre Ausstrahlung.

Die gemeinsam von Gert Reising und mir konzipierte Ausstellung verdankt den Gesprächen mit vielen Kundigen Anregungen und Erkenntnisse. Unter den Zeitzeugen sind besonders Franz Bernhard, die Professoren Rolf-Gunter Dienst, Klaus Gallwitz, Klaus Jürgen-Fischer, Dieter Krieg und Lothar Quinte hervorzuheben, unter den Kennern der Region und der Zeit vor allem die Kollegen und Galeristen Frau Dr. Erika Diruf-Rödiger, Karlsruhe, Frau Suzanne Fischer, Baden-Baden, Herr Dr. Klaus Gerriet Friese, Stuttgart, Frau Margot Fuerst, Stuttgart, Herr Dr. Helmut R. Leppien, Hamburg, Frau Dr. Ursula Merkel, Karlsruhe, Frau Helgard Müller-Jensen, geb. Rottloff, Karlsruhe, Herr Dr. Kuno Schlichtenmaier, Grafenau, Herr Hans Strelow, Düsseldorf, und Herr Bogislav von Wentzel, Wachtberg. In den Archiven gaben uns Frau Angelika Sauer, Stadtarchiv Karlsruhe, und Herr Dr. Kurt Hochstuhl, Hauptstaatsarchiv Stuttgart, entgegenkommend Auskunft.

Durch vielfältige, für unsere Unternehmung neu erarbeitete Beiträge verschiedener Autoren konnte das Thema im Katalog so facettenreich ausgeleuchtet werden: Die Stuttgarter Szene stellt Frau Dr. Ursula Zeller dar, während Herr Dr. Dirk Teuber auf Baden-Baden als Verlags-, Ausstellungs und Künstlerzentrum mit internationalen Verflechtungen eingeht. Am Beispiel des ersten baden-württembergischen Kunstpreises wirft Herr Dr. Kurt Hochstuhl ein besonderes Licht auf Beziehungen zwischen Staat und Kultur im Lande. Herr Alexander Mohr schildert auf lebendige Weise das damalige kulturelle Umfeld in Karlsruhe, während Herr Dr. Reising und Herr Dr. Wilfried Rößling in ihrem gemeinsamen Beitrag vor allem den Karlsruher Impulsen und ihrer Rezeption nachgehen. Frau Eva Studinger hat die Künstlerbiographien bearbeitet. Zu danken ist auch Frau Signe Brunner für die Gestaltung des Kataloges. Die große Zahl der Neuaufnahmen haben in bewährter Weise unsere Fotografin Frau Ellen Frank und ihre Mitarbeiterin Frau Heike Kohler bewältigt. Die umfangreiche Textverarbeitung leistete in kurzer Zeit Frau Gerlinde Beisch. Mein Dank schließt die Verwaltung, den haustechnischen Dienst und alle Mitarbeiterinnen und Mitarbeiter der Kunsthalle ein, die im Hintergrund am Gelingen der Ausstellung mitgewirkt haben.

Ein ganz besonderer Dank gebührt den öffentlichen und zahlreichen, zumeist ungenannt bleibenden privaten Leihgebern dafür, daß sie sich fast ein Vierteljahr von ihren Werken trennen. Sie machen es uns möglich, ein bedeutendes Kapitel der jüngeren Kunstgeschichte vor Augen zu führen, zentrale Arbeiten einer Zeit, als der Südwesten Deutschlands ein Zentrum der Avantgarde war.

Siegmar Holsten

Horst Antes

Hans Baschang

Bernd Berner

Franz Bernhard

Emil Cimiotti

Rolf-Gunter Dienst

Peter Dreher

Hans Martin Erhardt

HAP Grieshaber

Otto Herbert Hajek

Erich Hauser

Peter Herkenrath

Bert Jäger

Klaus Jürgen-Fischer

Herbert Kitzel

Fritz Klemm

Dieter Krieg

Thomas Lenk

Wilhelm Loth

Georg Meistermann

Günter Neusel

Georg Karl Pfahler

Markus Prachensky

Lothar Quinte

Heinz Schanz

Felix Schlenker

Emil Schumacher

K.R.H. Sonderborg

Walter Stöhrer

Inhalt

Zur Avantgarde in der südwestdeutschen Kunst der sechziger Jahre

Ursprung im Formlosen

Nachdem der Ausbruch der frühen Moderne aus der sichtbaren Wirklichkeit zwischen den Weltkriegen durch Realismen unterschiedlichster politischer Couleurs konterkariert worden war, setzte sich nach 1945 in der westlichen Kunst die Gegenstandslosigkeit durch. Darstellungen äußerer Wirklichkeit wurden fast tabu. Selbst wenn Lehrer der älteren Generation ihren gegenständlichen Traditionen treu geblieben waren – für die meisten ihrer Schüler wurde die Abstraktion zur selbstverständlichen »Weltsprache der Kunst«.

Innerhalb der Vielfalt der Richtungen gingen vor allem diejenigen Künstler über die Traditionen der Klassischen Moderne entscheidend hinaus, die die herkömmliche Bildvorstellung in sich selbst ruhender Kompositionen in Frage stellten. Bahnbrechendes Vorbild dafür war Jackson Pollock, dessen flächendeckende Bewegungsspuren Bildgeviert und Bildraum sprengen. Auf solche Entfesselung des Selbstausdrucks und der Grenzöffnung zielten in bescheideneren Dimensionen – beispielhaft für die Pariser und die deutsche Szene der frühen fünfziger Jahre – auch Georges Mathieu und Karl Otto Götz. So ging die junge Avantgarde der späten fünfziger Jahre – Günther Uecker in Düsseldorf z.B. nicht weniger als die Aufrührer in Karlsruhe und Stuttgart (Abb. S. 71, 77 und S. 75) –

Georges Mathieu: Uranus II. 1953

zunächst durchweg vom Tachismus, Informel und Abstrakten Expressionismus bzw. deren Mischformen aus. Die Bildstrukturen im Frühwerk der meisten Künstler, auf die die Ausstellung die Aufmerksamkeit lenkt, muten wie eine brodelnde Ursuppe an, aus deren Chaos sich verschiedene individuelle Gestaltungswege bildeten. Wer die Formensprache des Formlosen zum Ausgangspunkt nahm, hatte in besonderem Maße der

Jackson Pollock malend. 1950

Karl Otto Götz: Bild vom 3. 2. 1953. 1953

Gefahr der Routine gewärtig zu sein und war umgekehrt dem Vorwurf solcher Erschöpfung ausgesetzt. Solches Ringen darum, die Beliebigkeit offener Form zu bannen, spricht beispielhaft aus einem Satz Emil Schumachers über die Paradoxie von Chaos und Gestalt: »Alles, was ist, hat die ihm gemäße Form oder ist bestrebt, Form anzunehmen: die Inselbildungen nach Überschwemmungen, die Schneereste nach der Schmelze, die Schlacke nach dem Brand. Die Form, die das Leben zur Voraussetzung hat – die das Leben enthält – ist formlos und doch Form.« (Emil Schumacher, Aphorismen, in: Ein Buch mit sieben Siegeln, Heidelberg 1972). Aus derselben Erkenntnis heraus hatte bereits Jean Dubuffet in den fünfziger Jahren als Einzelgänger das Informel vereinnahmt und auf vitale Weise überwunden, indem er Bildstrukturen des Formlosen mit Zeichen surrealer Anspielungskraft verband.

Revolten andernorts

Damit ist schlaglichtartig die Spannungslage um 1960 angedeutet, die – gleich einem explosiven Gemisch – bei den jüngeren Künstlern unterschiedliche Reaktionen auslöste und Kräfte freisetzte – vom provokativen Traditionsbruch bis zur Zuspitzung und Umwandlung gewachsener Positionen. In Südwestdeutschland überwog die Evolution, auch wenn es Quantensprünge gab. Selbst öffentliche Eklats wie Grieshabers Bauzaun-Aktion in Karlsruhe (Abb. S. 16) setzten künstlerisch mehr auf Kontinuität als auf Zäsur.

Diese Erneuerung vollzog sich nicht in regionaler Abkapselung, sondern dank Zeitschriften wie »magnum« und »das kunstwerk«, der »documenta« und durch Begegnungen vor dem Hintergrund und im Dialog mit mannigfaltigen internationalen Kunstrevolten. Sie seien kurz in Erinnerung gerufen, ehe von Entwicklungen im Südwesten die Rede ist.

Im Unterschied zur amerikanischen und englischen Avantgarde, wo sich als Aufstand banaler Alltagswelten und plakativer Werbesignale die Pop-art Bahn brach, blieb im Südwesten die Abstraktion als zeitgemäße Ausdrucksform so gut wie unangetastet. Auch die Pariser Revolte des »Nouveau Réalisme«, die – nicht zuletzt dank Paul Wembers Wirken im Krefelder Museum – durch Yves Klein und Arman in das Rheinland hineinwirkte und Verwerfungen herkömmlichen Kunstverständnisses auslöste, blieb hier – bei aller Nähe zur französischen Metropole – ohne Auswirkung.

Die rheinischen Kunstrevolution kündigte den ontologischen wie den gesellschaftlichen Konsens gleichermaßen auf. So radikalisierten die Zero-Künstler die Ansätze des Informel durch Farbverweigerung und überwanden sie durch Monochromie und serielle Reduktion. Mit Joseph Beuys und dem Koreaner Nam June Paik setzten gleichzeitig Fluxus-Aktionen im Rückgriff auf Duchamp durch Schocks von Ding und Ereignis das Tafelbild außer Kraft. Im Vergleich dazu waren im Südwesten die Schübe des Neuen stiller. Sie sprengten nicht die Vorstellung vom autonomen Werk des Tafelbildes und der Skulptur. Und doch gab es auch hier – gleichsam von innen heraus – eine weithin und anhaltend wirksame Erneuerung. Sie vollzog sich, ausgelöst durch bestimmte Katalysatoren, in verschiedenen künstlerischen Richtungen von der geometrischen Konkretion über Farbräume bis hin zur abstrahierten Figürlichkeit.

Günther Uecker: Informelle Struktur. 1957

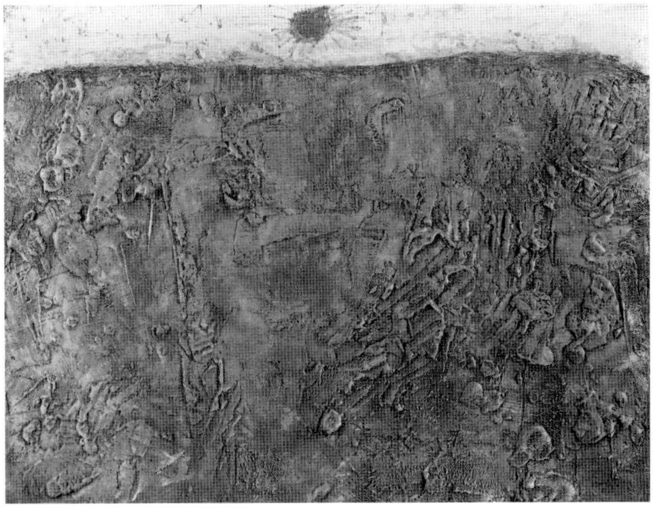

Jean Dubuffet: Paysage d'informe. 1952

Georg Karl Pfahler: ›A 8‹. 1956

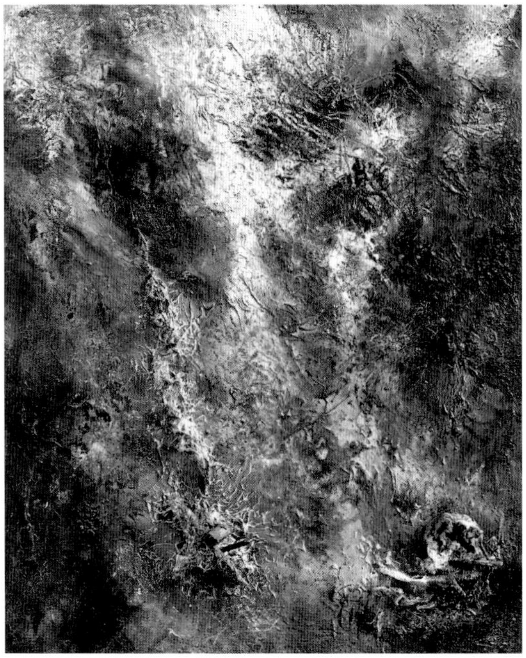

Bernard Schultze: neelt. 1958

Vom Mahlstrom zum Winkel

Die Herkunft vom Informel überrascht besonders bei solchen Künstlern, die als Hard-edge-Maler und Konstrukteure der Geometrie bekannt sind. Das gilt z.B. für den damals in Stuttgart tätigen Georg Karl Pfahler, dessen erste Gemälde Ausschnitten strudelnder Lavaströme oder ihren schrundigen Verhärtungen gleichen. Sie stehen noch den Kosmogonien Bernard Schultzes nahe. Auch in Pfahlers farblich reich orchestrierten Gemälde von 1959 (S. 103) züngeln noch urweltliche Energien. Sie zerströmen nicht mehr in alle Richtungen, sondern verdichten sich zu pastosen Farbfeldern und scheinen sich an deren aufeinanderprallenden Rändern als flackerndes Farblicht zu entzünden. Die Entladung solcher Energiespannungen an Nahtstellen blieb Pfahlers Generalthema, wie die Ausstellung in exemplarischen Schritten deutlich macht (S. 110, 111). In den sechziger Jahren reduzierte Pfahler die brodelnde

Lothar Quinte: Gestik Schwarzlack auf Schwarz. 1958

Durchdringung von Farbströmen mehr und mehr zum Aufeinandertreffen monochromer Hard-edge-Felder (S. 133): Malerei, die durch die Kraft optischer Wirkungen vom Lesbaren zum Erfahrbaren vorstieß, die am Puls einer fortschrittsgläubigen Zeit dem Bild signalhafte Schärfe verlieh.
Im ähnlicher Richtung vollzog sich auch die Entwicklung Lothar Quintes. Er war zu Beginn der fünfziger Jahre an der Bernsteinschule in Sulz durch HAP Grieshaber zu Offenheit und Experiment ermuntert worden und hatte bereits eine eigenständige Formensprache entwickelt, als er sich 1960 in Karlsruhe niederließ. Seine Phase des »Formlosen« ist durch den Vergleich mit chinesischer Tuschpinselkalligraphie und Pariser Tachisten (Abb. S. 8) nur teilweise charakterisiert. Was Quinte in spontan und flüssig gesetzten Farbbündelungen und -gittern anstrebte, war in erster Linie die gestische Schlagkraft lebendiger Malerei. Fetzen, Gitter und Geflechte gesetzter Farbe sind bei ihm zu allererst eine Funktion des Raumes und des Lichtes. Sie öffnen die Bildfläche in die Tiefe und machen den Widerstreit von Licht und Dunkel zum eigentlichen Thema. Das mag schon für die abstrakten Kompositionen des Parisers Pierre Soulages in der Mitte der fünfziger Jahre zutreffen, die indes noch zeichenhaft Raumillusionen erzeugen, während Quinte in seinen Farbmembranen Licht viel unmittelbarer, konkreter ins Auge zwingt.
Daher griff er später eigenwillig die Möglichkeiten der Op-art auf. Über gestisch beruhigte Schleierbilder, Meditationstafeln atmenden Raumes und pulsierenden Lichts (S. 108), gelangte er um die Mitte der sechziger Jahre zu geometrischen Keil- und Kreisformen, die jegliche Handschrift verleugnen (S. 112). Ihre scharfen Farbgrenzen machen das Wechselspiel von Licht und Dunkel desto prägnanter wirksam (S. 134). Aus verhaltenen Schwingungen wurden im allgemeinen Trend lauter werdender Op- und Pop-art-Signale unausweichliche, die Retina bedrängende Vibrationen.
Erst 1965 stieß als Stuttgarter Akademielehrer ein Maler zur südwestdeutschen Szene, der kaum auf die neueren Richtungen reagierte und – dem Düsseldorfer Kollegen Götz vergleichbar (Abb. S. 8) – seinem sehr persönlichen informellen Ansatz der fünfziger Jahre treu blieb: K.R.H. Sonderborg, der im Stuttgarter Raum ebenso herausragt wie in den Jahrzehnten

Pierre Soulages: Komposition. 1955

zuvor Willi Baumeister und Oskar Schlemmer. Seine in Hamburg und Paris entwickelte Bildkonzeption dynamischer Raumeroberung ist bis heute vital geblieben. Sie beruht auf der Sicherheit sekundenschneller Bewegung, deren Spuren das Bildgeviert rasant durchmessen (S. 105). Hier geht es weniger um den Ausdruck psychischer oder physischer Erregung als um ein abgründiges Verhältnis von Raum und Zeit. Im Südwesten war diese künstlerische Position bereits zu Beginn der sechziger Jahre durch den Wiener Markus Prachensky vorbereitet worden. Manche seiner damaligen »Blottings« ähneln den offensten Arbeiten Sonderborgs, doch im ganzen neigte Prachensky eher zu einer zeichen- und signalhaften Verfestigung malerischer »Würfe« (S. 114, 116).

Den Schritt vom Informel zur geometrischen Reduktion vollzogen um 1960 nicht nur Maler, sondern mit besonderer Schärfe auch einige Bildhauer bzw. Objektemacher. Otto Herbert Hajeks Raumknoten und -schichtungen z. B. (S. 72) stehen in ihrer Wucherung noch den weich modellierten, Körper und Hohlräume verflechtenden Gebilden Emil Cimiottis nahe (S. 83). Während dieser jedoch ein Plastiker vegetabilischer und landschaftlicher Formationen blieb, setzte sich Hajek zu Beginn der sechziger Jahre mit der aktuellen Diskussion über die gesellschaftliche Relevanz der Kunst auseinander. Konsequent zielte er nun auf den öffentlichen Raum und vollzog eine Wendung zum Zeichenhaften: Skulpturen als Wegmarken, Richtungsachsen und Orientierungsbaken (S. 112). Sie erschöpfen sich nicht in autonomer Selbstgenügsamkeit, sondern nehmen, geometrisch einfach und buntfarbig klar erfaßbar, auf den Betrachter als gesellschaftliches Wesen Bezug – Signale eines auch die Kunst erfassenden demokratischen Aufbruchs. Auch Wilhelm Loth, der um eine elementare Gestaltung des Körperlichen rang (S. 70), brachte sie später zur Synthese mit geometrischen Figuren (S. 141).

Eine ähnlich radikale Wende vollzog in Württemberg Thomas Lenk. Wer sein Werk nur von den typischen Schichtungen aus quadratischen Platten mit abgerundeten Ecken her kennt, wird überrascht sein, daß auch auch er vom prozeßhaften Bilden geomorpher Strukturen ausging. Seine frühen Bronzen gleichen Strömen magnetisch gelenkter Kraftfelder. Sie wichen erst um 1963 einer strengen Disziplinierung durch geometrische Konstruktion, und im Jahre 1964 – für viele Künstler ein Wendepunkt im Zeichen internationaler Pop-art-Impulse – der Erfindung seiner Reliefschichtungen (S. 124). Monochrome Signalfarben steigern das einprägsame serielle Formprinzip.

Farbräume

Aus der Rückschau verdient die Tatsache Beachtung, daß nicht nur im Rheinland, sondern auch in Südwestdeutschland einige herausragende Maler aus der Abstraktion der fünfziger Jahre heraus zu konkreten Farbraumbildern gelangten. Das Beispiel der Amerikaner Ellsworth Kelly, Barnett Newman und Mark Rothko hat zwar in Europa nirgends zu so erhabenen, in ihrer Dimension den Betrachter überwältigenden Lösungen geführt, doch war es als folgenreicher Anstoß wirksam, abstrakte Raumillusionen in konkrete Farbräume zu überführen. Unabhängig von den Düsseldorfern Gotthard Graubner und Gerhard Hoehme näherten sich im Südwesten verschiedene Maler auf sehr individuelle Weise diesem Problem.

Die Berufung Georg Meistermanns an die Karlsruher Akademie im Jahre 1960 war hier gewiß wegweisend gemeint. Und doch erscheinen gerade Meistermanns abstrakte Kompositionen in ihrer sakralen Feierlichkeit (S. 106) eher wie Nachklänge eines Pathos der fünfziger Jahre. Im Bemühen, schwingendes Farblicht zu erzeugen, vertraute er nicht der Wechselwirkung reiner Farben, sondern einer fein modulierenden Pinselzeich-

Thomas Lenk: Landschaft 17. 1959/60

nung. Vielleicht ist es die Kultiviertheit solcher Feinstabstufungen, die dem großen Wurf mächtiger Vibrationen im Wege stand.

Folgenreicher war der Impuls der Jüngeren, deren Erfindungskraft durch die ausgelebte Freiheit des Informel von vornherein ungehemmter war. Maler wie der erwähnte Lothar Quinte und Bernd Berner hatten bereits in ihren Anfängen die Fesseln der Komposition abgeschüttelt und das Eigenleben der Farbe, die unmittelbare Kraft ihrer Erscheinung erfahren. Schon vor 1960 malte Berner, in Stuttgart tätig, »Flächenräume«, die Farbe in ihrer Substanz und Strahlkraft zur Erscheinung bringen (S. 109). Er entwickelte dabei Flächenformen, die in ihrer voluminösen Präsenz die Bildträgergestalt der prallen »Farbraumkörper« Gotthard Graubners vorwegnehmen. In vielfältigen Schichten übereinandergelagert, werden unterschiedliche Farben zu einem Unisono verdichtet, um ihre Schwingungen an den Rändern als aufgestaute Energie oder – ohne akustische Metapher – als Ausströmen in den Raum hinein sichtbar zu machen.

Von einem anderen Farbraummaler war schon im Zusammenhang mit dem Weg vom Informel zu geometrischer Abstraktion die Rede: Lothar Quinte, der um 1960 mit den Schleiernbilder seine wohl bedeutendste Werkgruppe geschaffen hatte (S. 108). Er überwand die Phase spontaner Pinselergüsse durch ein Verfahren vertikal gestrichener Übermalungen noch flüssiger Farbe. Durch solches Wegblenden faßlicher Motive erfand er seinen membranartig zwischen Bild und Betrachter erscheinenden Farbschleier, der im Auge den Eindruck verhaltener Vibration erzeugt. Konkrete Farbmalerei, in der nicht nur das Licht, sondern auch sein dämpfender Gegenspieler Schwingungen hervorruft – nichts bedeutend und doch Ausdruck einer hohen, meditativ zu nennenden Konzentration. Nicht zufällig ist Quinte in jüngerer Zeit zur Sparsamkeit seiner frühen Farbraumbilder zurückgekehrt, in der weniger die Form als die Erscheinung von Licht und Dunkel Gegenstand der Farbe ist.

In diesen Zusammenhang gehört als besonderes Zentrum gegenstandsloser Malerei auch die 1965 in Baden-Baden konstituierte Gruppe »Syn«. Beispielhaft steht hier als herausragende Position die Malerei von Rolf-Gunter Dienst. Ihre Eindringlichkeit beruht auf einem malerischen Verfahren, welches das Bildfeld als Tagebuch von Augenblicken mit zeilenweise fortgeschriebenen Zeichen füllt und belebt (S. 120). Ihre kleinste Einheit ist ein stetig wiederholtes, mit feinem Pinsel gesetztes Linienbündel, Zellkern eines auch im Betrachten nachvollziehbaren additiven Wachsens. Zeit ist ein wesentlicher Faktor dieser durchaus ornamentale Reize bietenden, aber durch ihre beharrliche Selbstvergewisserung vitalen Malerei.

Durch keine Gruppe getragen war schließlich der Einzelgänger Fritz Klemm. Sein Unterricht an der Karlsruher Akademie hatte für seine Malerei nur sekundäre Bedeutung. Fritz Klemms pastose Malerei wird überdauern, weil sie – in Deutschland

Gotthard Graubner: Farbleib. 1962

ohne Beispiel – nicht vom Informel, sondern vom stillebenhaften Ding her, zu einer Konkretion gefunden hat, die Ding und Bild zur Deckung bringt (S. 128). Weit über den regionalen Kontext hinaus orientierte er sich früh an Paris, wo Jean Dubuffet, Antoni Tapies und Nicolas de Staël Maßstäbe setzten, reagierte aber in den sechziger Jahren auch auf die amerikanische Minimal-art. Ihre Intensität verdanken seine Bilder der philosophischen Konzentration auf nahezu ein Motiv: die Wände des Ateliers, die in äußerster Reduktion eins wird mit der ikonenhaften Tafel, die es malerisch verkörpert (S. 129).

Neue Figuration

Der wichtigste Schub ging – einer Explosion gleich – um 1960 von der jungen Studentengeneration an der Karlsruher Akademie aus.

Daß Akademieschüler wie Heinz Schanz, Horst Antes, Walter Stöhrer und Franz Bernhard sich zur Avantgarde einer als »Neue Figuration« bekannt gewordenen Richtung entwickeln konnten, verdanken sie vor allem den Lehrerpersönlichkeiten HAP Grieshaber und Wilhelm Loth. Deren Lehrstil zeichnete sich dadurch aus, daß er die Schüler nicht in die eigenen Bahnen zwang, sondern ihre jeweils persönlichen Möglichkeiten zur Entfaltung brachte.

Anders als in Berlin, wo das Figurenbild wiederbelebt wurde, und anders als 1989 eine deutsch-amerikanische Wanderausstellung (in Toledo/Ohio, New York, Williamstown, Düsseldorf und Frankfurt) zu zeigen suchte, die den für die Karlsruher Szene geprägten Begriff der »Neuen Figuration« im Sinne neuer Gegenständlichkeit verwässerte, ging es hier um eine existentielle Neubestimmung der Kunst. Man diskutierte Sinnfragen, las Albert Camus und André Malraux. In den neuen Bildern taucht Figürliches nur in abstrahierter Form auf, denn das Interesse zielte nicht auf die Gestalt des Körpers, sondern auf seine Befindlichkeit. Kompromißlos machte man die eigenen körperlichen und psychischen Energien bewußt und bildhaft. Der Mensch wurde als Kraft- oder Spannungsfeld begriffen und entsprechend das Kunstwerk als dessen Zeichen.

Man berief sich auf expressionistische Vorbilder, aber es war weniger die Tradition der Brücke-Maler, die mit Erich Heckel als Karlsruher Lehrer nach dem Zweiten Weltkrieg und mit den Neuerwerbungen der Kunsthalle Karlsruhe ohnehin noch gegenwärtig war; bezeichnend ist vielmehr, daß Grieshaber als Beispiel einer existentiellen Kunst ein Bild von Paul Kleinschmidt als Ansporn in seinem Dienstatelier stehen hatte. Präsent waren aber auch die jüngeren Bewegungen, von der figürlichen Expression der Cobra-Künstler Karel Appel und Asger Jorn oder das Beispiel Willem de Koonings bis hin zum Abstrakten Expressionismus der Amerikaner (Abb. S. 14). Wichtiger als die nun leicht zugänglich gewordene umfassende Information durch Kunstzeitschriften und Literatur war für Initialzündungen die Begegnung mit Originalen internationaler zeitgenössischer Kunst. Besonders wirksam war die Ausstellung Francis Bacon 1962 in der Kunsthalle Mannheim. Nicht weniger forderten die Ausstellungen der Wiener Arnulf Rainer und Markus Prachensky (S. 116) der Karlsruher Galeristin Rottloff zur Auseinandersetzung heraus. In diesem Spannungsfeld verbot sich die Fortführung malerischer Strukturen des Informel ebenso wie ein bloßer Rückgriff auf den Expressionismus.

Wo Malerei so radikal in Frage gestellt war, entstand ein Nährboden für die Entwürfe eines neuen Menschenbildes, das weit über die Dynamisierung des Körpers hinaus zum Ausdruck seines Bewußtseins vordrang. Körper und Psyche, Außen und Innen wurden als Einheit erfahren. Sie forderte als Thema Künstler heraus, mit dem totalen Risiko des freien Falls die eigene Bewußtheit auszudrücken.

Kaum jemand hat dieses neue Selbst- und Werkverständnis treffender als Wilhelm Loth formuliert: »Indem also der Maler oder Bildhauer ein Spannungsfeld oder einen Spannungsraum aus Linien, Farben oder Massen herstellt – eine Energie-Sendestation also – bildet er die Natur nicht mehr ab. Er schafft neue Wirklichkeiten, die den Anspruch auf ihr Dasein nicht mehr von der Ähnlichkeit mit der »Wirklichkeit« (der Natur, des Lebens) herleiten. Der Mensch, so müßte man fordern, ist heutiger Wahrheit gemäß nicht mehr die deutlich umrissene Gestalt, sondern ein in stetiger Veränderung befindlicher Spannungsraum von Energien. Wir werden uns angewöhnen müssen, ihn so zu sehen.« (Wilhelm Loth, Zum Problem des Naturstudiums für Künstler – heute. Vortrag 1964, Karlsruhe 1965, S. 12).

Loth hat diesen Anspruch wohl in keinem Werk zwingender zum Ausdruck gebracht als 1959 in dem Torso einer sitzenden bzw. stürzenden Frau (S. 73). Während Rumpf und Schenkel kubisch blockhaft erscheinen, sind Arme und Haare als waagerecht ausgreifendes Gestängebündel abstrahiert. Es ist dieser hohe Abstraktionsgrad, an den fünf Jahre später sein Schüler Franz Bernhard anknüpfte, um mit einfachen Eisenstangen und Holzplatten menschliches Liegen und Lehnen, Aufrichten und Balancieren bildhaft zu machen (S. 137).

Asger Jorn: Orientation extrême. 1955/56

Arnulf Rainer: Übermalung ›Platschek‹. 1961. Galerie Rottloff

Noch größer war die Wirkung und Ausstrahlung Grieshabers – vor allem als Vorbild einer Haltung und durch sein unmittelbares Eingehen auf jeden Schüler. So hielt er keinen Klassenunterricht ab, sondern suchte seine Schüler reihum in ihren jeweiligen Ateliers auf. Die Intensität der Gespräche brachte in den malerischen Experimenten der Schüler Neues zum Durchbruch. Ihre Werke erinnern nicht an die des berühmten Holzschneiders der Nachkriegszeit. Analogien zu den Werken der Jüngeren mag man einzig in Grieshabers kaum für die Öffentlichkeit bestimmten Gouache-Malereien finden, deren lockere Kürzel den Geist der »Neuen Figuration« spüren lassen (S. 74). Doch den Keim dazu findet man im Werk eines anderen: Heinz Schanz, der wie Lothar Quinte mit dem Lehrer Grieshaber als einer der ältesten Schüler 1956 von der Hohenzollernschen Bernsteinschule an die Karlsruher Akademie überwechselte, malte schon 1958 Bilder von besonderer Intensität. Ihr Widerstreit von spontan gesetzten Figurenkürzeln und heftig sie übermalenden Pinselhieben (S. 71) nimmt vorweg, was Horst Antes nach 1960 zu eindrücklichen Akten verdichtete (S. 95).

Den inspirierenden Einfluß, den Schanz mit seinen frühen Bildfindungen auf alle Künstler um Grieshaber ausübte, bekennt Walter Stöhrer noch heute. Zugleich ist er derjenige, der diesen künstlerischen Ansatz expressiver Figurenabstraktion konsequent durchgehalten hat, ohne an malerischer Vitalität einzubüßen. Seit jeher begreift er in besonderer Weise das Bildgeviert als einen Ausschnitt aus einem Raumkontinuum. In den späten fünfziger Jahren kämpfte er zunächst mit Gittern heftiger Pinselhiebe, die im Auseinanderstieben den Blick zu verstellen scheinen, gegen den Kleinmut herkömmlicher Engmaschigkeit (S. 77). Anfänglich dürften ihn dabei die splittrigen Kompositionen des Venezianers Emilio Vedova und mehr noch die mächtig in den Raum greifenden Farbbahnen des Amerikaners Franz Kline beflügelt haben, dessen Werke ihn 1959 auf der »documenta« beeindruckten. In diesen Kompositionen der späten fünfziger Jahre kündigt sich bereits die Sprengkraft seines späteren malerischen Aufruhrs an. Noch in Karlsruhe entwickelte er die charakteristischen rotierenden Konvulsionen elementarer organischer Formen (S. 88), doch erst nach der Übersiedlung nach Berlin bekommen sie die inhaltliche, Malerei, Zeichnung und Schrift vereinende Schärfe, die ihn immer wieder zu einem abgründigen Selbstausdruck im Wechselspiel von Trance und Konzentration befähigen (S. 89).

Einen besonderen Weg ging der 1958 aus Halle nach Karlsruhe übergesiedelte Herbert Kitzel. Nach 1945 in der Kunstschule Burg Giebichenstein ausgebildet, ging er vom Figurenbild aus. In der Auseinandersetzung mit Anregungen durch die Karlsruher Szene entwickelte er Bilder von Körpern, die das Innere nach außen kehren und – nicht ohne Züge der Selbstauflösung – dem Lothschen Verständnis des Menschen als Spannungsfeld von Energien besonders nahekommen (S. 92). Im Unterschied zu den in westlicher Tradition geprägten Kollegen behielt für ihn die Formauflösung in viel höherem Maße einen auf die dingliche Realität bezogenen Sinn als Metapher kreatürlicher Verletzlichkeit.

Getrennte Wege nach 1964

Nie bildeten die mit der »Neuen Figuration« verbundenen Künstler eine Gruppe, und doch erscheint ihre Entwicklung von

Emilio Vedova: Dal Ciclo della Protesta ›53-5‹. 1953

Franz Kline: Four Square. 1956

etwa 1964 an wie deren Auflösung. Die älteren profilierten sich individuell, die jüngeren mieden von vornherein kollektive Bindungen. Einen besonderen Ansporn bildete die Pop-art mit ihrem Verzicht auf Zwischentöne, der Bildwürde des Banalen und plakativer Allgemeinverständlichkeit. Sie provozierte Auseinandersetzungen und Reaktionen.
Stärker als andere nahm Horst Antes seit 1964 Anregungen vor allem der englischen Pop-Art auf und stellte sich damit dem internationalen Vergleich. Seine nervigen Figurenabstraktionen (S. 75) wichen nun signalhaften Farben und festen Umrissen. Mit dem zu Flächenformen verknappten Kopffüßler erfand er die Formel für ein Menschenbild, das in seiner Deformation so irritierend wie eingängig erscheint. Die »Maskierte Figur« von 1965 (S. 87), im selben Jahr auf der Biennale in Venedig ausgestellt, wurde hieraus von der Hamburger Kunsthalle nicht als südwestdeutscher Sonderfall, sondern als herausragendes Werk deutscher Gegenwartskunst erworben. Anklänge an Picassos kubistische Verschränkung unterschiedlicher Körperansichten verbinden sich mit einer Silhouettierung, die an Richard Lindner erinnert. Eine zerlegte menschliche Gestalt fügt sich gleich einem Puzzle zur Kunstfigur zusammen. Gegenüber Pop-Künstlern gab Antes dabei zunächst die Dimension des Ausdrucks, in diesem Fall einer ironischen Mischung aus Bedrohung und Mißtrauen, nicht auf. Im Zenit der Pop-art ging aber auch er – weiter als andere im Südwesten – zum spielerisch heiteren Umgang mit einfachen Formen und signalhaften Farben über. Seine ironisch als Liege konzipierte Skulptur »Familie oder die Lust der Lust« z. B. (S. 97) schockierte als Teil eines bunten Ensembles 1967 durch erotische Anspielungen manchen Besucher der Karlsruher Bundesgartenschau.
Entgegengesetzt reagierte ein anderer Schüler Grieshabers auf die fortschrittsgläubige Zeit. Zugleich von Herbert Kitzel geprägt, unterläuft Dieter Krieg Virtuosität malerischer Illusion durch irritierende Störungen. Was sein Pinsel zu Zwittern von Dingen und Figuren vereint, sträubt sich gegen leichte Bekömmlichkeit (S. 96). Vertrautes wird zu Ausschnitten oder Arrangements verfremdet, die – weit über die Tradition der Surrealisten hinaus – allein schon durch die Materialität ihrer Farbe beunruhigen und abstoßen können. Die souveräne Beherrschung malerischer Illusion gibt den Bildern ihre besondere Kraft, und die List, mit der die Suggestion des Pinsels durchkreuzt wird, ihre verunsichernde Doppelbödigkeit. Ging solche Irritation in den sechziger Jahren noch von Zwittern aus Dingen und Figuren oder von der Wirkung verkrusteter Lackfarben aus, so lag sie später in der Diskrepanz zwischen nahsichtigem Stilleben und monumentaler Pastosität, Malerei und Schrift.
Einen besonderen Höhepunkt verdankt die südwestdeutsche Kunstszene der Berufung eines Malers an die Karlsruhe Akademie, der sich gegen alle Einflüsse aktueller Kunstströmungen, besonders der Pop-art, resistent verhielt. Auf eine sehr persönliche Weise führte Emil Schumacher in der zweiten Hälfte der sechziger Jahre weiter, was den Lebensnerv der »Neuen Figuration« ausgemacht hatte: Malerei als existentielle Aussage, aus der Bewegung und dem Atem des Körpers heraus realisiert und – bei aller zeichenhaften Abstraktion – noch bezogen auf die Themen Mensch und Natur (S. 139). Anders als Stöhrer und Krieg bedarf er keiner Dialektik von Bild und Text und baut allein auf die physische und optische Energie der Farbe in Verbindung mit zeichenhaften Kürzeln. Sie stellen Körper nicht dar, abstrahieren nicht ihre Gestalt, sondern sind als Ausflüsse seiner Bewegung Ausdruck physischer und psychischer Kraft. Die Formen, zu denen sie gerinnen, bleiben offen für mannigfaltige Assoziationen. Die Bögen und Doppelbögen auf Rot in der Ausstellung sind dafür in ihrer Bündelung geballter Vitalität besonders markant.

Richard Lindner: Plakat für die ›Paris Preview‹. 1965

Nur mit wenigen Beispielen konnte hier der Blick auf ein Jahrzehnt südwestdeutscher Kunst gelenkt werden. Die ganze Breite zu zeigen, war nicht das Ziel der Ausstellung. Aus der Perspektive des saturierten Jahrhundertendes erscheint diese Kunst wie ein explosiver Kraftausbruch der Neugier. Während damals Kosmonauten den Blick aus dem All auf die Erde lenkten, suchten die Künstler nach Selbsterfahrung und Selbstverwirklichung – jenseits aller Konventionen. Der Impuls war im Südwesten nicht weniger mächtig als im experimentierfreudigeren Rheinland. Gewiß, hier fehlte ein ausreichender Markt, der die Produktion langhin trug, und den mannigfaltigen internationalen Anregungen stand die Abwanderung mancher Hochbegabter gegenüber; aber die Werke sind geblieben und können als »Energie-Sendestationen« ihre Kraft jedem weitergeben, der sich ihnen offen stellt.

Anregungen verdanke ich Gesprächen mit Franz Bernhard und Klaus Gallwitz

ohne anfang ohne ende · Bilder zur deutschen Demokratie

Es mutet eigentümlich an: Die Tageszeitung Badische Neueste Nachrichten leitete ihre Berichte zu den Veranstaltungen anläßlich der 100-Jahr-Feier der Staatlichen Akademie der bildenden Künste Karlsruhe 1954 mit der Überschrift »Hüterin der badischen Kunsttradition« ein. Ihre Aufgabe sei es, »fundamentale Einsichten«, etwa die »Umformung der Naturform in die Kunstform« zu vermitteln und eine »möglichst universale Ausbildung zu garantieren«.[1] Kein Wort verlor der Verfasser über die Leistungen der Karlsruher Schule in den zwanziger Jahren, über die Kunst seit 1930 oder wenigstens seit 1945. Ganz selbstverständlich wurde Erich Heckels Spätwerk, obgleich es »etwas Nazarenisches bekommen«[2] hatte, mit dem Expressionismus der »Brücke« zu einem Kontinuum verbunden und den Akademiestudenten als vorbildliche Grundlage für die eigene Entwicklung anempfohlen. Der Verfasser G. schloß sich hierin dem breiten Strom der nationalen Kunstempfindung an, die via Max Beckmann, 1946 (!) und 1951 in München retrospektiv ausgestellt, zur deutschen Avantgarde des beginnenden 20. Jahrhunderts zurückfand.[3] Daß Heckel zu Baden – außer seiner Übersiedlung nach Hemmenhofen am Bodensee im Jahre 1944 – keinerlei Beziehung hatte, störte nicht weiter! In demselben Artikel wurde jedoch vor den »Einflüssen von außen«, die die »schöpferische Unruhe« im Innern stören, gewarnt. Welche »Einflüsse« von außen« mag G. wohl im Sinne gehabt haben: unbadische, undeutsche Vorbilder? Man möchte im Hinblick auf Heckels 71. Geburtstag, auf seinen besonderen Status als Lehrbeauftragter mit jährlich erneuertem Vertrag seit dem 1. Januar 1952 und den von ihm für das Wintersemester 1954/55 avisierten Ruhestand[4] fast an Warnungen vor einer Berufung des falschen Künstlers als Nachfolger, vor dem zunehmenden Einfluß der Pariser Schule und vor den dirigistisch verstandenen Entscheidungen des Kultusministeriums in Stuttgart denken. Wie berechtigt G.'s Sorge war, erwies für die badische Traditionalisten Grieshabers Berufung zum Sommersemester 1955. Auch der abwertende Blick auf die Stuttgarter Akademie als »Werkschule« wurde nicht versäumt, während sich die Karlsruher Akademie gerne als Schule der »freien Kunst« sah und ansehen ließ und somit ein Qualitätsgefälle zwischen Karlsruhe und Stuttgart suggerierte.

Just zur gleichen Zeit, als die Karlsruher Akademie ihr 100jähriges Bestehen feierte, wurde die Kunsthalle Baden-Baden dem Kultusministeriums Baden-Württemberg unterstellt, und ihrer Leitung ein paritätisch besetzter Beirat zugeordnet.[5] Damit war, zumindest formal, der Anspruch des »Verbands bildender Künstler Baden«, verbunden mit dem Hinweis auf die vom Stifter Engelhorn gedachte Zweckbestimmung der Kunsthalle,

Walter Stöhrer: Blumenstilleben. Um 1955

HAP Grieshaber (mit Lothar Quinte): Bauzaun, Akademie Karlsruhe. Um 1956/57

nach einer »nordbadischen Ausstellung« hinfällig geworden.[6] Zuvor hatte der unermüdliche Altmeister des badischen Porträtfachs und Karlsruher Vertreter der »Gemeinschaft Deutscher Künstler«, Oskar Hagemann, vergeblich eine »tolerantere Auffassung« und den Verzicht auf eine politische Abrechnung gefordert.[7]
Nach der Gründung des Bundeslandes Baden-Württemberg waren »altbadische« Forderungen allemal unklug geworden – wenigstens in der öffentlichen Meinung. Folgerichtig schlossen sich die »älteren prominenten Künstler des gesamten Landes« am 7. Februar 1955 zum »Künstlerbund Baden-Württemberg« zusammen. Seine erste Ausstellung wurde zwei Monate später in der Kunsthalle Baden-Baden eröffnet.[8] 85 Künstler, darunter 18 ehemalige Mitglieder der Badischen Secession, die auch die Hälfte des Vorstands stellte, allesamt wenigstens 40 Jahre alt, beteiligten sich mit 233 Werken. Die »Jungen« sollten erst einmal zeigen, was sie können, und wurden auf den Kunstpreis der Jugend 1955 verwiesen. Im Katalogvorwort lesen wir: Der Künstlerbund Baden-Württemberg »will auf baden-württembergischer Ebene, das heißt über das ganze neue Bundesland hinweg, jene schöpferischen Kräfte [...] sammeln, denen Qualität das vordringlichste Anliegen ist und die darum auch bereit sind, über die verschiedenen, in unserer Gegenwart besonders divergierenden Kunstrichtungen und Kunstbekenntnisse hinweg Qualität zu sehen und anzuerkennen, wo sie wirklich ist.« Die gemeinsame Plattform zur Lösung der regionalen Kunstkonflikte schien geschaffen zu sein. Ein Streitobjekt war und blieb jedoch weiterhin der Kunsthallenleiter Erwin Heinrich. Er hatte sich als treibende Kraft der Badischen Secession bis 1936 und nach 1945 hervorgetan und war 1952 nach Baden-Baden berufen worden.[9] Kurz zuvor hatte er mit Kurt Martins Unterstützung die zweite Nachkriegsausstellung der Secession in der Kunsthalle Baden-Baden eingerichtet. Hier auszustellen strebte die Künstlergruppe zwar schon seit ihrer Gründung im Jahr 1927 an, realisieren konnte sie sie jedoch erst jetzt.[10] Die auf Emil Bizers und Erwin Heinrichs Initiative hin von Leo Wohleb 1949 politisch durchgesetzte Gründung der Freiburger Akademie mit sechs Lehrern, deren vier der Badischen Secession angehörten, ist ebenfalls aus der bereits vor dem Krieg formulierten Absicht einer Aufwertung Südbadens gegenüber Nordbaden zu verstehen.[11] Insofern war der Secession nun ein unerwartet hoher Sieg gelungen, eine mehrfache Rehabilitation widerfahren – und ebendies war der entscheidende Ansatzpunkt der Kritik an Heinrich: Der Verband bildender Künstler Baden und einzelne Künstler, wie etwa Theodor Butz (Freiburg) und Oskar Hagemann (Karlsruhe), lehnten ihn wegen »Parteilichkeit« ab.[12] Die Formulierung ist sicherlich auch in politischem Sinne zu verstehen, denn Heinrich galt als »belastet«.[13] Selbst das Stuttgarter Ministerium, vertreten durch Wolf Donndorf, wollte die Nachfolge Heinrichs, der die Altersgrenze längst überschritten hatte, vorantreiben[14] und nominierte 1954 den von Kurt Martin empfohlenen Kunsthistoriker Ulrich Gertz (Darmstadt), der bis 1951 Leiter des Badischen Kunstvereins in Karlsruhe gewesen war. Im selben Jahr beschloß der Landtag die Auflösung der selbständigen Freiburger Akademie.[15] Zwei Jahre später wurde sie tatsächlich geschlossen, um als Außenstelle der Akademie Karlsruhe weitergeführt zu werden: Je eine Akademie pro Landesteil sei genügend! Natürlich empfanden die »Alt-Badener« diesen Eingriff als zerstörerischen Hieb der »Stuttgarter Zentralisten«, die um die gleiche Zeit die Bernsteinschule im ehemaligen Bezirk Südwürttemberg-Hohenzollern auflösten und ihren Lehrer HAP Grieshaber nach Karlsruhe beförderten.[16] In Baden-Baden fiel nach einer Stellenausschreibung und Heinrichs unerwartetem Tod am 3. Juli 1956 die Entscheidung für den Wahl-Baden-Badener Dietrich Mahlow gegen 16 Mitbewerber.[17] Mit ihm schloß sich der für die Freiheit der Kunst engagierte Kreis: Weder Stuttgart, noch Karlsruhe oder Freiburg waren zur Bühne für internationale Kunstabenteuer geworden, sondern das gleichsam unbedarfte Baden-Baden, dessen Kunsthalle zum Ausstellungshaus Baden-Württembergs erklärt wurde. Hier hatte sich im Grenzbereich der Besatzungsmächte, im Windschatten des savoir vivre und vor der polyglotten Historie der Stadt ein Zirkel aufgeschlossener Kunstfreunde gebildet, die in ihrer Begeisterung für junge Kunst geradezu ansteckend gewirkt haben mußten. Ungefähr ein Drittel aller Ausstellungen in der Kunsthalle von 1955 bis 1967 wurde unter der Mitwirkung der Gesellschaft der Freunde junger Kunst[18] oder von ihr federführend veranstaltet. Die unvergleichliche Zeitschrift Das Kunstwerk, herausgegeben in Baden-Baden, hatte bereits mit ihrer ersten Nummer im Jahr 1946 begonnen, sich kompromißlos für moderne und junge Kunst einzusetzen: Hans Kuhn, Kurt Martin und der Verlag stellten im Herbst 1947 unter dem Protektorat des Baden-Badener Oberbürgermeisters Dr. Ernst Schlapper »Deutsche Kunst der Gegenwart« vor. Immer wieder und fast überall begegnen wir Kurt Martin als unermüdlichem Verfechter einer neuen Kunst ohne heimattümelndes Gehabe: als Leiter des Landesamts für Museen, Sammlungen und Ausstellungen (1946–1953) in Freiburg, als Beiratsmitglied der Staatlichen Kunsthalle Baden-Baden (bis Februar 1957)[19], als federführender Berater für deutsche Ausstellungen im Ausland (veranstaltet von der Notgemeinschaft Deutscher Künstler, vom Deutschen Kunstrat, vom Auswärtigen Amt) und für die Dankspende des deutschen Volks an hilfreiche Personen und Institutionen im Ausland.[20] Theodor Heuss holte ihn 1951 in den Beraterausschuß, der die Festausstellung zum 100jährigen Bestehen des Germanischen Nationalmuseums vorbereitete;[21] 1955 wirkte er bei der Planung der ersten documenta in Kassel mit. Er war Mitbegründer des Internationalen Museumsrats ICOM und hielt neben der konservatorischen Aufgabe des Museumsbeamten seine pädagogische Arbeit in der Öffentlichkeit für besonders wichtig.[22] Hierin deckte sich sein Anspruch mit den politisch motivierten Vorstellungen der

Erich Hauser: Betonwände, T.H. Karlsruhe. 1960/61

O. H. Hajek: Ev. Pfingstbergkirche, Mannheim. 1962/63. (Arch.: C. Mutschler)

westlichen Besatzungsmächte: Demokratieverständnis spiegle sich im Umgang mit Kunst wider; je freier die Kunst, desto freier die Menschen – wie es ähnlich auch im Gründungsmanifest des Deutschen Künstlerbunds 1950/1951 formuliert worden war. Trotz aller Aktivitäten blieb Kurt Martin außerhalb des Rampenlichts.[23] 1958, nach seiner Übersiedlung nach München, wird er, gemeinsam mit dem ehemaligen Akademiedirektor und Architekten Otto Haupt, als »Kunst-Globke« bezeichnet, die beide »schon einmal [im Dritten Reich – Anm. der Verfasser] am Niedergang unserer Kultur mitgewirkt« haben.[24] Sind derartige Vorwürfe als typische Reaktion der verspäteten Antifaschisten und der bodenständigen Traditionalisten auf die Erfolge der jungen Kunst ausgangs der fünfziger Jahre gerade noch zu verstehen, so kann es aber heute nur noch als Verbohrtheit angesehen werden, wenn diese Rufmordorgien im Jahre 1993 abermals herangezogen werden, um die angeblich fatalen Folgen für den kulturellen Wiederaufbau im Südwesten aufzudecken.[25] Das öffentliche Desinteresse am künstlerischen Werk der »Unzeitgemäßen« und der »Realisten« kann freilich auch als Martyrium der Ausgeschlossenen verstanden werden.

Es schien schon etwas wunderlich, aus der ehemaligen Residenzstadt, die seit 1951 Sitz der beiden höchsten Gerichte war, eine Industriestadt entwickeln zu wollen. Karlsruhe suchte das Wirtschaftswunder, wollte den Anschluß an das Aufblühen der jungen Republik, und Karlsruhe wurde in den mittleren fünfziger Jahren zu einem der Motoren westdeutscher Industrialisierung. Günther Klotz, seit 1952 Oberbürgermeister, trieb die Industrialisierung voran, und 1956 sollten 267 Industriefirmen, davon 100 Neugründungen seit dem Krieg, Karlsruhe ein neues Image geben.[26] Es blieb das erzwungene Zusammengehen mit Württemberg als einem Land, und damit der Verlust des Karlsruher Hauptstadtcharakters. Dennoch blühte die Stadt auf, gewann an Selbstbewußtsein, doch künstlerisch wurden es vorerst Rückblicke aus badischer Sicht; dies spiegelten die Ankäufe der Stadt wider.[27] Auch die Ausstellung »100 Jahre Akademie Karlsruhe« galt eher der Rückwendung auf Badi-

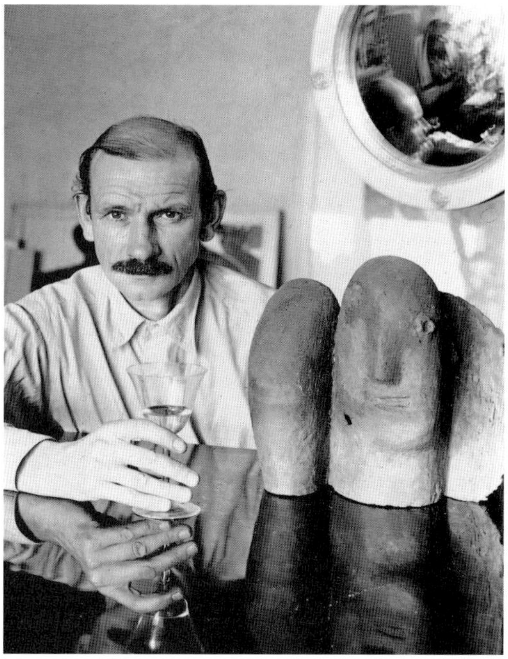

HAP Grieshaber mit der Büste ›Kopf 5/54‹ von Wilhelm Loth

sches,[28] boten doch allenfalls die Gemälde Fritz Klemms in ihrem an de Staël erinnernden Stil, Helmut Rehmes Abstrakta und Otto Laibles an Braque orientierte Gemälde etwas Modernität.[29]

Als HAP Grieshaber berufen wurde, konnte das Stuttgarter Kultusministerium annehmen, es werde nun endlich frischerer Wind in die hiesige Kunst geblasen[30] – sicher zur Freude des Direktors der Kunsthalle und Kosmopoliten Kurt Martin.

Diesem im Dritten Reich umsichtigem Verwalter und geschicktem Verhandler war es bis dahin vorbehalten, im amerikanisch besetzten Karlsruhe und im französisch besetzten Freiburg eine relativ moderne Kunstpolitik zu betreiben. So hatte er es mit Hilfe seiner Cousine Hilla Rebay geschafft, sogenannte gegenstandslose amerikanische Kunst nach Karlsruhe zu bringen.[31] Bis heute ist jedoch wenig dokumentiert, welche Rolle Kurt Martin im Kunstgetriebe der Zeit spielte.[32] Der von ihm sicherlich befürwortete Aufbruch kam in Grieshabers Person[33] über die Schwäbische Alb nach Karlsruhe hinunter.[34] Er nahm Heinz Schanz von der Bernsteinschule im Schwäbischen mit,[35] zog Lothar Quinte aus Reutlingen ab und an zu Aufgaben heran; und nun durchwehte mit seinen neuen Schülern die Akademie ein Zeitgeist, der sich am Badischen nicht orientierte, sondern auf Internationalität sann.

Es muß ein seltsamer Widerspruch gewesen sein: Statt der spätexpressionistischen Gemälde des Altmeisters Heckel stand nun im selben Dienstatelier ein expressionistisches Gemälde des von den Nationalsozialisten gejagten Paul Kleinschmidt.[36] Noch in der Bernsteinschule hatte es zwischen Grieshaber und Quinte des stilistischen Vorbilds wegen einen nicht mehr auszuräumenden Krach gegeben: »Der wollte aus uns allen deutsche Expressionisten machen«, so Lothar Quinte.[37] Die Akademie schuf sich damals einen Freiraum, der sie zum einen von der eher konservativen Stadtkultur abkoppelte, aber zugleich zum deutschen Kunstgeschehen beste Kontakte herstellte: Kurt Martin wußte geschickt seine Fäden zu knüpfen, HAP Grieshaber erhielt damit den notwendigen kulturpolitischen Spielraum.

Mit dem Kunstpreis der Stadt Karlsruhe wurden 1953 immerhin zwei moderne Künstler geehrt,[38] doch gelang es den traditionalistischen Kräften unter Führung Otto Gillens und Fritz Wilkendorfs, die unter badischer Fahne ihre Kleinmeisterei des Nationalsozialismus wieder hoffähig zu machen versuchten, weiterhin kulturell aktiv zu bleiben.[39] Ein zwittriges Klima also seit der Mitte der fünfziger Jahre: Auf der einen Seite eine industriell aufblühende Stadt, der das internationale Image gut getan hätte, auf der anderen Seite das Beharren im »Badischen« – Heile Welt und halb Wiedergutmachung in einem. Grieshaber spürte zwar das Wohlwollen des Kultusministeriums in seinem Rücken, aber die Kräche innerhalb der Akademie – zum einen die skandalöse Spindbemalung, die er mit seinen Schülern zum Ärger von Hausmeister und Direktion durchführte, zum anderen die Bemalung des Bauzauns mit Lothar Quinte 1956[40] rings um die Akademie, die er wegen des Einspruchs der Staatlichen Hochbauverwaltung wieder rückgängig machen mußte – machten ihm das Leben in Karlsruhe schwer.[41] Und innerhalb des Akademiekollegiums gelang es ihm nicht, Fernand Léger und Francis Bacon als mögliche Professoren durchzusetzen.[42]

Paul Kleinschmidt: Die Anprobe

Ernst Wilhelm Nay: Legende. 1943

Im Gegensatz zur Enge der Bernsteinschule hatte er in Karlsruhe keine unmittelbare Nähe zu seinen Schülern: Er stieg montags am Bahnhof in Karlsruhe ins Taxi und fuhr von Atelier zu Atelier, um bis Mittwoch über Kunst zu debattieren. Damit blieb das Atelier des ältesten Schülers, Heinz Schanz, Anlaufstation für die anderen, und Grieshaber wurde Diskussionspartner seiner Schüler, eher Anreger einer »Gruppe«, die letztlich keine sein sollte, da Grieshaber das System der Gruppe seit dem Faschismus suspekt war und Individualität einforderte. Es wuchs eine merkwürdige Mischung heran: Aus dem deutschen Expressionismus der zweiten Generation, aus dem Ende des Informel, aus den Anregungen der amerikanischen Kunst zwischen Jackson Pollock und Willem de Kooning wuchs eine Kunst, die sich bewußt vom europäischen Erbe abspaltete, da diese durch den Nationalsozialismus verbraucht worden war, und man absorbierte eher jene Kulturen, die verstärkt als außereuropäische Hochkulturen in Ausstellungen in Baden-Baden, in Zürich undundund gezeigt und in neuen Zeitschriften wie Das Kunstwerk publizistisch verbreitet wurden: präkolumbianische, chinesische, afrikanische Kunst[43] stillten den Hunger der jungen Leute nach dem Vakuum des Faschismus.

Die alten Schüler: unter ihnen Dreher, Wachter, Arnold, Baschang, Erhardt etwa, machten zum Teil den Wechsel mit, und Erhardt begann sich nach Heckel nun an Kleinschmidts Bildwelt zu orientieren.[44] Baschang ging einen Schritt weiter in die expressive Abstraktion, vor allem aber die »neuen« Schüler: Schanz, Antes, Stöhrer und Krieg wagten sich in Bereiche, die weit über das Grieshabersche Postulat hinausging, »Klee und Picasso zu meiden«:[45] Es entstanden damals aus jener Ursupppe abstrakter Gestaltung Bilder, die sich von allen historischen Bedingungen freimachen wollten und alle Ausdrucksformen zwischen einfacher Linie und fester Bildgestalt, Sprache und Stammeln, farbiger Fülle und terra ignota der weißen Leinwand umfaßten, kurz: aus dem allgemeinen Klima der Zeit und insbesondere in der Grieshaberklasse entstand eine Kunst, die man später mit dem falschen Begriff der Neuen Figuration belegte. Der Ausdruck war Teil der Strategie, aus dem Existentialismus der fünfziger Jahre auszubrechen und aus dem subjektiven Informel heraus eine neue Öffentlichkeit, damit mehr Objektivität zu entwickeln. Zwar wollte man durchaus das moderne, abstrakte Vokabular weiter benutzen, doch sollten die Bilder so wachsen, daß sie auf eine Allgemeinheit trafen, die Chiffren, Zeichen, Fragmente, Pictogramme und Strukturen lesen konnte. Damit entstand eine internationale Bildsprache. Sie nutzte schamlos, nämlich absichtsvoll, alle Möglichkeiten zum Kopieren, zum Umdenken, Vexieren, kurz, zum Lernen; sie zogen Kubistisches, Klassisches, Sprachliches, Sprachloses, Zeichenhaftes, Chinesisches, Psychisches in ihren Bann und bauten Bilder daraus: eindeutig, zweideutig, zwiedeutig innerhalb jenes Gemenges, das sich aus der neuen, globalen Weltsicht zu formen begann: Die Sprache der Demokratie: einfach und mehrfach zugleich zu sein, indem alles, wirklich auch alles verwendbar, wertbar wurde, ohne auf Wertungen alter Güte zu achten: positiv oder negativ, wer wußte es schon,[46] und aus dem Chaos, das einstmalen den Kubismus angesichts der erstarrten Welt bewegte, positiv herauszuwachsen.

Es ist zu konstatieren, daß Stöhrer, Antes, daß Krieg und Schanz bald künstlerisch weiter waren als Grieshaber, und Grieshaber suchte engagiert nach Möglichkeiten, seinen Schülern Ausstellungen und Verkäufe zu ermöglichen.[47] Grieshaber wünschte sich nun auch neue Professoren, und der in Halle eher »Beckmannsch« malende Kitzel wurde ebenso gewonnen wie der sicherlich von Kurt Martin empfohlene Wilhelm Loth, die dann beide die Neue Figuration in Karlsruhe mitentwickelten.[48] Bald waren Grieshabers Schüler und die neuen Professoren jenseits badischer Grenzen bekannt, in Karlsruhe hingegen kann man »sich des Eindrucks nicht erwehren«, schrieb Otto Gillen anläßlich der Professoren-Ausstellung im Kunstverein 1958, »als sei bei der Suche nach neuen Kräften für die Akademie allein der Grad der Abstraktion oder Deformierung maßgebend gewesen. Darauf ist es wohl auch zurückzuführen, daß man keinen badischen Künstler für wert und würdig erachtete, an die einzige badische Kunstakademie berufen zu werden, während man die meisten Professoren, die jetzt berufen werden sollen, hier nicht einmal vom Hörensagen kennt. Aber sie haben eins: sie sind moderner als modern.«... »Der Gesamteindruck ist der eines gewaltsam forcierten Avantgardismus, der manchmal bis an die Grenze des Chaotischen geht... In Frankreich, auf das man sich bei uns so gern beruft, ist man jetzt schon wieder weithin von der Abstraktion

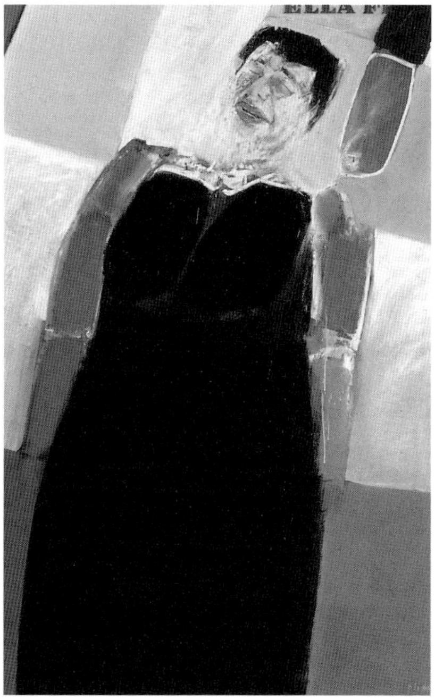

H. M. Erhardt: Ella Fitzgerald. 1960

abgekommen, deren Vertreter durchweg der älteren Generation angehören.«[49] Dieser journalistische Eingriff in Berufungsfragen der Akademie führte zur Forderung des Stuttgarter Kultusministeriums,[50] die neuen Lehrer sollten sich im Hinblick auf die negative Karlsruher Resonanz vor der Öffentlichkeit legitimieren.[51]

Um so deutlicher wurde, welchen Verlust für Karlsruhe der Wechsel Kurt Martins 1957 an die Bayerischen Staatsgemäldesammlungen in München bedeutete, Stöhrer etwa spürte diesen Stimmungswechsel so, daß er nach Berlin ging, denn insgesamt fehlte nun im Stuttgarter Ministerium der Fürsprecher Karlsruhes.

Heinz Schanz, seit dem Studium auf dem hohenzollernschen Bernstein mit Grieshaber, dann mit Quinte befreundet, hatte in Reutlingen bei den Schattenspielen und der Ausführung der Betonfenster von Lothar Quinte geholfen. Er war jedoch angesichts der politischen Aktivitäten Grieshabers und Quintes bei der Gründung DFU eher enthaltsam geblieben.[52] Er hatte allerdings bald eine eigenständige Malerei entwickelt, die sich schon damals dem näherte, was in Karlsruhe zu organischen Abstraktionen wurde.[53] Schanz wurde an der Akademie Zentrum der Aktivitäten, da er Grieshaber am besten kannte. Er entwickelte eine Selbständigkeit, die Antes, Baschang, Stöhrer und Krieg jene Distanz ermöglichte, ihrerseits einen eigenen Weg zu finden.[54] Er versuchte sich sogar bei Loth in der Bildhauerei, doch schienen ihm diese plastischen Experimente unergiebig.[55] So wurde Schanz auch künstlerisch zur Achse zwischen Grieshabers Figuration, dem neuen Lehrer Loth und dem heftig-deftigen Arbeiten seiner Mitschüler. Nach 1956 fand er zu einer grellen Malerei, die Expressives, Kubistisches und Primitives mischte: eher eine Malerei früher Hochkulturen als in der europäischen Tradition stehend. Es überrascht zunächst, daß sich die Motivik an Kindlichem orientiert: »Schreiendes Kind«, »Kinderspielplatz« usf. heißen die Titel. Diese grellen, kontrastreichen Bilder orientieren sich unerwartet stark an Klee, an Delaunay und Picasso. Sie stehen damit dem Verdikt Grieshabers entgegen, nicht hinter diesen herzulaufen. Es handelt sich zugleich um den »Vatermord« an Grieshaber, den dieser immer wieder gerne provozierte.[56]

Ein Jahr später wechselte Schanz in eine großflächige, derbe Malerei, der das Motiv mehr und mehr abhanden kam, er war erneut auf der Suche nach Möglichkeiten, wie COBRA und die amerikanischen abstrakten Expressionisten eine großflächige Abstraktion mit Rückgewinnung von quasiabbildlichen Zeichen zu finden. Hierin lag der Kern für die Ausprägung der Karlsruher Neuen Figuration, indem ungeschlachte Zeichen, Farbwirbel, Vernetzungen, Schlieren, Pinselhiebe und Psychogrammatisches auf der Leinwand entstand. Diese Malerei hatte Folgen für seine Mitschüler,[57] aber auch für Hans Baschang und dessen Lehrer Herbert Kitzel, den Kurt Martin 1957 als Hubbuchs Nachfolger empfohlen hatte.[58] Kitzels Malerei war zuvor von jener Tristesse bestimmt, die ihn rasch zum Existentialisten werden ließ, der seine seelische Spannungen in eine bedrückende Malerei übertrug. Unter dem Einfluß westlicher Lebensweise malte er in jenem Duktus Karlsruher Prägung, die seine Bilder grell leuchten ließ: eine offene, risikobereite Malerei,[59] die sehr schnell in eine bedrängende Motivik mündete.

Als Loth 1959 endlich in Karlsruhe eingetroffen war, zogen nun die meisten Professoren an einem Strang – der zwar konservative, doch immerhin kollegiale Schnarrenberger war damals bereits emeritiert –, man spürte wohl den Impuls, den man gemeinsam entwickelte. Auch Loth war noch von Kurt Martin lanciert worden, obgleich dieser damals bereits in München war.[60] Loth brachte bereits ein selbständiges Repertoire an offenen Formen und ein Formverständnis mit, das über Expressionismus und Kubismus weit hinaus ging, wie der Vergleich zur verehrten Kollwitz zeigt.[61] Bildhauer sind aufgrund ihres wenig erzählerischen, vergleichsweise engen Motivkreises gezwungen, Erzählformen in knappe Körpergesten zu übersetzen. Loth analysierte den menschlichen Körper kubistisch und schuf eine dynamische Körpersprache, die Expression und Symbolik so setzten, daß Bewegungskürzel und Körperteile zu einem abstrakten Vokabular aus Chiffren und Pictogrammen wurden. Aus Torsi schuf Loth idolhafte Figuren, deren Sensualistik sich freilich gegen die Tendenz zur völligen Abstraktion stemmte. Damals wurde Loth jener Bildhauer, der im Gegensatz zu Otto Herbert Hajek und Thomas Lenk im nahen Stuttgart, zu Norbert Kricke in Düsseldorf und Ernst Hermanns in Münster nicht in die kubische Abstraktion ging, weil er die menschliche Körperlichkeit fortführte[62], hier eher Joseph Beuys vergleichbar.

Käthe Kollwitz: Mutter und Zwillinge. 1927–1937

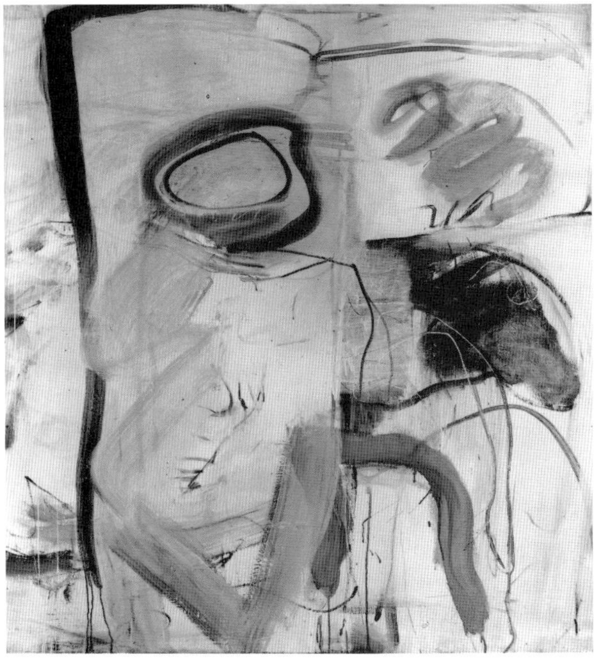

Dieter Krieg: Samantha. Um 1963/64

Peter Brüning: 49/63. 1963

In jenem Milieu körperhafter Abstraktion, das die drei Lehrer Grieshaber, Loth und Kitzel pflegten, gedieh eine Kunst, die sich bald von den Professoren, aber auch von Schanz löste. Sie wurde von Horst Antes, Walter Stöhrer und Dieter Krieg getragen, und sie begannen wie Schanz, suchten wie Schanz und kehrten, wie Schanz, in die Figuration ein, die sie allesamt nicht als Rückkehr in die feste Gestalt begriffen. Sie sahen Gestalt als offenes Feld. Auch untereinander wurden bald deutliche Unterschiede erkennbar, indem Antes den nahenden Strukturalismus begrifflich faßte, Stöhrer jede Form auflöste und deren Grundbestandteile als psychisches Alphabet formulierte,[63] Krieg eher abstrakte Landschaften schuf.[64] Damals begann bei Dieter Krieg jenes Vexieren zwischen Motivgebundenheit und freier Malerei, das seine Kunst bis heute auszeichnet. Die Malerei in Karlsruhe wurde avantgardistisch, doch blieb Karlsruhe selbst provinziell.

An der Karlsruher Akademie orientierte man sich nun nach Inhalten jenseits Badens und sucht Gleichgesinnte dort, wo man sie fand: 1959 auf der documenta II, bei der Gruppe Spur in München, bei der Gruppe Junger Westen im Düsseldorfer Raum um Gerhard Hoehme und Peter Brüning, nicht jedoch innerhalb von Kreisen des Konservatismus, so sehr auch neue Gruppierungen wie der Künstlerbund Baden-Württemberg Möglichkeiten des Austauschs außerhalb Badens geboten hätten. Der Künstlerbund oder die Badische Secession und andere Landesgruppierungen standen nicht zur Debatte,[65] die Diskussion verschob sich ins unbelastete Baden-Baden.

Der regionale Kunstpreis der Jugend wurde, auf Mahlows Betreiben hin, 1959 erstmals als Deutscher Kunstpreis der Jugend ausgeschrieben und durch eine international besetzte Jury vergeben. Träger des Preises waren das Kultusministerium Baden-Württemberg, die Städte Mannheim, Stuttgart und Baden-Baden; zwei zusätzliche Preise stifteten die Firma Josef Pankofer (München) und die Gesellschaft der Freunde junger Kunst (Baden-Baden). Der Pressespiegel war umwerfend: »Die totale Leere in der Badener Kunsthalle« (Stuttgarter Zeitung, 11. 9. 1959); »Die Gegenstandslosigkeit ist ein Zeichen für die Weltbildlosigkeit unserer Gesellschaft« (ebenda), »Man spürt den Leerlauf«, aber auch: »Sie [die jungen Künstler – Anm. der Verfasser] wollen das autonome Bild, die bildnerische Freiheit, den handschriftlichen Ausdruck, das Psychogramm« (beide Zitate Stuttgarter Zeitung, 12. 9. 1959); »Diese Jugend bringt nichts Neues, nichts Revolutionierendes. Sie zwitschert das, was die heute tonangebenden Alten sungen. [...]. Wir möchten vorschlagen, daß der Kunstpreis der Jugend in Zukunft auf das Land Baden-Württemberg beschränkt bleibt. Das Land selbst hat genügend qualifizierte Künstler, um ein optimales Ergebnis zu erzielen. Vorbedingung aber müßte sein, daß alle Richtungen, die unserer Zeit gemäß sind, zu Wort kommen.« (BNN, 14. 9. 1959); »Man muß schließlich der Jury das Zeugnis ausstellen, daß sie den Mut zu einer Wahl hatte, die Widerspruch erwecken wird« (Die Welt, 22. 9. 1959); »Abstrakter Nihilismus in Reinkultur« mit einigen passenden Leserbriefen, die entrüstet gesundes Volksempfinden widerspiegelten (Badische Neueste Nachrichten, 26. 9. 1959). Hatte man nicht gerade Ruinen, Hunger und Todesangst überwunden und zu einem neuen Heimatbild gefunden?! Wie anders hätten denn die despektierlichen Werke eines 23jährigen Horst Antes oder eines 21jährigen Walter Stöhrers wirken sollen? Gerade sie besaßen ja die subjektive Unvoreingenommenheit, die es

ihnen ermöglichte, ihre Vorbilder dort zu suchen, wo sie es für richtig hielten. Die Welt dieser Künstler bestand nicht nur aus Religion, Politik oder Kunstgewerbe, denen sich andere andienten, um gleichsam auf der sicheren Seite zu stehen, vielmehr wollten sie das Universum erobern, indem sie sich übermütig hineinwarfen – und dabei nicht untergingen. Dieser Aufbruch ins Universum schlug sich literarisch, musikalisch und technisch nieder: Jack Kerouac, ein professioneller Tramp, mit Allan Ginsberg Ziehvater der Beatniks, schrieb seine Pseudoreiseberichte »On the Road« (1957), von der Literaturkritik auch als »spontane Prosa« bezeichnet. Der erste Sputnik meldete sich 1957 von seiner Umlaufbahn um die Erde. Der Saxophonist Ornette Coleman veröffentlichte 1959 seine mit Don Cherry u. a. aufgenommene Langspielplatte »Change of the Century«, verglich im Plattentext die »ohne Anfang ohne Ende« konzipierte Musik mit Jackson Pollocks spontaner Malerei und markierte damit den Beginn des Free Jazz.
Franz Roh sprach vom »Decrescendo der Nationalkonstanten«[66] und betonte die Internationalität der modernen Kunst. Doch spüren wir heute auch die unterschwellige Sorge, die

Markus Prachensky: Rouge sur gris – Karlsruhe II. 1962

K.R.H. Sonderborg: »...abors von Karlsruhe«. Zeitungsausriß 1966

junge deutsche Kunst entspräche nicht der angestrebten Position gleichberechtigter Teilnahme im »Finger hakeln« der Großmächte:[67] Künstlerische Freiheit als Spiegelbild westlichen Demokratieverständnisses konnte sich nur in der Abstraktion niederschlagen, während der »Gänsemarsch der Realisten«[68] als Kennzeichen sozialistischer Kunst des sogenannten Ostblocks galt. Gerade diese Polarisierung aber führte die Kunst, mehr noch die Kunstbetrachtung in ein gesellschaftspolitisches Dogma, in dem sich das Wort von der Freiheit der künstlerischen Richtungen als Lippenbekenntnis erwies.[69]
Antes' preisgekröntes Gemälde »Bildnis« war in den Augen seiner Zeitgenossen zweifellos abstrakt, denn es folgte nicht dem gewohnten Porträttypus. Bezeichnenderweise wurde es aber als gegenständliches Bild beschrieben, als eine »vergröberte und unziemlich vergrößerte Kinderzeichnung« charakterisiert,[70] der Einsatz der Farbe als Brutalität empfunden.[71] Es ist in der Tat erstaunlich zu sehen, wieviel Wahrheit in den negativ gemeinten Beschreibungen steckt, wie sehr ideologische Verurteilung und emotionales Entsetzen ungewollt zugleich die

K.R.H. Sonderborg: Paris, 2. 4. 1966

Eindringlichkeit der jungen Kunst demonstrieren: Sie hatte sich schnell von den west-östlichen Vorgaben befreit und war in Karlsruhe zunächst unter Grieshabers, dann auch Loths und Kitzels Anleitung zu einer Sehweise gelangt, der später die Begriffe »Neue Figuration« und »Abstrakter Expressionismus« zugeteilt wurden. Folgen wir der von Jutta Held[72] am Beispiel Hofer-Grieshaber dargestellten Entwicklung zu einer »rudimentären Menschlichkeit«, einer »beherrschten Reduzierung« und ergänzen sie einerseits durch Hans Thoma, andererseits

z. B. durch Horst Antes, dann hat sich sogar die von Otto Gillen geforderte Funktion der Karlsruher Akademie als »Hüterin der badischen Kunsttradition« trotz aller Einflüsse von außen erfüllt; wenn auch im anderen Sinne als von Gillen gehofft: Nicht die »Kunstrichtung« wurde tradiert, sondern der élan vital, der es schaffte, akademische Trampelpfade zu verlassen, unversöhnliche Positionen zum Streit von gestern zu machen, und zugleich einen neuen Traditionsstrang schuf, der über Berlin nach Karlsruhe zurückfinden wird.[73]

In Karlsruhe hatte derweil eine neue Galerie ihre Arbeit aufgenommen: die Galerie Gallwitz,[74] die sich der Kunst im südwestdeutschen Raum verschrieb und als willkommne, weil moderne Ergänzung der Kunstangebote in der Stadt gesehen wurde, sicher auch deswegen, weil dies nach dem Weggang Kurt Martins als notwendig erkannt wurde. Und als Gallwitz dann seit 1959 bis 1966 den Badischen Kunstverein Karlsruhe übernahm, wurde auch dieser aus seinem Provinzialismus gerissen.[75] Auf diese Weise behielt Karlsruhe Anschluß an die Moderne, zumal Helgard Rottloff 1961 in Karlsruhe wiederum eine Galerie für zeitgenössische Kunst eröffnete, deren Anspruch noch weiter als jener der Galerie Gallwitz der Internationale galt, ein Ansatz, der sich leicht aus Rottloffs Studium bei Grieshaber und dem Bekanntenkreis auch ihres Mannes, Lothar Quinte, verwirklichen ließ.[76]

Georg Karl Pfahler und Helgard Rottloff, Galerie Rottloff. Um 1962

Galerie Rottloff, Karlsruhe. Um 1962

In diesen wenigen Jahren vor 1960 hatte sich eine Gruppe gebildet, die Grieshaber später als »meine Schule« bezeichnete und in der ein offenes Experimentieren möglich wurde.[77] Doch das mühsame Gleichgewicht zwischen den alten und neuen Professoren zerbrach bald, nachdem Kurt Martin Karlsruhe verlassen hatte. Grieshaber sah dies voraus[78] und erwog seitdem auch den Gedanken an einen Verzicht auf die Professur.[79] Die Schelte während der Professoren-Ausstellung 1958 war eher nur ein Vorgeschmack auf die Ereignisse des Jahres 1960: Der durch die nationale Presse bekannt gewordene Skandal an der Karlsruher Akademie bestand zunächst darin, daß das Prüfungsergebnis einer Prüfung Grieshabers von der Direktion der Akademie ablehnt und so die Prüfungsbefähigung Grieshabers bestritten wurde. »Man wollte ihm die Meinung sagen, daß er nicht König sei«,[80] war die spätere Einschätzung von Heinz Schanz über das Vorgehen des Akademiedirektors Gaensslen und wohl auch Fritz Klemms, die gegen Grieshaber Stellung bezogen.[81] Ein anderer Vorfall, der Grieshaber kurz zuvor in Rage gebracht hatte, bestand darin, daß Josua Reichert, den er als neuen Schüler aufgenommen hatte, der Arbeitsplatz verweigert worden war. Kurt Martin schilderte, Grieshaber sah dadurch »die Freiheit der Lehre in Karlsruhe nicht gewährleistet, und er gab deswegen seine Professur auf«.[82] Viel bedeutsamer war jedoch Grieshabers energische Absicht, die hieratische Form des vom Ministerium eingesetzten Direktors durch ein Rektorat zu ersetzen, um so die Selbstverwaltung der Akademie zu erweitern – und damit hätte er zugleich Gaensslen entmachtet.[82a] Da Grieshaber nun bei beiden kleineren Problemen keine Unterstützung vom Ministerium erfuhr, befürchtete er um so mehr, daß die Umwandlung der Direktionsstelle in ein Rektorat scheitern würde.

So wurde 1960 ein für die Karlsruher Kunst folgenschweres Jahr, indem der Motor für die Auseinandersetzungen um eine neue Kunst in Karlsruhe letztlich stehenblieb. Lothar Quinte zog sich nach Lauterburg zurück,[83] Walter Stöhrer ging nach Berlin.

Georg Meistermann, Vorsitzender des Deutschen Künstlerbundes und wie Grieshaber ein kulturpolitisch sensibler und aktiver Zeitgenosse, kam an dessen Stelle als Professor für Monumentalmalerei; er wurde zugleich vom Kollegium in die Position des Rektors gewählt. Damit hatte die Akademieverwaltung die Autonomie gegenüber dem Stuttgarter Ministerium erlangt, die von Grieshaber so lange angestrebt worden war: Er hatte letztlich gewonnen.

Es hätte nun ein ähnlich innovativer Schub erfolgen können, wenn Meistermanns Schüler Gotthard Graubner und Raimund Girke mit ihrem Lehrer nach Karlsruhe gekommen wären,[84] doch allein Karlheinz Overkott zog mit in den Süden, einer der ersten aus dem deutschen Westen, die wie Peter Herkenrath (1962) und Emil Schumacher (1966) nach Karlsruhe kamen – freilich mit relativ geringem innovativem Schub. Bert Jäger blieb in Freiburg, und ihn hat Karlsruhe nur randläufig interessiert.[85] Er reist schon früh nach Paris, wo er sich fürs Cabaret und den Jazz interessierte, weniger für die »Ecole de Paris«, eher noch für die klassische Moderne und für Soutine.[86] In den frühen fünfziger Jahren lebte in Freiburg Gunter Fruhtrunk, vor allem aber Walter Schelenz, und die Aktivitäten des dortigen Kunstvereins wirkten befruchtend – weniger die Akademie. Und Jäger, dessen Malerei sich zusehends zur Avantgarde hin bewegte, fand seine Interessen daher eher auf Reisen in die Schweiz, nach Italien und nach Frankreich. 1960 wurde er Mitbegründer der Freiburger »Galerie 61«, in der Horst Antes

Galerie Rottloff, Karlsruhe 1962 (mit Springer, Quinte, Rottloff, Dorazio, M. Prachensky, Müller, Prachensky)

präsentiert wurde, und 1962 besuchte er mit Willy Kiwitz, mit dem er befreundet war, die Biennale in Venedig: er hatte schon vorher in Freiburg Emilio Vedova kennengelernt, hatte dort auch die Gruppe »Geflecht« mit den Münchner »Spur«-Leuten um Heimrad Prem kennengelernt, kurz, es hatte sich um diesen wie Stöhrer eher strukturalistisch arbeitenden Künstler ein Kreis entwickelt, der keinesfalls badisch, sondern international dachte – bei Jäger ebenso wie bei Grieshaber aus den Erfahrungen des 2. Weltkrieges heraus.

An Karlsruhe ging ein Gutteil der künstlerischen und politischen Aktivitäten vorbei. Die Schwerpunkte verlagerten sich nach Baden-Baden und auch nach Stuttgart, wo sich zum Beispiel um die Galerie Müller ein neuer Brennpunkt ent-

Galerie Rottloff: Piero Dorazio und Helgard Rottloff

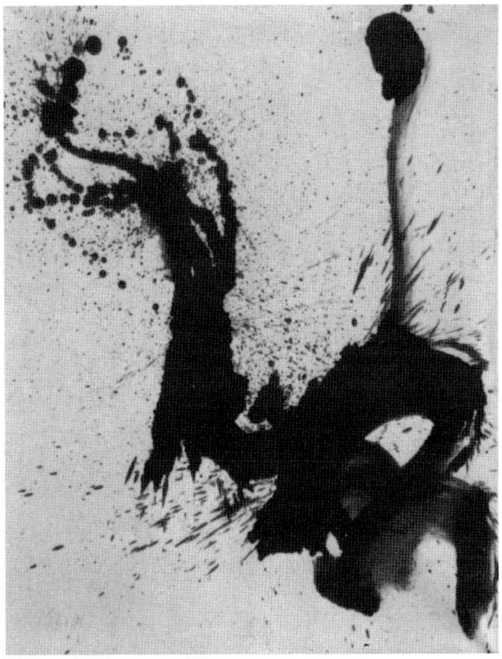

Markus Prachensky: Rouge sur gris – Karlsruhe 1. 1962

Galerie Rottloff: Heiner Ruths spricht

wickelte. Es erwies sich für die Karlsruher Galerie Rottloff mit ihrem durchaus ambitionierten Programm als immer schwieriger, in Karlsruhe ein nennenswertes Publikum zu finden, ihre Käufer kamen eher von Stuttgart als aus der eigenen Stadt. Allein durch die Entwicklung eines ebenso ambitionierten wie heute fast unbekannten Graphikprogramms gelang es Helgard Rottloff, sich auf dem Markt zu etablieren und zugleich mit ihren Massen-Auflagen in ein Programm zu kommen, das später über den Kaufhof vertrieben wurde – und letztlich aus Ärger anderer Galerien zur Entstehung des ersten Kunstmarktes in Köln beitrug:[87] »Ich stellte eine komplette Edition von 50 Auflagen à 50 Exemplaren für den Konzern zusammen mit Künstlern außer den bereits genannten (Quinte, Pfahler, Piene, Mack, Uecker, Gaul, Hauser, Lenk, Richter, Dorazio, Hajek) wie Antes, Schultze, Hoehme, Dahmen, Schumacher, Geiger, Stöhrer, Kitzel, Brüning usw. Im Mai 1966 wurde gleichzeitig in Düsseldorf, Köln und München in den Häusern des Kaufhofes die neue Abteilung eröffnet. Womit ich damals nicht rechnete, war die Empörung der Kollegen. Rudolf Zwirner, Köln: ›Wir können es nicht zulassen, daß die Konzerne mit Kunst handeln – zuerst Graphik – dann Bilder. Uns fehlt das Kapital, konkurrenzfähig zu bleiben.‹ Er setzte sich mit den Galeristen Müller, Springer, Brusberg, Ricke, Thomas, Stünke, Schmela zusammen – es entstand der erste Kunstmarkt in der ganzen Welt überhaupt im Herbst 1967 in Köln.«[88]

Wie ein i-Punkt wirkt die peinliche Auseinandersetzung mit dem »Garten der Lüste« von Horst Antes zur Bundesgartenschau 1967, bei der sich sowohl der Leiter des Kunstvereins, Klaus Gallwitz, als auch der Künstler vor einem städtischen Publikum legitimieren mußte. Es wurde eine Hetzkampagne, die jener anläßlich der Professorenausstellung 1958 in nichts nachstand und ebenso von Otto Gillen ausgeschlachtet wurde.[89] Karlsruhe war fast ins künstlerische Abseits geraten – dies zu einem Zeitpunkt, als Horst Antes an der Akademie Professor werden sollte, und Emil Schumacher gerade Professor geworden war.

Für Karlsruhe ging eine wichtige Ära zu Ende: Die Ära Klotz, in der aus der Verwaltungsstadt ein Industriezentrum wurde, brachte den Einzug der Moderne in die so konservative Stadt. Er hatte mit Grieshabers Elan begonnen und wurde mit der Kraft vor allem seiner Schüler und Wilhelm Loths weitergeführt, und letztlich konnten die Provinzpossen dieser Entwicklung insgesamt nichts anhaben – Karlsruhe jedoch war betroffen, da sich hier kein Kunstzentrum mehr etablierte. Die Öffentlichkeit, sei es in Baden, sei es in Deutschland insgesamt, nahm denn auch letztlich vom Kulturstreit zwischen Baden und Württemberg kaum mehr Kenntnis: Diskussionen über die Kunst in den Metropolen und in der Provinz nahmen innerhalb des deutschen Föderalismus einen anderen Verlauf.

Ausstellung O. H. Hajek: Farbwege. (op)art Galerie Esslingen 1966

O. H. Hajek: Universität Saarbrücken. 1965–70. (Arch.: K. Schrempf)

Impuls Südwest?

Seit Mitte des letzten Jahrhunderts die damalige politische Linke damit scheiterte, vom Südwesten aus Deutschland zu republikanisieren, ist diese Region im Bewußtsein der deutschen Öffentlichkeit mehr und mehr an den Rand gerückt. Das galt für die Epoche des Kaiserreichs, verstärkt für die Zeit der Weimarer Republik und änderte sich auch nicht während des »Tausendjährigen Reiches«, was allerdings kein Unglück ist. Die Randlage Badens, die sich bis weit ins 19. Jahrhundert durch den engen Kontakt mit Frankreich und der Schweiz zumindest in kultureller Hinsicht vorteilhaft erwiesen hatte, war in den folgenden Jahrzehnten der Konfrontation mit dem zum »Erbfeind« erklärten Frankreich immer deutlicher ins Negative umgeschlagen. Die Folgen des Ersten Weltkriegs trafen diese Region besonders hart. Die Rückgabe des Elsaß an Frankreich, mit dem Baden vorher eng verflochten war, und die wiederholte Besetzung durch die Siegermacht sorgten für einen Exodus bei Wirtschaft und Bevölkerung, von dem sich das Land vor 1945 nicht mehr erholen sollte. Wer etwas werden wollte, Ideen hatte, ging damals besser nach Berlin.

Die Jahre nach der deutschen Niederlage im Zweiten Weltkrieg veränderte diese Situation jedoch grundlegend. Sowohl die Aussöhnung wie das neuerwachte Interesse am Nachbarn Frankreich, ja die Westorientierung der entstehenden Bundesrepublik überhaupt, führten Baden aus der Isolation und gaben ihm seine natürliche Funktion als Vermittler zwischen den südlichen und westlichen Nachbarn einer- und Deutschland andererseits zurück. Erst auf Grundlage dieser veränderten Nachfrage und wiedererwachten Aufmerksamkeit waren Impulse aus dem Südwesten überhaupt wieder möglich. Denn Aufnahmebereitschaft beim Adressaten ist eine der wesentlichen Voraussetzungen dafür.

Aber war die bundesdeutsche Gesellschaft der fünfziger Jahre nicht mit anderem beschäftigt? In gesellschaftlicher Hinsicht gelten die ersten Jahrzehnte der Republik heute weithin und nicht zu Unrecht als »bleierne Zeit«, die sich jenseits politischer Sonntagsreden nur so weit mit der nationalsozialistischen Epoche auseinandersetzte, wie es notwendig erschien, um sich das Wohlgefallen der – westlichen – Sieger zu sichern. Auf Homosexuelle, Kommunisten und andere mißliebige Gruppen oder Personen machte man hingegen fröhlich weiter Jagd wie zu Hitlers Zeiten, teils sogar noch mit dem seinerzeit geschaffenen rechtlichen Instrumentarium. Reichlich brauner Mief und Stammtischspießigkeit waberten unterm Petticoat, das zu lüften sich nur hin und wieder Kabarettisten, etwa die Berliner »Stachelschweine« oder die Münchner »Lach- und Schießgesellschaft« trauten. Die als Teepuppen verkleideten Damen und die Herren im dunklen Anzug mit Hornbrillen verschluckten sich da höchstens am Sekt.

»Hier kommt das Wirtschaftswunder! Der deutsche Bauch saniert sich auch und ist schon sehr viel runder...«, sang Wolfgang Neuss und die Gesichter strahlten selbstzufrieden. Man war wieder wer und zeigte es, ob mit dem Urlaub an der Riviera, Borgwards Isabella oder schlichter Teilhabe an der Freßwelle. Konsum lautete das Bekenntnis jener Tage, und bitte schön, ungestört. Die ideale Voraussetzung also, um eine Wahl mit dem Spruch »Keine Experimente!« haushoch zu gewinnen. Ein Bundeskanzler, der auf Eseln reiten und Boccia spielen konnte, soviel Weltläufigkeit hätte man uns gar nicht zugetraut, was? Zeiten der Selbstzufriedenheit sind jedoch äußerst ungünstig als Basis kultureller Impulse. Das gilt für nahezu alles, was damals die Massen in seinen Bann schlug: den Heimatfilm a la »Geierwally«, den deutschen Schlager a la Rudi Schurike oder den Traum vom eigenen Auto.

Dennoch gab es in dieser Zeit Impulse in der kulturellen Entwicklung, die über die Rezeption des in den zwölf braunen Jahren Versäumten und Verpaßten ebenso hinauswiesen, wie über die staatlich geförderte Tendenz der Wiedergutmachung an den einst davongejagten Künstlern der klassischen Moderne von Erich Heckel bis Mies van der Rohe, die lediglich ein Anknüpfen an den Status Quo Ante ermöglichte. So bedauerlich es ist: Ihre Präsenz in wichtigen Positionen des kulturellen Lebens wirkte überwiegend bremsend auf die weitere Entwicklung. Oft war es erst die Emeritierung dieser Dinosaurier, die eine zeitgemäßen Tendenzen entsprechende Neuorientierung ermöglichte.

Die wesentlichen Impule gingen hingegen wie so oft in der Geschichte nicht von der Begegnung mit der eigenen Vergangenheit, sondern der mit dem Fremden aus: die Amerikaner brachten eben nicht nur den Chewing-Gum und Rock'n'Roll, sondern auch den Jazz mit. Die Amerikahäuser mit ihren Bibliotheken und Veranstaltungen waren in den ersten Nach kriegsjahren die wichtigsten Kulturinseln im Meer der Verwüstung. Schwarze amerikanische Soldaten ließen den bislang als Inbegriff unheimlicher Exotik geltenden »Neger« zum selbstverständlichen Bestandteil des alltäglichen deutschen Straßenbilds werden. Amerikanische Filme vermittelten unter anderem den Prototyp des zornigen jungen Mannes, wie ihn Marlon Brando in »Endstation Sehnsucht« verkörperte, ein Vorbild, das von den »Halbstarken«, wie man die nicht konformen Jugendlichen damals nannte, begeistert nachgeahmt wurde – selbst wenn man dafür die weiter ausgeschnittenen deutschen Unterhemden verkehrtherum tragen mußte.

All das Fremde, Neue, Unbekannte wurde besonders von der jüngeren Generation nach den Jahren der Abschottung förmlich aufgesogen. Man drängte sich in den Ausstellungen und in den Jazzkellern, aber auch die Medien befriedigten den Hunger nach ausländischen Themen und Schauplätzen. »Internationalität« war angesagt. Die Zeitungsfeuilletons quollen über von Berichten über andere europäische und sogar exotische Länder, im Radio besang man mindestens Capri oder den Seemann und dessen Heimat, das Meer. Der deutsche Film begab sich höchstselbst auf die Jagd nach dem »Tiger von Eschnapur« und im nagelneuen Fernsehen hießen die Lieblinge des noch raren Publikums Catarina Valente oder Vico Torriani. Hieß man hingegen nur Peter Frankenfeld, so bedurfte es zumindest auffällig karierter Jacketts, damit sich die Zuschauer fühlen konnten »wie in Amerika«.

Gerade die damals viel intensiver als heute gepflegte Begegnung mit dem ehemaligen Feind und jetzigen Freund Frankreich erwies sich als produktiv. Hier war mit Schriftstellern wie Sartre, Camus und St. Exupéry, Dramatikern wie Anouilh oder Ionesco, Filmemachern wie Jean Renoir und René Clair längst eine Generation herangewachsen, die die Moderne der zwanziger Jahre alt aussehen ließ. Mit dem Nihilismus kam, nach der abstrakten Kunst der Moderne, nun die gegenstandslose Kunst. Aber auch der italienische Neorealismus vermittelte hauptsächlich über die Filme Rossellinis, de Sicas und Viscontis wesentliche Anregungen. Die fünfziger Jahre sind eben nicht nur die »bleierne Zeit«, sondern auch die Epoche, in der sich die Revolte der sechziger vorbereitete, aus deren ungelösten Spannungen sie ihre Sprengkraft bezog.

Die Distanz hat uns gelehrt, daß nicht alles, was damals geschaffen und später unter den Nierentisch gekehrt wurde, wirklich so kleinbürgerlich spießiger Tand war. Von den ›Fliegenden‹ Dächern bis zur Melitta-Kanne wurde vieles geschaffen, das erst aus dem Abstand in seiner ganzen ästhetischen Kraft und Gültigkeit erkennbar wird.

Impuls aus Karlsruhe?

»Karlsruhe kennen...« so begann ein Spruch, mit dem die Stadt Karlsruhe in den siebziger Jahren für sich warb. Ähnlich wie der Slogan »Partner der Welt« einer gewissen Landeshauptstadt deckte er jedoch eher Defizite auf. Um Karlsruhes Bekanntheit war und ist es in der Republik und darüber hinaus nicht zum besten bestellt. Lediglich auf juristischem Gebiet bringt sich die Stadt bei spektakulären Entscheidungen der höchsten Gerichte der Bundesrepublik hin und wieder in Erinnerung. Doch selbst wenn man großzügig ist und das spektakuläre Kruzifixurteil der jüngsten Zeit als Anstoß zu einer ästhetischen Grundsatzdebatte über die Gestaltung von Klassenzimmern wertet, ist Karlsruhe im allgemeinen kein Schauplatz überregional beachteter kultureller Produktion.

Der heute allenthalben gern herbeizitierte »Genius loci« verspricht ja auch nicht gerade Spektakuläres. Karlsruhe gilt seit langem als »Beamtenstadt«. Was immer sich die Anwender dieses Begriffes konkret darunter vorstellen mögen, man assoziiert automatisch das Flair eines gediegenen Seniorenstifts, behaglich, aber fade und ein wenig stur. Innovative oder gar avantgardistische Impulse für das kulturelle Leben »draußen im Lande« stehen nicht zu erwarten, eher die etwas verspätete Rezeption dessen, was einmal Trend war, längst Allgemeingut ist und deshalb gern als »klassisch« bezeichnet wird. Heiße Themen läßt man in dieser Atmosphäre erst einmal abkühlen, bevor man sie in kleinen Schlückchen goutiert.

Die Kontinuität des Konservativen ist tatsächlich ein vorherrschender Zug in der Karlsruher Stadtgeschichte. Die bürokratische Tradition der geborenen Residenz und der zu ichbezogener Bequemlichkeit neigende badische Charakter ergänzen sich hierbei vortrefflich. Auf Karlsruhe färbte weder 1789, 1849 oder 1919 die revolutionäre Aufgeregtheit der Zeitgenossen ab, taten sich weder die einheimischen Politiker noch die Künstler je mit innovativen Großtaten hervor, immer wieder nur die Techniker: Karl Friedrich Drais, Johann Gottfried Tulla, Emil Kessler oder Carl Benz heißen typischerweise die Söhne dieser Stadt. So wie im Grundriß ihres Gemeinwesens scheint den Karlsruhern der Zirkel oft im Hirn zu stecken, bestimmen Sachlichkeit und Wirtschaftlichkeit die Tagesordnung.

Wenn schon Kunst, so war es in dieser Residenz meist die große (in Quadratmetern), laute (Richard Wagners Opern) und repräsentative (im oft falschen Glanz einer Theaterdekoration), die wohlgelitten war.

Gerade zum Theater hatte man stets ein enges Verhältnis. Mangels langer Geschichte und Bedeutung wurde in Karlsruhe ja von Anfang an inszeniert. Von den in Ziegelrot gestrichenen Holzhäusern der Frühzeit über die (für eine Stadt mit damals 8000 Einwohnern bombastische) Marktplatzplanung samt »Via triumphalis« bis zur neogotischen Bernhardskirche: Symbolik in Übergröße. Was zu Weinbrenners Zeit meist an knappen Finanzen scheiterte, brach sich im letzten Drittel des Jahrhunderts Bahn in der unproportionierten Neorenaissance des Architekten Josef Durm oder den so virtuosen Historienschinken des Malers Ferdinand Keller, der stilvollerweise in einer transsylvanisch angehauchten Phantasie des Stararchitekten hauste. Das Pathos jener Jahre wirkt heute so überzeugend wie der Empire-Thronsaal im Schloß oder die badische Krone: Pailletten und Goldbrokat auf Pappmachee.

Avantgardistisches war beim Karlsruher Publikum hingegen meist einen Skandal wert, etwa 1910, als im Badischen Kunstverein Werke von Picasso, Braque, Jawlensky, Kanoldt und Kandinsky präsentiert wurden, oder Ende 1929, ausgelöst von dem aus aktuellen Produktionen bestehenden Zyklus »Zeittheater« des Landestheaters. Der Neues meist abweisende Karlsruher Charakter zeigt allerdings Aufgeschlossenheit in einem Punkt: dort, wo Technik und Ästhetik einander berühren und durchdringen, ist man offen für Zukunftsweisendes. Das gilt von Weinbrenners minimalistischem Klassizismus über

die Dammerstocksiedlung von 1929 – vorgestellt unter dem Titel »Die Gebrauchswohnung« – oder die Schwarzwaldhalle bis hin zur Konzeption des in den achtziger Jahren entstandenen Zentrums für Kunst und Medientechnologie ZKM.
Auch wenn diese Phänomene nur sporadisch zu nennen sind, sie haben eines gemeinsam: alle entstanden in einer Umbruchphase, in der die Stadt sich gezwungen sah, Weichen für eine veränderte Zukunft zu stellen. Am deutlichsten und radikalsten war der Umbruch in den fünfziger Jahren. Sein »Leitfossil« ist die von Schelling 1953 erbaute Schwarzwaldhalle, deren Konstruktion ein wesentliches Stück deutscher Architektur-Avantgarde nach dem Zweiten Weltkrieg darstellt und international Beachtung fand. Auch wenn wir die Halle heute als ebenso typisches Produkt der Nierentisch-Ära empfinden wie den Coctailsessel oder die Tütenlampe: sie war avantgardistisch, und zu Recht hat kein anderes Karlsruher Bauwerk seither auch nur entfernt das Echo gefunden wie sie. Ein echter Impuls aus Karlsruhe. Gab es weitere?
Blenden wir zurück ins Karlsruhe der fünfziger Jahre. Der Krieg ist seit zehn Jahren vorbei, die Bombenkrater längst aufgefüllt und der Schutt weggeräumt. Karlsruhe ist als eine der ersten Städte Deutschlands »enttrümmert«, vielleicht auch eine der am radikalst aufgeräumten. Es ist die Zeit der Nachtaufnahmen: beleuchtete Schaufenster und Leuchtreklamen in der Innenstadt spiegeln sich im üppigen Chromzierat blankpolierter Pontonkarosserien. Der abendliche Schaufensterbummel auf dem »Glitzerboulevard Kaiserstraße« (BNN) hat sich als fester Punkt der Freizeitgestaltung etabliert. Wirtschaftswunder, das ist Verheißung plus Elektrizität, das Glück zukünftigen Besitzes hinter den Panoramascheiben der Auslagen.
Bei Tage betrachtet regt die Szenerie weniger zum Träumen an. Statt der üppigen Steinfassaden der Gründerzeit rahmen ärmliche ein-, höchstens zweistöckige Provisorien die Kaiserstraße. Teerpappegedeckte Scheunen, die sich erst gar nicht die Mühe machen, den Charakter des Vorläufigen zu verbergen. Einige, leider zu viele, wird man später dennoch nur aufstocken und so die Notstandsarchitektur in einen anhaltenden Architekturnotstand verwandeln.
Man hat sich bereits angewöhnt, die konservierten Ruinen des Schlosses, des Hoftheaters oder des Ständehauses für einen pittoresken Bestandteil des Stadtbildes zu halten; in Karlsruhe erleichtern einem die Grünanlagen, in die die meisten von ihnen eingebettet liegen, diese falsche Illusion von Romantik. Zwar sind die Zeiten bereits wieder vorbei, in denen man ernsthaft den Abriß des Schlosses zugunsten innenstadtnaher Wohnbebauung erwog, doch sollte die Zahl der Ruinen, in die wieder Leben einzieht, begrenzt bleiben. Was fehlt ist Bedarf, ist auch nur die Spur einer sinnvollen Nutzungsmöglichkeit.
Das Stück, für das die meisten dieser Gebäude gedacht waren, wird hier nicht mehr gespielt. Wie überflüssige Theaterkulissen stehen sie noch eine Weile herum, bevor man sie zerlegt. Karlsruhe ist nicht mehr Residenz und Landeshauptstadt. Was will man da mit einem Parlamentsgebäude, noch dazu einem, das speziell für diesen Zweck errichtet wurde?
Der Unterschied ist augenfällig. Während das kommunale Zentrum, der Marktplatz größtenteils nach leicht retuschierten Plänen Weinbrenners wieder hergerichtet wird, geschieht dies genau bei den zerstörten ehemals staatlichen Bauten nicht, die ihre Funktion verloren haben: den Ministerien, dem Ständehaus und dem Hoftheater als Ort staatlicher Repräsentation. Weder in Württemberg-Baden noch im späteren Baden-Württemberg verspürt man Bedarf nach einer »Lohengrin-Regierung«. Für Karlsruhe reicht das umgebaute Konzerthaus im Stadttheaterzuschnitt, keine Logen für den Landesherrn und seinen Hof mehr, bloß noch Parterre und Balkon.
Was die Stadt getroffen hatte, war mehr als ein beliebiger Zentralitätsverlust. Dem glanzvollen Aufstieg, den ihr das 19. Jahrhundert beschert hatte, drohte im 20. bereits das Gegenteil zu folgen.
1918 hatte man bereits den Titel »Residenz« ablegen müssen. Mit dem großherzoglichen Hof verschwand das Gepränge höfischer Selbstdarstellung, das bisher Mittelpunkt des gesellschaftlichen und kulturellen Lebens in der Stadt war. Schon damals fiel die angemessene Nutzung des republikanisierten baulichen Erbes offenbar schwer: im markgräflichen Palais am Rondellplatz beispielsweise wurden nun Möbel verkauft.
Der Rang einer Hauptstadt und die Aufgabe der Regierungszentrale waren Karlsruhe jedoch geblieben, die »raison d'etre« seines Bestehens, seit Karl-Wilhelm Bäume roden ließ.
Hitlers Machtantritt läutete dann das Ende ein. Reichsstatthalter und Gauleiter Robert Wagner erschien das »Klein-Bayreuth« des wilhelminischen Kaiserreichs nicht der richtige Rahmen für seine Interpretation des Weihespiels zu sein. Gegen diesen negativen Eindruck halfen offenbar weder Eingemeindungen noch Autobahnanschluß oder ein in Speerschen Dimensionen geplantes »Gauforum« im Bereich des Festplatzes. So hatten die braunen Machthaber bereits 1940 ihre Residenz im eroberten Straßburg aufgeschlagen und einen bedeutenden Teil der ehedem badischen Zentralverwaltung dorthin verlegt. In den Kriegsjahren war das nur nicht in aller Konsequenz deutlich geworden.
Endgültige Weichenstellungen brachte dann die Nachkriegszeit. Schnell wurde nach der Teilung Badens zwischen den Siegermächten USA und Frankreich klar, daß es keine zentrale gesamtbadische Verwaltung mehr geben werde, schon gar nicht mit Sitz in Karlsruhe. Dies drohte die Stadt in eine existenzielle Krise zu stürzen, denn genaugenommen war Karlsruhe eine »Regierungsbeamtenstadt«. Die Schicht, aus der sich die leitenden Beamten der Ministerien und der übrigen Zentralverwaltungen rekrutierten, war ein wesentlicher Bestandteil des Karlsruher Bürgertums und ein wichtiger Wirtschaftsfaktor. Familien wie die Eisenlohr, Turban, Vierordt oder Bürklin prägten über Jahrzehnte den badischen Staat, die Stadt und das kulturelle Leben gleichermaßen.

Auf die Rezeption von Kunst und Kultur hatte der Geschmack dieser Schicht immer entscheidenden Einfluß gehabt. Das avantgardistische Experiment war, wie gesagt, ihre Sache nicht, Zeitgeist und möglichst repräsentative Wirkung waren die Fixpunkte, an denen sich künstlerisches Schaffen zu orientieren hatte. Vor dem Ersten Weltkrieg verstanden es Künstler wie Hans Thoma oder Ferdinand Keller, der »badische Makart«, vollendet, sowohl in ihrem Werk wie ihrer Selbstinszenierung den Wünschen dieses Publikums gerecht zu werden. An dieser Orientierung änderte sich auch in der Zwischenkriegszeit nur wenig, es fehlte lediglich am nötigen Geld, die früheren Dimensionen beizubehalten.

Mit dem Ende des Zweiten Weltkrieges begann nun jedoch wirklich eine neue Epoche. Die Folgen des Krieges hatten die alte kommunale Gesellschaftsordnung aufgebrochen. Karlsruhe, die Entthronte, stand vor der Herausforderung, sich auf fast allen Gebieten neu zu orientieren, eine neue Identität und Zukunftsperspektive zu finden. Eine Aufgabe, für deren Bewältigung sich die Bevölkerung der Stadt 1952 den Mann als Oberbürgermeister wählte, der bereits mit ihren Trümmern aufgeräumt hatte: einen der Geschäftsführer der »Aufräumungs-Arbeitsgemeinschaft Karlsruhe«, Günther Klotz. Seine Wahl dokumentierte gleichzeitig, daß das Bewußtsein, vor neuen Herausforderungen zu stehen, in der Bevölkerung weit verbreitet war. Anders als in Bonn war man bereit zu Experimenten, zumindest unter Leitung einer derart charismatischen Persönlichkeit wie Klotz.

Und Klotz schrieb zunächst und vor allem Bewerbungen. Was die Stadt angesichts der wachsenden Bevölkerungszahl dringend brauchte, waren neue und mehr Arbeitsplätze als bisher. Das wesentliche Ziel des neuen Oberbürgermeisters war, aus der »Beamtenstadt« eine »Industriestadt« zu machen, die verlorengegangenen Arbeitsplätze in der Landesverwaltung durch die gezielte Ansiedlung zukunftssicher erscheinender Industrien zu ersetzen. Und er hatte Erfolg. Neben dem Siemens-Werk gelang es ihm, von Ölraffinerien bis zu Schönheitspflege-Firmen die unterschiedlichsten Sparten in Karlsruhe anzusiedeln. Doch ging es Klotz ganz offenbar nicht nur um den wirtschaftlichen Aufschwung, sondern auch darum, die Stadt ins Scheinwerferlicht der Öffentlichkeit zu rücken. Dies zeigt sich deutlich an der Bewerbung um den Sitz der beiden höchsten Bundesgerichte und ein damals kaum fragwürdiges Projekt, den Forschungs-«Atommeiler«, das spätere Kernforschungszentrum, mit dem die Bundesrepublik den Einstieg in die Nutzung der Kernenergie vorbereiten wollte.

Gleichzeitig betrieb Klotz – mitunter sogar rücksichtslos – die Modernisierung der Stadt. Überall wurde in Straßen- und Wohnungsbau investiert, ganze Stadtviertel im Westen und Norden der Kernstadt aus dem Boden gestampft, Mühlburgs Rheinstraße zum Großstadtboulevard umgebaut, futuristische Pläne wie der einer Rheinstadt am Knielinger See entworfen, obwohl dort damals sicher hundert Schnaken auf einen Bewohner gekommen wären. Die Karlsruher Architekturfakultät genoß internationalen Ruf. Schelling und Eiermann sind hierbei die überragenden Persönlichkeiten. Ihre Pläne müssen sie allerdings zumeist außerhalb verwirklichen. Denn nicht nur auf die BNN wirkten ihre gewagten Pläne »schockierend«, wie die Zeitung 1960 anläßlich ihrer Entwürfe zum Theaterneubau-Wettbewerb schrieb. Insbesondere Eiermann kam in Karlsruhe über einige Privathäuser nicht hinaus, lediglich für die Universität konnte er ein einziges Institutsgebäude verwirklichen. Meisterwerke wie die Gedächtniskirche sucht man am Ort seines Wirkens hingegen vergeblich.

Klotz war sich jedoch auch darüber im klaren, daß eine Stadt für Investoren, auch wenn man sie damals noch nicht so hochtrabend bezeichnete, nur interessant sein konnte, wenn sie sich auch auf kulturellem Gebiet ins rechte Licht zu rücken verstand. Seit 1953 gab die Stadt einen jährlich erscheinenden Kulturbericht heraus, die zweite Nummer beschrieb die aktuelle Situation des Kunststandorts so:

»Wenn hier der Boden bis zu einem gewissen Grad für moderne Formen aufgeschlossen ist, so bringt er selbst doch keine zahlreichen kühnen Erscheinungen hervor. Das Spätwerk der großen Meister der zwanziger Jahre hat Hoheit und Reife erlangt, und die Nachfolgenden variieren und verfeinern, was jene erschaffen haben. Es liegt nichts Beunruhigendes mehr in den guten Arbeiten, die überall zu finden sind. Dennoch bietet Karlsruhe der bildenden Kunst einen unschätzbaren Vorteil für die Zukunft: Es leben hier Menschen, die Begabungen zu erkennen vermögen, und man ist allenthalben bereit, der großen Künstlerpersönlichkeit, die durch ihr Werk zu bezaubern versteht, zu huldigen. Die Maßstäbe sind hier freilich gegeben durch eine fortwirkende Tradition und nur Ebenbürtiges kann sich in Karlsruhe behaupten. Akademie und Kunsthalle, Kunstverein und Stadt selbst sind aufmerksame Beobachter der Tendenzen und vermitteln Karlsruhe den Anschluß an die allgemeinen Kunstrichtungen unserer Zeit.«

Neben den durchgängig im Tone betulicher Schöngeistigkeit formulierten Berichten trat die Stadt just im gleichen Jahr 1953 als Mäzen hervor und verlieh erstmals den mit mehreren tausend Mark für die damalige Zeit beachtlich dotierten »Karlsruher Kulturpreis«. Bei der Auswahl der Preisträger zeigte man sich allerdings ganz auf der Linie der Kulturberichte: »Beunruhigendes« wurde hier tatsächlich in keinem Fall prämiert. Schon die Wahl der Sparten, für die der Wettbewerb ausgeschrieben wurde, verhinderten allzu Schrilles, ebenso wie die Zusammensetzung der Jury aus städtischen Honoratioren und die Zielsetzung, die Preise dem Nachwuchs, also vor allem Studenten von Musikhochschule und Kunstakademie zukommen zu lassen.

Kompromißlos moderne Wege beschritt Klotz hingegen in der Präsentation der Stadt. Ein Film wurde gedreht, und für die Landesausstellung 1955 in Stuttgart ein vom Stadtplanungsamt entworfener und dennoch futuristischer, transportabler Pavillon verwirklicht. »Die 100 000 Mark dürften kein hinausgeworfenes Geld sein, denn hier hat Karlsruhe einmal die Chance, der Welt zu zeigen, daß es sich durch den Verlust seiner Eigenschaft als Residenz und Landeshauptstadt nicht unterkriegen ließ, sondern auf dem besten Wege ist, sich zu einer bedeutenden deutschen Wirtschafts- und Kulturmetropole zu entwickeln«, meinte die BNN auftrumpfend zu diesem Vorhaben. Den staunenden Stuttgartern sollte hier ein Theaterstück präsentiert werden mit dem programmatischen Titel: »Karlsruhe, die Stadt mit Zukunft!«

Mehr als die Berichte, die allerdings viel über die Geisteshaltung der Zeit aussagen, und die städtischen Kulturpreise rückte Karlsruhe in diesen Jahren eine Veranstaltung zunehmend in den Mittelpunkt des öffentlichen Interesses, die mit dem Massenmedium der Fünfziger, dem Film in engster Verbindung stand.

Obwohl der Historiker Adolf v. Grolmann, der in jenen Jahren die Stadtgeschichte beackerte, die Auffassung vertrat, »diese Dinge gehören zur Vergnügungsindustrie und haben mit dem kulturellen Leben der Stadt wenig zu tun«, sah die Realität anders aus. Der Film genoß in Karlsruhe wie überall in der Republik eine heute kaum mehr vorstellbare Aufmerksamkeit. Jede Tageszeitung betrieb feuilletonfüllende Filmberichterstattung, den Premieren neuer Filme fieberte das Publikum wochenlang entgegen, der Auftritt bekannter Filmstars in der Öffentlichkeit rief riesige Menschenmengen auf den Plan. Und in diesem Trubel hatte sich ausgerechnet Karlsruhe einen Balkonplatz gesichert.

Seit 1948 verlieh die in der »Karlsruher Neue Verlagsgesellschaft« von Karl Fritz erscheinende Zeitschrift »Film-Revue« einen Preis an die beliebtesten Filmschauspieler des Jahres. Die Trophäe stammte – wie könnte es anders sein – aus der Majolika-Manufaktur: eine kleine Rehplastik aus weißer Keramik, wohl in Anlehnung an den Disney-Erfolg des Jahres '48 »Bambi« genannt. Die Jüngeren kennen meist nur noch den zum Fernsehpreis mutierten, goldglitzernden Nachfolger, der in München vergeben wird.

Während sie es in den ersten Jahren kaum zu mehr als einer Zeitungsnotiz brachte, mauserte sich die Bambi-Verleihung im Laufe der Zeit zu einem gesellschaftlichen Ereignis ersten Ranges. Der spektakuläre Aufstieg dieses Preises zu einer der wichtigsten europäischen Filmauszeichnungen läßt sich besonders deutlich an der Teilnahme der erwählten ausländischen Künstler an der Preisverleihung ablesen. Ab Mitte der fünfziger Jahre ließ es sich fast keiner der Ausgezeichneten mehr nehmen, das weiße Rehlein eigenhändig in Obhut zu nehmen. Mit Jean Marais, Gina Lollobrigida und anderen Stars gelangten Ende der Fünfziger Berühmtheiten in die Stadt wie nie zuvor (und nicht wieder), Klotz mit der Lollo oder der Schell auf dem Rathausbalkon oder am Ort der Verleihung – natürlich der Schwarzwaldhalle – waren in allen deutschen Kinos zu sehen und brachten gleichzeitig etwas vom Schaueffekt großherzoglicher Zeiten in die mediatisierte Residenz zurück. Karlsruhe wurde beliebt als Schauplatz von deutschen Uraufführungen, zu denen die Hauptdarsteller anreisten, der Erfolg beim Karlsruher Filmpublikum galt gar als zuverlässiger Gradmesser für das Bundesgebiet. Die in ihrer Grundstruktur erhaltenen Kinopaläste »Schauburg«, »Kamera« und »Kurbel« künden heute noch von dieser, leider kurzlebigen Glanzzeit. 1962 erhielten Klotz und Fritz die »Ehrenmedaille der Deutschen Filmwirtschaft«, wenige Jahre später sollte es letztere bekanntlich nicht mehr geben, und das Bambi mußte künftig bei den Helden des Pantoffelkinos sein Gnadenbrot verdienen. Doch noch sonnte sich Karlsruhe im Glanz internationaler Besetzung, und die Stadt ließ jenen bereits erwähnten Film über sich drehen mit dem Titel, der über der gesamten Epoche stehen könnte: »Stadt im Umbruch«, dem die Filmbewertungsstelle in Wiesbaden sogar das berühmt-berüchtigte Prädikat »besonders wertvoll« verlieh, denn »... als Städtefilm nimmt sich der Film als eine Spitzenleistung aus«.

Auch in fast allen anderen Bereichen des kulturellen Lebens der Stadt waren die Jahre zwischen 1955 und 1965 Jahre der Veränderung und des Neubeginns. Unabhängig von den großen Kinoverleihern hatte sich der Film-Club konstituiert und brachte in Zusammenarbeit mit dem »Resi«-Kino anspruchsvolle Filme in die Stadt, oft auch experimentelle, die kein Massenpublikum ansprachen.

Im Bereich der Literatur erregte ein kleiner Karlsruher Verlag bundesweites Aufsehen: Ingeborg Stahlberg hatte Autoren unter Vertrag, die heute zur Creme der Literatur der Fünfziger gerechnet werden, allen voran Malaparte und Arno Schmidt. Gerade sie fehlen kennzeichnenderweise in der kurzen Vorstellung des Verlags im Kulturbericht von 1954, allerdings genossen Bühnenschriftsteller damals auch wesentlich mehr öffentliche Aufmerksamkeit, als sie anderen Literaturbereichen zuteil wurde.

Gerade im Bühnenbereich tat sich im Verlauf dieser Jahre Wesentliches, entstanden die bis heute bestimmenden Eckpfeiler der städtischen Theaterlandschaft.

Im Dezember 1950 hatten Erich Schudde und Werner Wedekind das Privattheater »Die Insel« gegründet. Es war, wie 1955 die BNN schrieb, »die einzige und letzte der zahlreichen Theatergründungen im Karlsruhe der Nachkriegszeit, die die Krisen der Anfangszeit überstand. Die Theatergründer stellten sich dabei die Aufgabe, »den Spielplan des Staatstheaters nach der Seite der modernen Dramatik, des Problemstücks zu ergänzen und gleichzeitig jungen noch unbedeutenden Autoren eine Chance zu geben«. Erster Spielort war der Saal des Kunstvereins, später der »Munz-Saal« in der Waldstraße. Karlsruhe wurde durch die »Insel« zum Ort zahlreicher Ur- bzw. deutscher Erstaufführungen, etwa 1954 von Thornton Wilders »Unsere kleine Stadt«. 1958 zeigte die »Insel« erstmals Ionesco, 1959 wurde John Priestleys »Die Folter« uraufgeführt.

Noch kleiner, aber damals mindestens ebenso ambitioniert war das 1956 entstandene »Kammertheater«. Sartres »Geschlossene Gesellschaft«, Cocteaus »La Voix humaine«, »Eurydikes Hände« von Bloch oder Strindbergs »Totentanz« standen hier auf dem Programm, das ursprünglich in einem Keller an der Waldstraße über die Bühne ging. »Das Kernproblem des modernen Theaters, die Kommunikation zwischen Bühne und Publikum versuchen Bühnen wie das Karlsruher Kammertheater auf absolute Art zu lösen: es wird inmitten der Zuschauer gespielt, die unmittelbar angesprochen sind und sich ohne Schranken mit dem Dargestellten auseinandersetzen. Diese Theaterform verlangt eine kompromißlose künstlerische Linie...« Der Erfolg beider Theater, die sich beide der modernen Dramatik verschrieben hatten, die damals gern unter dem Schlagwort »Experimentiertheater« zusammengefaßt wurde, war im Hinblick auf die Karlsruher Theatertradition und das diese bis heute repräsentierende und dominierende Staatstheater bemerkenswert. Er zeigt jedoch auch, wie hoch damals die Nachfrage des Publikums nach »zeitgemäßen«, die eingefahrenen Bahnen des Rampentheaters verlassenden Theaterformen war. Ein Vergleich der damaligen Spielstätten samt Repertoire von »Insel« und »Kammertheater« mit der heutigen Situation zeigt außerdem, wie sehr sich die einstigen Experimentierer (sowohl Theatermacher wie Publikum) inzwischen wieder zu den Konventionen des Etablierten zurückbewegt haben und wies um so deutlicher auch auf den Ausnahmecharakter jener Epoche.

Die bildende Kunst hatte es schwerer, die konservativen Bahnen zu verlassen. Allzu mühsam und oberflächlich hatte sich das Publikum gerade erst mit der klassischen Moderne abgefunden. Diesen Stand der Dinge dokumentierte sehr schön die 1961 stattfindende Ausstellung »Kunst aus Karlsruher Privatbesitz«. Auch unser bester Seismograph für traditionelles Karlsruher G'schmäckle, die BNN, stellten als »Kunstwerke des Monats« aus Beständen der Kunsthalle so gut wie nichts aus der Zeit nach der Jahrhundertwende vor.

Die Stadtverwaltung war zwar etwas progressiver, schielte jedoch beim Ankauf von künstlerischen Werken immer auf den breiten Publikumsgeschmack. Wie stand es im Kulturbericht: »Das Spätwerk der großen Meister der zwanziger Jahre hat Hoheit und Reife erlangt, und die Nachfolgenden variieren und verfeinern.« Der Kanon der Gestaltungsmöglichkeiten schien festgelegt, die Schüler sollten ruhig noch ein paar andere Farben hineinmischen.

Als 1954 die Kunstakademie auf ihr hundertjähriges Bestehen zurückblicken konnte, tat man das mit drei Ausstellungen: »Die Lehrer«, »Ehemalige Schüler« und zuletzt »Die Schüler heute«. Zwei zu eins für die Vergangenheit also, denn die Lehrer, auch die gegenwärtigen, waren ja Denkmäler längst vergangener Zeiten. Erich Heckel, der ein Jahr später ausschied ebenso wie Karl Hubbuch und Otto Haupt. Die Berufung HAP Grießhabers 1955 war der erste Ansatz, diese Phalanx der Tradition aufzubrechen und endete bereits fünf Jahre später im Skandal. 1955 allerding veranstaltete die Akademie eine Ausstellung über die Gruppe der »Tachisten«. Bei der Eröffnung war ein Teil der Künstler anwesend, und Grieshabers Klasse führte Schattenspiele auf.

Ähnlich das Verhältnis bei den Ausstellungen der Kunsthalle. Von den zwölf 1953 durchgeführten Präsentationen waren lediglich drei der Gegenwartskunst gewidmet: eine über das Werk von Willy Meyer-Amden, dann »Farbgrafik der Gegenwart« und »Moderne italienische Keramik«. 1955 präsentierte die Kunsthalle »Kunst unserer Zeit«, in der »Neuerwerbungen zeitgenössischer Künstler« erstmals dem Karlsruher Publikum vorgestellt wurden. Und welche Maler empfand man offenbar als Zeitgenossen? Kirchner, Franz Marc und August Macke!

Die Progressiven unter den wirklich zeitgenössischen Künstlern konnten sich denn auch nur außerhalb der staatlichen und kommunalen Institutionen präsentieren und suchten diesen Weg. Immer wieder entstanden Galerien, die meisten nicht von hoher Lebensdauer. Ständig änderten sich Adressen und Namen, teilweise wurden auch nur für eine Ausstellung Räume angemietet. Der damalige Kunstbetrieb in Karlsruhe gruppierte sich so weitgehend um vier bis fünf dauernde Einrichtungen: den mal mehr mal weniger zu Gewagtem aufgelegten Kunstverein, die privaten Galerien Gallwitz, Rottloff und Apfelbaum sowie die »Tangente«, ein überwiegend von Studenten frequentiertes Etablissement, dessen offenbar teils spektakulären Veranstaltungen die zeitungproduzierende Öffentlichkeit jedoch so wenig Aufmerksamkeit widmete, daß nur spärliche Zeugnisse seiner Aktivität aufzuzeichnen sind.

1965 quasi zum Abschluß des Umbruch-Jahrzehnts und im selben Jahr, in dem sich die Bundesrepublik, ausgelöst vom Schah-Besuch, in den Umbruch der Studentenrevolte hineinbewegte, formierte sich hier die Gegentendenz in der konservativen Bewegung der »Karlsruher Künstler-Genossenschaft«, die »entgegen den modernen und umstrittenen Richtungen in der bildenden Kunst von heute, die vielfach von Managern inszeniert werden, ein Schaffen zu dokumentieren, das auf der Natur aufbaut und nicht außerhalb derselben steht«.

Dieses an sich zufällige Ereignis der Sammlung unter konservativem Vorzeichen könnte man allerdings auch als Sinnbild der Veränderung betrachten, die Mitte der sechziger Jahre Karlsruhe erfaßte. Die Stadt im Umbruch lenkte in ihre alten Bahnen zurück, die »Ära Klotz« neigte sich unaufhaltsam dem Ende zu. Das Umgestaltungsprogramm hatte die finanziellen Reserven erschöpft, wie ein potemkinscher Riese ragte das neue technische Rathaus jahrelang als Bauruine in den Himmel. Die Bundesgartenschau von 1967 war das letzte Fest, in dessen Glanz sich die Stadt und ihr OB sonnen konnten.1968 trat Günther Klotz als Oberbürgermeister zurück, weil der Stadtrat nicht mehr bereit war, seiner Linie zu folgen. Impulse sind seither selten geworden in Karlsruhe.

Stuttgart – Die goldenen Jahre

Die solide Beschaulichkeit, die bis heute Stuttgarts Außenwirkung trägt, läßt kaum erahnen, daß an diesem Ort in den sechziger Jahren eine Gruppe avantgardistischer Künstler versammelt war. Als äußeres Zeichen und gleichzeitig als Höhepunkt dieser kulturellen Blüte sind die Beiträge Georg Karl Pfahlers und Thomas Lenks zur Biennale von Venedig 1970 zu werten. Im Rückblick bezeichnete ihr damaliger Galerist Hans-Jürgen Müller diese Zeit als die »goldenen sechziger Jahre«[1], denn über der zeitgenössischen Kunstszene lag die Aufbruchsstimmung der »Stunde Null«. Eine neue Künstlergeneration war angetreten, nachdem Anfang der sechziger Jahre die ersten Wirtschaftswundererfolge das Bewußtsein der Katastrophe und die Kriegserinnerungen aus den Köpfen gedrängt hatten. Die Künstler sprengten die Grenzen der überkommenen Techniken und gingen mit Aktionen an die Öffentlichkeit. Galeristen und Vermittler setzten sich enthusiastisch für die zeitgenössische Kunst ein. Die Diskussionen aktueller Kunstereignisse in den Feuilletons belegten, daß die Kunst damals eine bewegende, manchmal sogar provozierende Kraft besaß.

Stuttgart wurde zum Kristallisationspunkt einer aufregenden Entwicklung. Bevor die wichtigsten Künstler vorgestellt werden, sollen zunächst die besonderen kunsttopographischen Bedingungen beleuchtet werden, auf denen die hiesige Szene beruhte. Die erste Erwähnung gebührt Willi Baumeister, dem prominentesten Wortführer in der Auseinandersetzung um die Moderne: dem Kampf zwischen Gegenständlichkeit und Abstraktion im Nachkriegsdeutschland. Der Stuttgarter Baumeister trug das Thema der Abstraktion über die dreißiger Jahre und entfaltete es von hier aus nach 1945 neu. In seinen Schriften formulierte er das Fundament einer nicht mehr abbildlichen Kunst, die ihre Begründung nicht aus formalästhetischen, sondern aus ethischen Motiven zieht. In den fünfziger Jahren erreichte sein Werk eine beispiellose öffentliche Wirkung im In- und Ausland. Baumeister paßte in die optimistische Aufbaustimmung, selbst unbelastet von der Vergangenheit und begünstigt durch sein abstraktes Frühwerk seit 1920. Die Vertreter der gegenständlichen Kunst hatten es schwer, gegen die Faszination seines Werkes anzukommen, und gerieten, auch in Stuttgart, ins Abseits. Als Gegenbewegung wurde bereits 1947 die »Stuttgarter Sezession« wiedergegründet, und Alfred Wais initiierte 1952 die »Freie Gruppe« als Nachfolgeorganisation der »Stuttgarter Neuen Sezession«. Er versuchte auf diese Weise, die gegenständliche und abstrakte Kunst in der Region miteinander ins Gespräch zu bringen.

Willi Baumeister: Phantom und gelber Tisch. 1952

Theodor Heuss, nach dem Kriege erster Kultminister in Württemberg-Baden und später erster Bundespräsident, hatte aus liberaler Einstellung heraus bei der Berufung der Stuttgarter Professoren ganz bewußt, wie er sagte, die »polaren sachlichen Spannungen hier zusammengebracht, das sogenannte Abstrakte neben das Realistische gestellt, dem Expressiven neben dem Naturalistischen einen Lebensraum angewiesen«.[2] Diese Weichenstellung für die Akademie mag die Tatsache begründen, daß in Württemberg, anders als in den meisten Bundesländern, beide Richtungen im öffentlichen Kunstleben präsent und bis in die sechziger Jahre virulent blieben. Die Wogen im Streit um gegenstandslose und gegenständliche Kunst gingen gelegentlich so hoch, daß sie selbst den Stuttgarter Landtag beschäftigten. So entzündete 1967 die 1965 im »Deutschen Kunstpreis der Jugend« prämierte Plastik »Elefantenkot« von Jochen Hiltmann eine Parlamentsdebatte: Der Maler Hans Münch hatte dem Kultusministerium wegen dieser Entscheidung »einseitigen Kunstdirigismus zugunsten der ›gegenstandslosen Kunst‹« vorgeworfen.[3]

Aller Polemik in der öffentlichen Meinung zum Trotz fand die neue Kunst in Stuttgart einen guten Nährboden. Neben Willi Baumeister, der bis zu seinem Tod 1955 an der Akademie lehrte, wirkte hier die Tradition des Bauhauses besonders stark nach: zum einen in der Weißenhof-Siedlung, dem gebauten Musterbuch avantgardistischer Architektur der zwanziger Jahre, zum anderen im Einfluß der 1950 in Ulm gegründeten Hochschule für Gestaltung. Neben deren Rektor Max Bill unterrichteten dort der ehemalige Bauhauslehrer Josef Albers, Friedrich Vordemberge-Gildewart und der Philosoph Max Bense, der seine neuentwickelte »Informationsästhetik« auch an der Stuttgarter Universität vertrat. Zudem hatte sich Anton Stankowski schon 1948 dauerhaft in Stuttgart niedergelassen. Als ihr geistiger Mittelpunkt machte er Stuttgart zu einem Zentrum konstruktiver Kunst. Nach seiner Ausbildung an der Folkwang-Schule in Essen war Stankowski zunächst nach Zürich gegangen. Dort führte ihn seine bildnerische Konzeption einer rationalen Bildgestaltung mit dem Kreis der jungen Grafiker, Fotografen und Künstler zusammen, in deren Umfeld die konkrete Kunst heimisch wird. Damals wie heute ist er überzeugt, daß sich freie und angewandte Kunst im Wesen nicht unterscheiden. Seine systematische Gestaltungslehre, sein Nachdenken über die Beziehung von Abbild und Wirkung mündeten in sein künstlerisches Verfahren der »Visualisierung«. Stankowski entwickelte sich in Stuttgart als Gestalter, Typograf, Fotograf und Theoretiker zum Generalisten auf dem Gebiet der freien Malerei und der Grafik, ranggleich der Gebrauchsgrafik und der visuellen Kommunikation.

In Stuttgart waren nicht nur vielfältige künstlerische Traditionen verfügbar, auch die Kritik war der neuen Szene aufgeschlossen. Neben dem jüngeren Günther Wirth, der sich bis heute publizistisch für die Kunst des deutschen Südwestens einsetzt, ist vor allem der Schriftsteller und Kritiker Kurt Leonhard hervorzuheben. Nach Kriegsende ließ er sich in Esslingen nieder und verhalf mit seinen Beiträgen vielen jungen Künstlern zu Beachtung. Leonhards eigenwillig typografierte Lyrik-Bände, die er als Lektor im Esslinger Bechtle-Verlag veröffentlichte, beeinflußten auch die damalige Literaturszene, besonders den Kreis um Max Bense. Bense scharte in Stuttgart Literaten und Vertreter der Konkreten Poesie um sich, die später als »Stuttgarter Gruppe« bezeichnet wurden. Mit Reinhard Döhl, Manfred Esser und Helmut Heißenbüttel sind ihre wichtigsten Mitglieder genannt. Sie waren den jungen Künstlern, die sich von dem guten Ruf der Akademie nach Stuttgart locken ließen, kongeniale kritische Begleiter.

In den Stuttgarter Verlagen, Editionen und Druckereien fanden sich aufgeschlossene Mitstreiter. Luitpold Domberger druckte zusammen mit Willi Baumeister 1950 den ersten Siebdruck in Deutschland. Domberger verfeinerte die ursprünglich amerikanische Technik so weit, daß in den folgenden Jahren Josef Albers, Victor Vasarely, Robert Indiana und viele andere das Können seiner Werkstatt in Anspruch nahmen. Durch seine Editionen lernten die Jungen neue, ihnen unbekannte künstlerische Konzepte kennen. Walter Cantz, ein anderer Stuttgarter Drucker, war für seine gestalterisch anspruchsvollen Bücher berühmt. Museumsleiter und Künstler aus ganz Deutschland arbeiteten mit ihm. Verlag und Galerie von Hansjörg Mayer bildeten wie die Buchhandlung Wendelin Niedlichs einen Schnittpunkt zwischen visueller und literarischer Kultur in Stuttgart. Gerade Hansjörg Mayer zog viele Autoren und Künstler hierher: Diter Roth, André Thomkins, George Brecht und Robert Filliou. 1967 war er Mitherausgeber der »anthology of concrete poetry«. Die Bedeutung der Verlage in dieser Zeit beleuchtet Reinhard Döhl 1986: »Was die in Stuttgart lebenden Künstler in toto trieben, ließe sich etwa an dem von Mayer und Domberger gemeinsam publizierten Mappenwerk ›16 4 66‹ gut illustrieren.«[4]

Kunst kann aber nicht gedeihen ohne die Unterstützung von Museen, Galerien und Sammlern. In Stuttgart spezialisierten sich einige private Kunstfreunde auf Werke der übernationalen Moderne.[5] So besorgte vor allem der Arzt Ottomar Domnick mit seiner Kollektion und ausgedehnten Ausstellungstätigkeit der abstrakten Kunst in Württemberg eine beispiellose Vertretung. Dieter Keller, der aus einer Verlegerfamilie stammte, kümmerte sich um das Werk Oskar Schlemmers und entwickelte eine besondere Vorliebe für Marcel Duchamp, Max Ernst und Alexander Calder. Auch Ursula und Gerd Hatje, der den ersten Kunstbuchverlag nach dem Krieg gründete, sammelten klassische und zeitgenössische Kunst: Willi Baumei-

Josef Albers: Homage to the Square. 1954

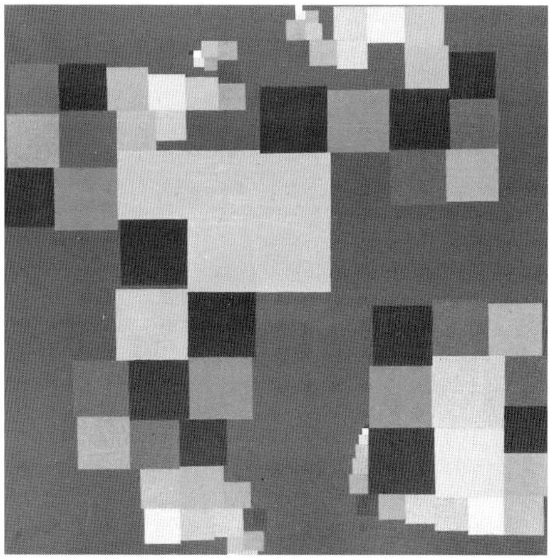

Anton Stankowski: Quadratprogression. 1959

Dieter Roth: Fernsehturm. 1967

ster und Norbert Kricke, Julius Bissier und K. R. H. Sonderborg, Fernand Léger und Paul Jenkins. Die Stuttgarter Künstler fanden auch Eingang in jüngere Sammlungen, die wie die des Fotohändlers Rolf H. Krauss und des Verlegerpaares Renate und Günther Hauff in den sechziger Jahren entstanden. Letztere stellten amerikanische und deutsche Kunst einander gegenüber.

Während die 1961 wiedereröffnete Galerie der Stadt Stuttgart sich sammlerisch um figurative Künstler wie Otto Dix kümmerte, trat die Staatsgalerie ihrerseits Ende der fünfziger Jahre mit dem Ankauf der Sammlung Moltzau aus provinzieller Enge. Die Aufnahme von Werken der überregionalen Moderne gab den Auftakt, das Haus ab den sechziger Jahren für aktuelle europäische und amerikanische Strömungen zu öffnen. Eine treibende Kraft hinter den Direktoren Erwin Petermann und Peter Beye war der Restaurator und Konservator Siegfried Cremer, der dank seines Urteils und seiner guten Kontakte zu Künstlern und Galerien früh auf neue Strömungen aufmerksam wurde.

Traditionell zeigten die Kunsthandlungen Valentien und Fischinger moderne Kunst. Dazu kamen in den sechziger Jahren weitere Galerien, die sich gezielt aktueller Tendenzen annahmen: die Galerien Lutz & Meyer, Senatore, Maercklin, Behr und die Op art-Galerie von Hans Mayer im benachbarten Esslingen. Die bedeutendste in dieser Zeit war aber sicherlich die Galerie Müller, die, 1958 gegründet, noch vor der Staatsgalerie zu einem Zentrum für die neueste Kunst wurde. Hier konnten die Stuttgarter bereits amerikanische zeitgenössische Kunst sehen, als sich in Deutschland mit Ausnahme von Karl Ströher in Darmstadt, Kurt Fried in Ulm und Alfred Schmela in Düsseldorf noch kaum jemand für sie interessierte. Müller stellte neben anderen die Amerikaner Morris Louis, Cy Twombly, Franz Kline und Al Held aus. Im Gegenzug setzte er sich mit großem Erfolg im Ausland für die deutsche Kunst ein, die sich aus der Formensprache des Informel gelöst hatte. Eine 1967 von Dieter Honisch im Kunstgebäude organisierte Ausstellung »Formen der Farbe« brachte die von Müller gezeigten Gemeinsamkeiten deutscher und amerikanischer Kunst im neuen Umgang mit der Farbe auf den Punkt. Der Galerist konnte erreichen, mit Georg Karl Pfahler, Thomas Lenk, Erich Hauser, Lambert Maria Wintersberger und Lothar Quinte der Stuttgarter Szene im internationalen Konzert Gehör zu verschaffen.

Interessant ist, daß die meisten zu den »Stuttgartern« zählenden Künstlern nicht von hier stammen, sondern, vom reichen kulturellen Leben der Stadt gelockt, zuzogen. Anfänglich dominierte die informelle Kunst. Zwei der Künstler, die in Paris zur Zeit der École de Paris gearbeitet hatten, stießen in den sechziger Jahren als Professoren zur Stuttgarter Akademie. In den vier Jahren bis 1965, die Heinz Trökes hier lehrte, zog er zahlreiche Studenten nach Stuttgart. Er selbst war in Krefeld Schüler von Johannes Itten gewesen. 1939 siedelte er nach Zürich um und nahm Einflüsse des Surrealismus auf, die sich

Peter Brüning: Ohne Titel. 1960/61

noch deutlich in seinen Ruinenlandschaften der Nachkriegszeit zeigten. Die zwei Jahre in Paris ab 1950, in denen er Wols, Matta und Breton kennenlernte, wurden für Trökes‹ Stil entscheidend.

Auch K. R. H. Sonderborg, der von 1965 bis 1990 an der Stuttgarter Akademie lehrte, war von Paris geprägt. Sonderborg geht es in seinen Bildern nicht in erster Linie um den ungehinderten Ausdruck psychischer Gestimmtheit. Die Farbe darf deshalb nie unkontrolliert fließen. Der Künstler bestimmt Form und Farbigkeit des Bildes, die sich auf Schwarz und Rot konzentriert. Unabhängig von Gegenstand oder Motiv wird die Linie zum Träger von Kraft und Bewegung. Ihr Verlauf, Dichte und Volumen ändern sich mit der Empfindung. Insofern wird das Bild zum Selbstausdruck. Der Gestaltungsprozeß bleibt in den Spuren, die Spachtel, Rasierklingen, Rakel und Pinselstile in der Farbe zurückließen, erhalten und nachvollziehbar. Sonderborgs Malaktionen gleichen Attacken auf die Leinwand. Sie machen auch vor den Bildrändern nicht halt, denn das Bild entsteht aus der Spannung des ganzen Körpers, die in der Aktion schnell und konzentriert sich entlädt. Dauer und Ablauf der Malaktion sind bildbestimmend, deshalb wird das Datum oft zum Titel.

Markus Prachenskys kalligrafische Bilder stehen Sonderborgs aktionistischem Ansatz am nächsten. Prachensky, der 1962 bis 1966 in Stuttgart lebte, ist methodisch noch radikaler: Ein Bild zeigt eine Geste, ein Zeichen, hervorgegangen aus eruptiver Dynamik der Hand, die der flüssigen Farbe Eigenleben und Eigenbewegung zugesteht. In intensivem Rot leuchten diese Chiffren auf schwarzem oder weißem Bildgrund.

Emil Cimiotti studierte in Berlin und Stuttgart. Starke Einflüsse nahm er auch aus Baumeisters Werk. Cimiotti stellte in den fünfziger Jahren in seinen Skulpturen das geschlossene, glatte Kernvolumen infrage, indem er die Oberflächen aufbrach. Das Verhältnis von Innen- und Außenraum wird von nun an zu seinem Thema. Durch Öffnungen in der Oberfläche entsteht Verbindung von Innen nach Außen. Das Auflösen der plastischen Form vollzieht sich zeitgleich mit der gestischen Malerei. So entstehen zerklüftete Landschaften, die organischen und vegetativen Wachstumsstrukturen ähneln. Tiere und Landschaften, aber auch mythologische Themen bieten Cimiotti Anregungen, die er frei in Wachsmodelle umsetzt. Durch Ausschmelzen, im Verfahren der verlorenen Form, erhält das Modell in Bronze dauerhafte Gestalt. An Cimiottis Werk, das konsequent dem einen Thema verpflichtet bleibt, zeigt sich deutlich die Tendenz, den Monolith der bildhauerischen Tradition zugunsten von raumbezogenen Objekten aufzugeben.

Am Ende seines Studiums an der Stuttgarter Akademie zeigen die poetische Skulpturen und Reliefs von Paul Reich noch surreale Einflüsse. Ab 1960 gab er die Bronzeplastiken auf und kombinierte in seinen neuen Arbeiten Stein, Metall und Glas. Diese »Lichtplastiken« lassen den plastisch umschlossenen

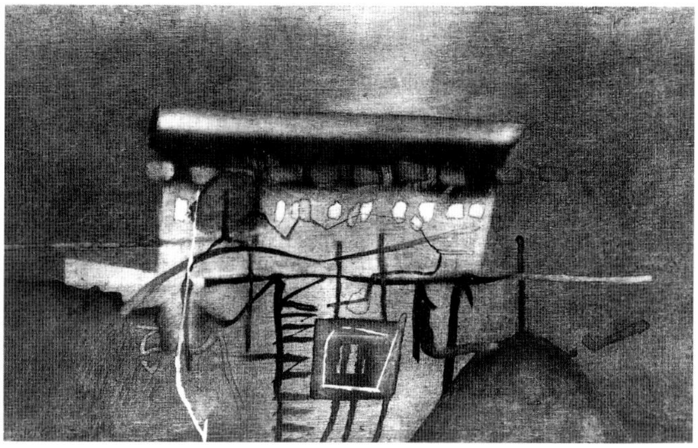

Heinz Trökes: Isolierte Station. 1962

Paul Reich: Skulptur. 1961

Raum sichtbar werden und heben ihn im Licht auf. Dazu bot sich Reich im Acrylglas ein ideales Material. Das Fließen des Materials, das ihn schon an den Bronzearbeiten interessierte, konnte er nun manuell in seinem Verlauf beeinflussen. Das Glas umschließt materiell Volumen und gibt es wegen seiner Transparenz zugleich frei. Reich kombiniert informelle Strukturen im Metall mit geformtem Glas, das ebenfalls Spuren seines Entstehungsprozesses zeigt. Das labile Gleichgewicht zwischen Metall und Glas bekommt Halt im Stein. Die Verknüpfungszonen der Materialien bilden die Spannungszentren der Plastiken.

Neue Ansätze gingen Anfang der sechziger Jahre von Mitgliedern der »Gruppe 11« aus, die 1955 in Stuttgart von den damals informell arbeitenden Künstlern Georg Karl Pfahler, Günther C. Kirchberger, Friedrich Sieber und Attila Biro gegründet wurde. Vier Jahre später hatten sie auf je individuelle Weise diese Werkphase überwunden, die Gruppe löste sich auf. Georg Karl Pfahler war sicher der eigenwilligste und erfolgreichste unter ihnen. Er fand als einer der ersten im Südwesten lebenden Künstler seiner Generation die Aufmerksamkeit einer übernationalen Kunstöffentlichkeit. Pfahlers frühe Arbeiten zeigen deutlich den Einfluß des Informel, sind jedoch nicht Ergebnisse gestisch-spontaner Malerei. In seinen Bildern verstärken sich die Ansätze einer konstruktiven Bildauffassung, verdichten sich die malerischen Strukturen zu großen Farbfeldern. Durch sein konsequentes Experimentieren und Erforschen der Farbe trug Pfahler maßgeblich zur Entwicklung der Farbformmalerei in Deutschland bei. Mit der Serie »Formativ« fand er 1960 zu der für ihn charakteristischen geometrisierten Bild- und Formensprache der Farbraummalerei. Farbe ist für ihn Bildmittel und Bildgegenstand zugleich. Pfahler schafft Raum ausschließlich durch das Nebeneinander unterschiedlicher Farbwerte in großen Flächenformen und bestimmt so die Relation von Bild und Grund, Farbe und Raum, Form und Bildgrenze vollkommen neu. Die Farben tragen sich gegenseitig. Pfahler begleitet und bereitet seine künstlerische Arbeit in den »Präkonzeptionen« vor: In diesen Bildideen auf Papier systematisiert er sein Formenrepertoire und spielt die Möglichkeiten der Farbe durch. Hier zeigt sich bereits das für ihn typische Arbeiten in Serien.

Bernd Berner war Mitglied der badischen Gruppe »SYN«, obwohl er bereits 1952 nach Stuttgart übersiedelte. Berner kam nach figurativen Anfängen um 1960 zur ganz aus der Farbe entwickelten »Flächenraum«-Malerei. Die Form, sehr häufig ein dem Bildformat einbeschriebenes Rechteck oder Quadrat, trat gegenüber der Farbe in den Hintergrund. Berners Bilder erscheinen als farbige Räume, die dem Betrachter entgegenwirken. Die Farbfelder ziehen sich fast über die gesamte Bildfläche, wobei nur eine schmale Randzone ausgespart bleibt. Jedes Feld besteht aus Schichten verschiedenfarbiger Flächen, die sich aus ungeordneten linearen Farbstrukturen zusammensetzen. An den Rändern erkennt man das gestisch-expressive Vorgehen. Hier werden die einzelnen Farben in ihrer ungemischten Reinheit sichtbar. Die Zone der farbigen Rinnsale trägt den Farbraum. Berner nutzt die räumliche Dynamik der gemalten Struktur und der Farben, die sich in der Überlagerung zu einer monochromen Farbform verbinden. Ohne gegenständliche Reminiszenz schafft sich das Bild eine eigene Wirklichkeit.

Auch Thomas Lenk hatte seine Anfänge im Informel. Mitte der sechziger Jahre kam er zu einer eigenwilligen Lösung auf dem Weg von der Kern- zur Raumplastik. Seine Skulpturen bestehen aus Hinter- oder Nebeneinanderreihungen genormter, zweidimensionaler Elemente, die nicht vorhandenes Volumen vortäuschen und gleichzeitig in den sie umgebenden Raum vordringen. Diese »Schichtungen« folgen, anders als die Reihungen der Minimal Art, einer Komposition, die oft in einer gedachten Mitte gegenläufige Bewegungen miteinander verbindet. Lenk setzt Farben ein, um die Raumwirkung der Skulpturen zu unterstützen oder abzuschwächen. Wie Pfahler und Hajek geht Lenk mit seinen Arbeiten in den öffentlichen Raum, den er als gesellschaftliches Phänomen und damit als einen Kontext von Kunst begreift, in dem sie sich beweisen muß.

Unter den Bildhauern der sechziger Jahre ist Erich Hauser hervorzuheben. Seine frühen Werke zeigen, dem Zeitgeist folgend, im Metall gestische Bearbeitungsspuren, später glättet er die Oberflächen. Früh sind die Themen angelegt, die Hauser zeit seines Lebens beschäftigen werden: Geschwindigkeit, Bewegung, von der Schwerkraft befreite, himmelstürmende Massen. Der Künstler wählt ein flaches Material, Stahlblech, das er durch Schneiden, Biegen, Schweißen, Hämmern und Schleifen zum Hohlkörper formt. So bildet er facettenreiche Konstruktionen mit kantigen Graten und Gruben. Hauser setzt sich mit geometrischen Grundformen und technoiden Bauelementen auseinander und interpretiert stereometrische Körper wie Kugel, Würfel oder Pyramide, indem er ihre regelmäßige Struktur in verschiedene Richtungen ausdehnt. Der Stahl wird immer mehr zur Hülle, die sich in Faltungen vertikal vom Boden aufrichtet. Daneben sind die röhrenartigen Säulen ein wichtiges Thema, auch sie als Hohlkörper aufgefaßt. Hausers Plastiken, oft nur auf wenigen Stützpunkten ausbalanciert, beziehen ihren Reiz aus dem schwebenden, labilen Gleichgewicht, in dem sie sich zu befinden scheinen.

Otto Herbert Hajek hat durch seine internationalen Aktivitäten den Namen Stuttgarts in die Welt getragen. Mit seinen frühen Arbeiten, den »Raumknoten« und »Raumschichtungen«, stand er in der Tradition des Informel: Bronzeskulpturen, die aus der Addition von Einzelstrukturen mit rauher Oberfläche entstanden waren. Die vertikal geschichteten Stäbe verbinden amorphe Strukturen in der Horizontale zu einem Gittersystem, das Raum locker umschließt. Mehr und mehr ließ Hajek den Umraum in die Skulptur eindringen. So entstehen begehbare Raumplastiken, die der Künstler mit ihrer Umgebung verschmelzen lassen wollte. Dazu bediente er sich auch raum-

O. H. Hajek: ›Frankfurter Frühling‹, 1962/63, auf der documenta III, 1964

plastischer Farbwirkungen: Hajek zog in den »Farbwegen« Farbbahnen durch die Umgebung und über die Objekte hinweg. Mitte der sechziger Jahre wurde seine Formensprache strenger. Er begann Konstruktionen aus geometrischen Elementen, in denen er waagrechte, senkrechte und diagonale Strukturen aneinanderreihte. Die Primärfarben Rot, Blau und Gelb setzten die übergeordneten Akzente und rhythmisierten die Raumgestalt. Ab 1973 arbeitete er neben den Raumstrukturen auch an Einzelplastiken, die als »Raumzeichen« ihre urbane Umgebung markieren. Hajeks Ansatz, Skulptur und Umraum als Einheit zu sehen, führt ihn zu intensiver Beschäftigung mit der Kunst im öffentlichen Raum. Gerade mit diesem Gebiet, das er im Sinne einer Kommunikation zwischen Kunst und Öffentlichkeit als demokratische Aktion sah, verbindet sich sein Name wie kein zweiter.

In den sechziger Jahren entfalteten sich auch neue figurative Tendenzen. Ihr Zentrum hatten sie in Karlsruhe, getragen von HAP Grieshaber, dem Reutlinger Holzschneider, und seinen Schülern. Die Zeit als Lehrer, zuerst an der Bernsteinschule, dann an der Karlsruher Akademie, die nach nur fünf Jahren 1960 im Eklat endete, war für ihn erfolgreich gewesen. Grieshabers Kunst, ein Sonderweg, war in Stuttgarts Öffentlichkeit stets gegenwärtig; seine spätexpressionistischen, politisch engagierten Holzschnitte haben ihm überregionale Beachtung eingetragen. Einer seiner talentiertesten Schüler stammt aus Stuttgart: Walter Stöhrer studierte von 1956–1960 in Karlsruhe und siedelte 1962 nach Berlin über. So nah er dem Lehrer stand, so kritisch sah er dessen Werk. Das zeigen auch die 1969 anläßlich der Grieshaber-Ausstellung in Stuttgart entstandenen Übermalungen von dessen Arbeiten: Stöhrer versuchte sich malend des Vorbilds zu entledigen. In der spontanen, den rauschhaften Malprozeß betonenden Arbeitsweise, nimmt er Einflüsse der informellen Malerei auf. Stöhrer setzt große, stark farbige Flächen gegen lineare, figurative Strukturen. Jede Setzung, jede Form fordert weitere ästhetische Entscheidungen heraus, die, sekundenschnell getroffen, über Gelingen oder Mißlingen eines Bildes entscheiden. Oft verbindet Stöhrer die gestischen Farbpartien mit literarischen Elementen, Textteilen, die der Malaktion als Inspiration dienen und als Schrift oder Collage Teil der Gestaltung werden. Anregungen können aber auch von sinnlichen Eindrücken der äußeren Wirklichkeit stammen, die im Bild sich mit Unbewußtem vermischen. Stöhrer selbst bezeichnet sein Verfahren als »intrapsychischen Realismus«, der seelische Prozesse visualisiert. Seine subjektiven Figurationen in leuchtenden, vitalen Farben stehen für eine persönliche, ausdrucksstarke Malerei.

Eine andere Richtung der figurativen Malerei wurzelte in der amerikanischen Pop Art und im Hyperrealismus, die ihren Weg nach Deutschland fanden. Die Pop-Artisten suchten ihre Themen und Gestaltungsmittel in der Werbung. Unter diesen Vorzeichen sind auch die realistischen Strömungen in Deutschland zu sehen: die Künstler nahmen den politischen und gesellschaftlichen Alltag ernst und hielten dem Wohlstandsfetischismus das private Leid derer entgegen, die aus dem Leistungssystem fielen.

Uwe Lausen, in Stuttgart geboren und auf der schwäbischen Alb aufgewachsen, hat die Pop Art sehr früh rezipiert. Als Autodidakt fand er im Umkreis der Münchner Gruppe SPUR zu Bildern, die nach Fotovorlagen entstanden. Seine Themen – Zerstörung, Verzweiflung und Tod – zeigen Nähe zur Bildwelt Lambert Maria Wintersbergers. Wintersberger, der 1969 zu den Künstlern der Galerie Müller stieß, ist wie Lausen Autodidakt. Ab 1965 entwickelte er in den »Kosmetikbildern« eine realistische Malerei auf surrealer Grundhaltung: es sind monu-

Uwe Lausen: Hervorragend. 1967

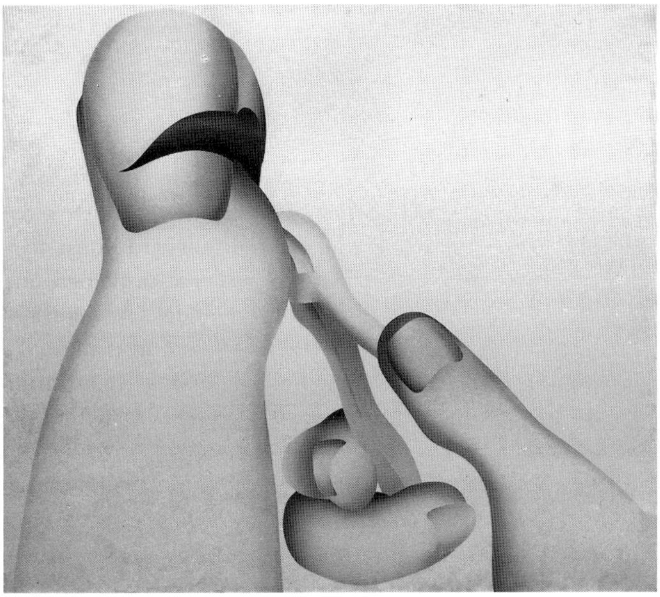

Lambert Maria Wintersberger: Maniküre. 1967

mentale Darstellungen von Fingernägeln und Mündern, die als Subjekte des Bildgeschehens ein Eigenleben entwickeln. Die latente Bedrohung, die diese überdimensionalen Gliedmaßen ausstrahlen, setzt Wintersberger im Motiv der Verletzung wenig später ins Bild: dicke Fingernägel, zerschnitten, verstümmelt, durchbohrt, verschraubt, gefesselt. Die Farben reduziert er auf Grauwerte. Diese Bilder sind Gleichnisse der Verletzung und der Verstümmelung von Menschen durch Menschen. In den großformatigen Porträts der siebziger Jahre zieht sich dieses Thema weiter. Die Zerstörung des Individuums wird deutlich in der Zergliederung der Gesichter. 1980 gibt Wintersberger die Nähe zur Wirklichkeit zugunsten einer malerischen Bildauffassung auf.

Die Bilder Ben Willikens', ab 1962 Schüler von Heinz Trökes in Stuttgart, kreisen um Architektur. Räume, genauer Innenräume, sind sein Motiv. Ihm liegt jedoch nicht an Architekturdarstellung, sondern an der emotionalen Wirkung und nihilistischen Bedeutung menschenleerer Räume: Bilder der Verlassenheit und der Kälte. Charakteristisch für die frühen Bilder von Fluren und Anstaltsräumen ist eine hyperrealistische Darstellungsweise. Ihre Perfektion erreicht Willikens durch feinste Farbnebel aus der Sprühdose, durch konstruktive Klarheit der Komposition und maßvolle Proportion des dargestellten Raums. Der Künstler zieht sich durch das fast mechanische bildnerische Verfahren scheinbar aus dem Bild zurück, indem er keine »Handschrift« erkennen läßt. Wer genauer hinschaut, bemerkt, daß Willikens sein fotografisches Vorbild in der Darstellung kritisch verändert: er klammert Menschen aus, läßt Nebensächliches weg und komprimiert Bildgegenstände und Bildaussage. In den aseptischen Anstaltsbildern wie in den späteren pathetischen Raumvisionen zitiert der Künstler die Architektursprache sakraler Bauten und setzt das Licht entsprechend pointierend ein. Die exakt nachahmende Wiedergabe äußerer Erscheinungen, wie sie die Renaissance im Entwurf eines möglichst wirklichkeitsnahen Sehbilds erstrebte, weicht bei Willikens der Transparenz des Dargestellten.

Ben Willikens: Anstaltsflur No. 3. 1973

1 Hans-Jürgen Müller: Kunst kommt nicht von Können, Nürnberg 1976, S. 265.

2 Zit. nach: Ausstellungskatalog Galerie Schlichtenmaier: 45 Jahre Malerei, Plastik, Graphik an der Stuttgarter Akademie, Grafenau 1990, S. 5.

3 Zit. nach: »Stuttgarter Zeitung«, Nr. 124 vom 2. 6. 1967.

4 Vgl. Reinhard Döhl: »Stuttgarter Gruppe« – nicht »Schule«, in: Flugasche, 6/1986.

5 Vgl. »Stuttgarter Leben«, 42/1967, Heft 4, S. 8ff. In seinem Artikel »Kunstsammler in Stuttgart« zeichnet Dieter Honisch ein interessantes Porträt aus zeitgenössischer Sicht.

»Wird die moderne Kunst gemanagt?« Kunst und Kunstpublizistik in Baden-Baden zwischen 1955 und 1965[1]

Ästhetische Botschaften können verstanden werden, weil sie auf Evolution beruhen, weil kein Kunstwerk ein »Etwas für sich« ist, sondern ein Beziehungswesen eben auch hinsichtlich seiner zeitlichen Herkunft und Zukunft.

Otto Stelzer[2]

Baden-Baden rückt gleich nach dem Ende des 2. Weltkrieges in den Mittelpunkt des internationalen Ausstellungsgeschehens. Als Teil der französischen – mithin westlich demokratisch freien – Kulturpolitik werden zunächst im Kurhaus anspruchsvolle Übersichtsschauen der benachbarten Kultur gezeigt. Programmatisch machte man seinen Einfluß und Anspruch in »Frankreich – Baden. Im Spiegel der Geschichte 1660–1860« geltend. Die später nach Mainz und Berlin weitergereichte Ausstellung »Moderne französische Malerei. Vom Impressionismus bis zur Gegenwart« (1946) zeigte auf höchstem Niveau mit nicht weniger als 130 Gemälden von über 100 Künstlern den Stand der französischen Malerei in diesem Jahrhundert. Überliefert ist diese hochkarätig ausgestattete Präsentation in einem kleinen Katalog[3] und in der Zeitschrift, die ab 1946 von Baden-Baden aus die Kunst der Welt nach Deutschland einführte.[4] Es ist »Das Kunstwerk«, jene legendäre das internationale Kunstgeschehen dokumentierende, analysierende und kritisch befragende »Monatsschrift über alle Gebiete der Bildenden Kunst«, die der Verleger Woldemar Klein begründet hatte. Bis heute ist dieses älteste Kunstmagazin der deutschen Nachkriegszeit dank seiner engagierten Redakteure Leopold Zahn (1949–1970), Klaus Jürgen-Fischer (1956–1988) und Rolf-Gunter Dienst (1964–1991) ein in der deutschen Kunstpublizistik einzigartiges Forum mit weitreichendem Einfluß.

Die 1909 gegründete Staatliche Kunsthalle Baden-Baden wird als Austellungshaus regelmäßig erst wieder ab 1953 genutzt.[5] Die Leitung lag zunächst in den Händen des »Kunsthallen-Ausschusses Baden-Baden«. Erst im April 1952 wurde der ehemalige Sprecher der 1946 neu gegründeten Badischen Sezession, der Maler Erwin Heinrich zum Direktor bestellt, mit der Aufgabe zeitgenössische badische Kunst und kunsthandwerkliche Erzeugnisse in regelmäßigen Ausstellungen zu zeigen. Heinrichs Neigung zur Kultur des südbadischen Landesteils forderte nordbadischen Widerstand heraus, mit Rückhalt in der noch nicht überwundenen tausendjährigen Vergangenheit in Karlsruhe – und in Stuttgart. »Neben dem 1. Vorsitzenden des ›Verbandes bildender Künstler e.V.‹ Kühlewein, war es vor allem der Maler Oskar Hagemann, Sprecher der ›Gemeinschaft deutscher Künstler‹, der als schärfster Kritiker der, wie er meinte, ›modernistischen Richtung‹ hervortrat.«[6] Er forderte, »...daß auch die politischen Hemmungen fallen und nicht mehr nach allen möglichen früheren Taten geurteilt wird. Kunst ist im Grunde immer unpolitisch und wird es sicher auch bleiben, und Künstler sind im Grunde immer politische Kinder...«[7] Künstlerische Qualität, vor allem aber der Öffnung der Kunsthalle in die Moderne standen unversöhnlich einflußreiche Seilschaften gegenüber, die bewirkten, daß die soeben eingerichtete Stelle von Erwin Heinrich bereits 1953 wieder gekündigt wurde. Zum Ausgleich der Konflikte zwischen den Künstlervereinigungen wurde ein Beirat eingerichtet, der Mitspracherecht beim Haushalt und der Berufung des Leiters erhielt. Nach dem Tod von Erwin Heinrich[8] wurde Dietrich Mahlow, promovierter Philosoph und Kunsthistoriker, u. a. mit Fürsprache des Freiburger Bildhauers Walter Schelenz, damals Ausschußleiter im südwestdeutschen Kulturring, und Georg Schmidt, Direktor des Baseler Kunstmuseums, zum Nachfolger gewählt, mit 26 Jahren einer der jüngsten Kunsthallendirektoren Europas. Er wird zwischen 1956 und 1967 durch sein engagiertes, in dieser Zeit bundesweit einmaliges differenziertes Programm die Kunsthalle zu internationalem Ansehen führen.

Dietrich Mahlow, der 1954 nach Baden-Baden zu Woldemar Klein gekommen war, trat sein Amt kommissarisch im September 1956 als ehemaliger Geschäftsführer eines Kunstvereins an, denn im Jahr zuvor hatte die »Gesellschaft der Freunde junger Kunst e.V.« sich konstituiert, nach dem gleichnamigen Münchener Vorbild – dort unter der Leitung des renommierten Kunsthistorikers und Kritikers Franz Roh und seiner Frau Juliane. »Die Gesellschaften haben sich zum Ziel gesetzt, das Verständnis zwischen Kunst und Publikum zu vertiefen und den Kontakt zwischen Freunden der jungen Kunst und zeitgenössischen Künstlern über ihre Werke aufzunehmen, um so der Urteilsbildung und der künstlerischen Arbeit zu dienen. Auf diesem Wege werden sie von Verlag und Redaktion der Zeitschrift DAS KUNSTWERK unterstützt.«[9] Präsident ist Dr. Leopold Zahn bis zu seinem Tod im Jahre 1970, der langjährige Herausgeber und Redakteur des »Kunstwerk«. Gründungsmitglieder sind Dietrich Mahlow und Klaus Jürgen-Fischer, Maler und Publizist, Sohn des Inhabers des AGIS-Verlag, Baden-Baden, Karl G. Fischer. Hinzu kamen die Kunstsammler Otto und Alice Schrag, der österreichische Honorarkonsul Prof. Dr. Philip Möhring und Fritz Borsi, Fabrikant in Offenburg. Die städtische Protektion vertrat der Oberbürgermeister von Baden-Baden Dr. Ernst Schlapper. Studienreisen, Vorträge, eine Leihbilderei, die Stiftung eines Kunstkritikerpreises und kleine Ausstellungen prägen den pädagogischen Impetus der Gesellschaft. Mit der Übernahme der Leitung der Kunsthalle

Gegenstand – selbst als Gegenstand der Weihe – verliert, ist damit nur noch Zeugnis künstlerischen Vermögens, nur mehr reines Kunstwerk; man kann sogar ohne Übertreibung sagen: ein künstlerischer Moment. Aber das ist es nun voll und ganz; mit Ausnahme einiger Werke, die der Funke künstlerischen Genies dem Historischen entreißt, sind diese so verschiedenen Kunstwerke Zeugnisse für ein immer gleiches Streben: als stieße ein imaginärer Geist der Kunst auf immer gleichem Eroberungszug von Miniatur zu Tafelbild, von Fresko zu Glasfenster vor... Die Reproduktion erweckt sie zum Leben und zwingt sie, sich in ihrem Sinngehalt zu offenbaren.«[35] Es hat den Anschein, daß der hier formulierte Werkbegriff, der die Form als genuin geistige Leistung und poetische Methode einer künstlerischen Sprache begreift, das Selbstverständnis des »Kunstwerk« durchwirkt, und seine Richtschnur wird.

Wege im »Kunstwerk« zwischen 1955 und 1965

1955 wird »Das Kunstwerk« zeitgleich mit der Gründung der Gesellschaft der Freunde junger Kunst« in den AGIS-Verlag übernommen. Leopold Zahn führt die Schriftleitung weiter. Klaus Jürgen-Fischer bestimmt mit ihm ab 1956 gemeinsam die redaktionelle Arbeit und das Erscheinungsbild. Die Übernahme bewirkt eine deutlichere Öffnung in die zeitgenössische Diskussion um Kunst und Kunstbegriffe.[36] Neben den monographischen Darstellungen einzelner Künstlerpersönlichkeiten sind Sonderhefte den großen Ausstellungen wie Biennale Venedig und documenta in Kassel gewidmet. Hinzu kommen ausführliche Themendarstellungen wie das Verhältnis zwischen informeller Kunst und Fotografie, der Einfluß Ostasiens auf die Moderne, dem Tanz und Bühnenbild, den außereuropäischen Kulturen, der Kunsterziehung. Ein gewichtiger Akzent ist die Würdigung der Architektur, die Diskussion um die Begrifflichkeit von Kunstkritik, Rezensionen, Berichte über Ausstellungsereignisse im In- und Ausland, nicht zuletzt birgt das Tagebuch der Redaktion, eine Erfindung des »Kunstwerk«, vielfältige intime Nachrichten, auch polemische Kommentare zur internationalen Kunstszene.

Das »Kunstwerk« leugnete nie den bildungsbürgerlichen Anspruch und das Fortschreiben der Moderne mit klassischem Bezug, dabei wurde eher ernsthaft diskutiert, auch anspruchsvoll und elitär, denn Wert auf eine unterhaltsame Journalistensprache gelegt. Stets waren die Hefte auf eine Fülle von Reproduktionen ausgelegt, auch solche, die nicht unbedingt sich in die redaktionellen Beiträge fügten. Zwar stellt Margit Staber im Januar 1961 Marcel Duchamp vor[37], doch findet die Erweiterung des Kunstbegriffs seit 1960, die systematische Entmaterialisierung des Kunstwerks und seiner sinnlichen Anschauung in Minimal Art, Fluxus und Konzeptkunst wenig Raum. Der »Ausstieg aus dem Bild« in Environment und Happening tangiert so erst verhältnismäßig spät das Interesse der Redakteure. Erstmals 1965 kritisiert Jürgen Morschel Wolf Vostells Happening »In Ulm, um Ulm und um Ulm herum« als eine durch Partitur und symbolische Bezüge den ästhetischen Raum zwar ausweitende, aber nie wirklich verlassende Form des künstlerischen Handelns, mithin letztlich eine untaugliche Form der ersehnten Vereinigung von Kunst und Leben.[38]

Parteilichkeit macht letztlich die Prägnanz des »Kunstwerk« aus. Man widmete man sich den Problemstellungen der abstrakten Malerei. Verfolgt man diese Position in der Zeit zwischen 1950 und 1965 kursorisch, so zeigt sich, daß Baden-Baden »Tatort des Informel« war, wie Albert Schulze-Vellinghausen schrieb,[39] und daß das »Kunstwerk« an der kritischen Würdigung seiner Grenzen und an der Weiterentwicklung der Malerei beteiligt war. Das »Kunstwerk« ist eine Institution für die Avantgarde, Ort der Verteidigung der Moderne durch Aufklärung. Die Frage nach der Berechtigung einer Kunst, die den Gegenstand verläßt, um in der Freiheit ihrer Mittel einen zeitgemäßen Ort zu formulieren, ist immer wieder analysiert worden. Sie ist in Teilen auch die Diskussion um die Stellung der Kultur im politisch historischen Kontext der jungen Bundesrepublik, wenn Realismus mit Sozialismus bzw. Faschismus identifiziert wurde und eine abstrakte Kunst als ausschließlich einer Demokratie würdig, die Autonomie des Individuums feiert.[40]

»Kunstpreis der Jugend 1959«: ein Streitfall

1959 wird das 50jährige Jubiläum zum Bestehen der Kunsthalle Anlaß für die großangelegte »Deutsche Kunstausstellung«. Man hatte diese Präsentation aus platztechnischen Gründen teilen müssen. Im späten Frühjahr zeigte man die ältere Generation, während im Herbst, diesmal als »Deutscher Kunstpreis der Jugend«, die Künstler bis 35 gezeigt wurden. Egon Vietta beobachtet in einer Ausstellungskritik hoffnungsfroh Neues zwischen Gegenständlichkeit in gestischer Abstraktion bei Horst Antes wie in minutiöser Perfektion bei Konrad Klapheck.[41] Hervorgehoben werden allerdings auch die neuen Bildformen, die sich in Düsseldorf zu ZERO abzeichnen. Mono-

Kunstpreis der Jugend, 1959. Jury mit Grochowiak, Kindermann, Apollonio, Jürgen-Fischer, Bachmann

chromie und Licht sind Ausgangspunkt systematischer ästhetischer Erfahrung. »...die Moderne ist bei der Jugend zu einer Grundlage geworden, mit der sie zu arbeiten weiß. Es ist kein blindes Tasten, sondern bereits ein behutsames Umgehen mit den neuen Mitteln zu beobachten (...). Wenn man darin den Nihilismus in Reinkultur sieht, wie es eine Karlsruher Zeitung formulierte, stört man den Arbeitsernst dieser Jugend durch nichtssagendes Ressentiment.« Von Vorteil sei es, daß der heutige junge Künstler nicht zu Abenteuern aufbricht, sondern etwas Neuem entgegenwartet. »Sein Interesse gilt der konsequenten Arbeit. Worin man diese Jugend bestärken muß.«[42] Doch die Frage nach dem Ort der Kunst kulminiert in einem Streit um den Preisvergabe der Baden-Badener Ausstellung. Aus den 1200 Arbeiten von 440 Künstlern hatte die Jury den Düsseldorfer Bildhauer Friedrich Werthmann (10000.– DM), den Pankofer-Preis erhielt Horst Antes, Karlsruhe (2000.–), Heimrad Prem, München (1000.– DM) und Otto Piene Düsseldorf (500.– DM) ausgewählt. Den Preis der Gesellschaft erhielt Emil Cimiotti (2000.–). Die öffentliche Ablehnung hatte nicht nur künstlerische Dimensionen: »Erstens: Die vom Senat der Staatlichen Akademie in Stuttgart geäußerten Bedenken gegen die Jury für den »Kunstpreis der Jugend« löste eine Zeitungsdiskussion zum Thema Dirigismus in der Kunst aus, dokumentiert in der Zeitschrift »Das Kunstwerk« 1959. Dieser Kunstpreis und seine Träger wurden von den Badischen Neuesten Nachrichten, schon damals konservativ, als Ausdruck des »abstrakten Nihilismus in Reinkultur« bezeichnet und damit abgelehnt. Zweitens wurde die Präsentation vorwiegend abstrakter Kunst auf der »documenta II« im selben Jahr Anlaß zum Aufstand der Provinzredakteure. Der Streit entzündet sich an dem Entscheid der Auswahlkommission, zu der bedeutende Künstler und Museumsdirektoren gehören[43], für den Preis an Horst Antes, dessen Werk pauschal als zu modern angesehen wird, wenngleich sich hier Neues zeigt, wie Egon Vietta lobend hervorhebt: »Der Mangel an gültigen gegenständlichen Lösungen war auch in Baden-Baden auffallend, da die Jury nur zu geneigt war, Talente auszuzeichnen, die dem Gegenstand neue Gesichtspunkte abgewinnen. (...) Maler, die Gegenständliches andeuten, sind schon auf dem halben Weg zur Abstraktion, was bei Heimrad Prem (...) und Horst Antes aus der Grieshaber-Schule sichtbar ist. Das brennende Rot ist zugleich Aussage über Reales, hier die Schwangerschaft.«[44] »Bei dem ersten Alarm wird das Beispiel eines Künstlers genannt, der mit gegenständlichem, halbgegenständlichem Bild nicht durchkommt und dann mit seinem »Sauftachismus« reüssiert. Einen Jux habe er sich machen wollen...«.[45] Die Antwort aus Stuttgart wiegelt ab: Man habe nur Sorge, daß schlecht gemalt würde, Sorge auch um die Qualität des Urteils über Kunst, wenn man Einseitigkeit in der Jury findet, die zumeist aus dem Bereich des Tachismus kämen. Egon Vietta antwortete: »Ich glaube nie und nimmer, daß wir mit dem aufgewärmten Streit, ob abstrakt oder nicht, weiterkommen. (...) Aber ich wehre mich ganz entschieden dagegen, daß der augenblickliche Mangel eines gegenständlichen Genies (...) den Nichtgegenständlichen zur Last gelegt wird.«[46]

Kunstgespräch Frankfurt 1960: E. Fiebig, K. Jürgen-Fischer, H. Wescher, W. Hofmann, C. Schweicher

Das Baden-Badener Kunstgespräch 1959

Diese Auseinandersetzung war ausschlaggebend für das Thema der Baden-Badener Kunstgespräche »Wird die moderne Kunst gemanagt?«, das vom AGIS-Verlag im Oktober 1959 im Kurhaus veranstaltet wurde.[47] Kritiker, Künstler, Kunsthistoriker und Verleger suchten den gesellschaftlichen Bezug darzulegen. Kunsthandel und Museums- und Ausstellungswesen als Partner, Basis und Widerpart, Sprachrohr und Nutznießer der Künstler wurden als Elemente eines Betriebssystem erstmals offen diskutiert. Doch mußte auch die Moderne als solche verteidigt werden, was die Zielrichtung der Tagung verunklärt. Nicht zuletzt macht die Diskussion politische Standpunkte offenbar, aus denen heraus Kunst und Kultur auch in Baden-Baden gefördert wird.

Henry Kahnweiler sah die Verbindung zwischen Kunsthandel und Mäzenatentum als Vermittlung aus Liebe und Freude an der Kunst und nicht aus Gründen der Spekulation. Handel mit junger Kunst heißt Investition und nicht Gewinn. Die abstrakte Kunst auf der documenta II ist für ihn Kunstgewerbe. Wie die Salonmalerei des 19. Jahrhunderts habe sie die klassische Moderne ausgebeutet, ohne sie zu verstehen.[48] Egon Vietta hingegen stellt fest, daß Künstler selbst sich des Gegenstandes entledigt hätten, und nicht ein Komplott von Kunsthändlern und Kunstkritikern, die publizistischen und kommerziellen Erfolge seien nicht an Stil und Haltung gebunden, sondern an künstlerischer Qualität.[49] Eher links orientierte Argumentationen fanden in Baden-Baden wenig Gegenliebe. Jürgen Beckelmann, Mitherausgeber der sozialistischen Zeitschrift »Tendenzen« konstatiert, daß mißverständlich Moderne nur mit ungegenständlicher Kunst gleichgesetzt werde, daß zudem das

Wort Management einen »üblen Beigeschmack« habe. »Es klingt nach Unlauterkeit, nach Manipulation.« Er sehe »viel ehrliche Begeisterung und ehrliches Mitgehen«.[50] Gegenstandslose Kunst stehe jedoch auch zwischen individualistischer Dekoration und kritikloser Akzeptanz gesellschaftlicher Verhältnisse, ohne selbst ein Wertsystem zu stiften,[51] und sei es die moralische Aufgabe der Kunst, sich der »gesellschaftlichen Untergrundwerte« zu versichern. Hoffnung liege in figurativ realistischer Kunst, die die Welt von heute widerspiegelt.[52] Beckelmanns Forderung nach einem Wertesystem wird in der Diskussion heftig kritisiert, weil gerade sein Fehlen die Freiheit der Kunst begründe. Konrad Farner sieht in der documenta II »bürgerliche Weltangst«. »Sie ist nicht Modellfall einer Weltkultur, sondern Modellfall einer problematisch gewordenen Klassenkultur, deren innerste geistige Situation von den subtilsten Seismographen, den Künstlern, exakt aufgezeigt wird.«[53] Dem auch aus dem linken Spektrum argumentierenden Farner hält Karl G. Fischer als Verleger entgegen, daß er als Manager der Moderne fungiere und daß »das Kunstwerk« zwar keine ausgesprochen kunstpolitische Publikation sei, aber wohl die einzige deutsche Zeitschrift, die unabhängig und ohne Rücksicht auf den Publikumsgeschmack die neue abstrakte, also moderne Kunst vertritt[54], eine Position die sich eher durch kritische Reflexion als durch materiellen Gewinn auszeichne. So verwehrt er sich entschieden gegen jede Wertehierarchie, denn dann würde »das Einschienensystem der Wertebefürworter proklamiert«, mithin ein Maß gefunden, das Dirigismus befördere. »Und sind die sozialistischen Verächter unsrer Kunst und die Befürworter neuer Werte im Grunde nicht identisch mit den konservativen Klageweibern um den Verlust der Mitte.«[55] Als Maler, Mitveranstalter und Redakteur macht Klaus Jürgen-Fischer nochmals entschieden deutlich, daß sich in der Abstraktion die aktuelle Kunst verkörpert. »Wer die letzten Bilder von Bernard Buffet, dem gegenständlichen Paradepferd, gesehen hat, kann bei wärmsten Vertrauen nicht mehr damit rechnen, daß aus dieser illustrativen Ecke noch etwas zu erwarten ist.«[56] Der Kunstbetrieb sei Teil der Gesellschaft, eine systematische, verschworene Gemeinde fehle: so seien Beziehungen und Korruption, Preisabsprachen und das Ausspielen von Rivalitäten auch Teil dieses Systems und damit Normalität in der Massengesellschaft. »Deshalb unsere Gesellschaft für an der Wurzel krank zu halten, ist auch meines Erachtens eine kulturpessimistische Vermessenheit.«[57] Für Theodor W. Adorno sind nicht die Gegnerschaften das Problem, sondern die normierten Reaktionen. »Man meint, über das herfallen zu dürfen, was man nicht versteht, weil in solchem Unverständnis ohnehin alle vernünftigen Leute übereinstimmten. Es ist die gleiche fatale Selbststilisierung wie die des deutschen Michel, der sich als naiv und tumb ausgibt, nur um daraus ableiten zu können, daß er immerzu über die Ohren gehauen werde, permanentes Opfer jener Manipulationen, an welche nach alter Väter Sitte ganz gewiß auch die denken, welche der neuen Kunst vorhalten, sie werde gemanagt.«[58] So empfiehlt er die Hotelbildmalerei, »eine umgekehrte Sezession sozusagen, mit nicht entarteter Kunst. (...) Eine solche Ausstellung, schräg gegenüber einer mit Winter und Nay, Emil Schumacher und Bernard Schultze, würde zwar die Frage nach dem Managertum nicht lösen, aber überflüssig machen.«[59]

Als Vertreter der vom Vorwurf der Manipulation getroffenen Künstler stellte HAP Grieshaber dar, wie sehr der Künstler auf Vermittlung angewiesen ist, da sein Arbeitsplatz im Atelier ist: Kunst bedarf der Öffentlichkeit. »Wer formt, erstrebt das Vollkommene, er denkt nicht an Bekanntes und auch nicht an den Kenner. (...) Ich bitte Sie geradezu darum, meine Damen und Herren, managen Sie, soviel Sie können. Das ist es nicht, was ein Künstler zu fürchten hat, er müßte schon ein schwacher Maler sein.«[60] Gefahr allerdings droht, wenn der Markt seine Bedingungen festlegt: Format, Technik, Regale, Verträge, doch sei der Markt Distributionssystem und Informationsbörse mit eigener Dynamik. Als Akademielehrer bereite er Studenten auf die Strukturen eines Lebens in einer von Normierungsmechanismen durchdrungenen Gesellschaft vor. »Wir leiden immer noch an der falschen Konfrontierung von 1945: hier moderne Kunst, hier Afterkunst des III. Reiches. Wir leiden am Plebiszit, einem über uns hängenden imaginären Fragebogen, der fragt: Wie stehen Sie zur modernen Kunst? Welche Gründe würden Sie dafür anführen? (...) Ausgerechnet wir leiden am meisten von allen Völkern an der Phrase vom unverbildeten Menschen, den es nicht gibt; es müßte ihn erst – durch Kunst – geben.«[61]

Argumente in Offsetlithographie

Daß die Frage nach dem Verhalten der Kunst zwischen Produktion, Innovation und Markt anders problematisiert werden kann, stellt HAP Grieshaber und seine Klasse mit einem Künstlerbuch für den »Kunstpreis der Jugend 1959« unter Beweis.[62] Aus Karlsruhe sind Horst Antes, Heinz Schanz und Walter Stöhrer beteiligt, aus Stuttgart treten als Typographen Manfred Kröplien und Iwar Radowitz hinzu. Das Buch wurde mit einem Sonderpreis ausgezeichnet, doch ergaben sich Turbulenzen. Denn Kröplin wurde wegen seines Engagements im Badischen von der Stuttgarter Akademie verwiesen.[63] Es ist die Zeit, in der es noch niemand wagte, gegen die Exmatrikulation vor laufenden Mikrofonen Stellung zu nehmen.

Der überformatige Band ist bewußt anspruchslos auf holzhaltigem Papier im Foto-Offset-Verfahren gedruckt, ein »sachlicheres Vervielfältigungsmittel als der Siebdruck« ohne die Aura des Künstlerischen, das die gestische Spontaneität und des Abdruckens von gefundenen Materialien und Gegenständen auf den Druckfolien zuläßt. »Was herauskam, war keine Graphik im eigentlichen Sinne, aber auch kein Fabrikat. (...) Die Materie ist allerdings völlig weggewischt, geblieben ist der élan und das Lebensfluidum einer guten Stunde. Immerhin, für einen Katalog, in dem eine Generation sofort und unmittelbar da sein muß, ein besseres und billigeres Verfahren, als Zinkätzung und Autotypie«, heißt es im Vorwort.[64] Zu dem Heft hatte Grieshaber einen vielfigurigen Holzschnitt beigetragen. Schanz und Stöhrer lassen energetisch ausgreifende Farbschlieren über die Bildflächen wuchern. Sie wechseln mit informell überarbeiteten Buchstabenfolgen von Manfred Kröplin. Horst Antes hingegen setzt klare Farben in entschiedenen Pinselzügen gegeneinander. Zudem: der Falz, der Seitenbeschnitt macht den informellen Fluß zur Bildfigur. »...so taten wir's, nur damit wir etwas täten, was eine Lust ist, weil es nicht erlaubt ist«[65] zitieren die Herausgeber den Heiligen Augustinus. »AN KUNSTHALLE BADEN-BADEN ALS UNVERLANGTE UND UNBEZAHLTE ANTWORT AUF DEN PRESSESTREIT ÜBER DEN KUNSTPREIS DER JUGEND« ist auf den programmatisch abgedruckten Brief von Albrecht Fabri vom 4. April 1959 an HAP Grieshaber gestempelt. Aber es ist nicht nur technisch sachliche Filterung seismographischer Unmittelbarkeit in existentieller Selbstfindung, sondern kritische, ehrlichere, realistischere Einschätzung, daß Kunst auch Ware ist, und nicht Fetisch sein muß. Der Warencharakter der Kunst verändert die Kunst, was nicht ohne Ausdruck, ohne inhaltliche Dimensionen sein muß: »Indem man die Sache von vornherein auf Reproduktion anlegt, selbst den Begriff des Originals vernichten! (...) Kunst ist entweder Magie oder Politik. Im ersten Fall genügt es, daß sie da ist, im zweiten muß sie gezeigt werden. Im ersten Fall läßt sich das Kunstwerk ins Meer werfen oder im Sand vergraben, im zweiten bedarf es der Katalogisierung und Ausstellung. Alternativ dementsprechend: Opferrauch oder Flugblatt, Gebetsfahne oder Plakat.«[66]

Zwischen Künstler und Konsument steht nicht die unmittelbare, menschliche Beziehung, der Warencharakter verdeckt diese Beziehung. Die Kunstlosigkeit der Offsetlithographie bedeutet neue Freiheit gegenüber dem singulären Original. Pop Art wird wenige Jahre später mit Multiples und dem Siebdrucken eine in diesem Jahrhundert einzigartige Demokratisierung der Kunst betreiben, eine Fortschreibung auch des Malraux'schen Gedankens zur Intellektualisierung des Kunstwerks durch Reproduktion.[67] Letztlich geht es um Botschaft ohne Aura und Ästhetisierung, eine weitere Antwort auf Walter Benjamin: »Die Entwicklung, die das Kunstwerk zur Ware gemacht hat, läßt sich nicht rückgängig machen. Man kann ihr höchstens dadurch begegnen, daß man den Warencharakter der Kunst noch übertreibt: ein in zehntausend Exemplaren und auf schlechtem Papier abgezogener Holzschnitt z.B. wäre keine Aktie mehr.«[68] Der Konflikt liegt im Kunstbegriff der bürgerlichen Gesellschaft, der den geistigen Gehalt zum Fetisch eines Kunstbetriebes macht, der darauf aus ist, Kapital zu mehren und damit Kunst im Sinne sozialisierender Konsolidierung ad absurdum führt, aber – contradictio in adjecto – eben ein Kunstbetrieb auch. »An sich übrigens durchaus logisch, die Entwicklung der Kunst als Ware. (...) Kultur halt! Unsere Feinde sind wahrhaftig nicht die Barbaren. Eher schon die, von denen wir leben und auf die zu schimpfen nicht sie ins Unrecht setzt, sondern uns.«[69] Albrecht Fabris Texte hatten in Köln einen engagierten Verleger gefunden, Heinz Stüncke, Inhaber der Galerie Der Spiegel.[70]

Figur: menschlich

Daß Sinnfindung noch aus der Gestalt gewonnen werden kann, beschreibt Kurt Leonhard im März 1961 in der erste großen Dokumentation über HAP Grieshaber: »Jede Idee, jedes Erlebnis, jeder Gegenstand, jede Form geraten ihm unter der Hand zu Gleichnissen, und es gibt kein noch so abseitiges Nebenwerk von ihm, das bedeutungsfrei, beziehungslos, inhaltleer oder gedankenarm wäre. So wenig er jemals ungegenständlich arbeitete, so wenig tritt er jemals unverbindlich auf. Er würde nie auf den Gedanken kommen, daß Kunst und Leben sich trennen ließen.«[71] Nicht mehr konkrete Realität des Bildes als autopoetische Sensibilisierung, sondern Bildersehen in der Verwandlung in archaisch mythischen Dimensionen. Erst verhältnismäßig spät, 1965, sieht Klaus Hoffmann im »Kunstwerk« die Grieshaber-Klasse als Vertreter eines überzeitlichen expressiven Stils, der an die Brücke, den abstrakten Expressionismus und Cobra figurativ anschließt. Horst Antes, Hans Baschang, Walter Stöhrer, Heinz Schanz und der seit 1958 an der Akademie lehrende Herbert Kitzel. Bei Horst Antes beschäftigt Hoffmann Figur und Auge, die Riesen-Gnom Gestalt »als muskelstarker Dämon und zugleich schwächlich-ohnmächtiger Geist«. Tragisch Expressives verbindet sich mit burlesker Komik. »Vom herkömmlichen Expressionismus unterscheidet ihn (...) der Anflug von Heiterkeit, genauer: von lustigem Ernst. Seine Mißgestalt im Spiel mit den tückischen Objekten seiner Welt. (...) Die neu, frei streunende Heiterkeit ist jedoch nicht in der Nähe von Verzerrung und Karikatur zu suchen. Dennoch kann man einige dieser tragisch-heiteren Figuren in die Familie grotesker und phantastischen Erfindungen stellen...«[72] In den stürzenden Figuren Herbert Kitzels sieht Hoffmann eine Aufhebung des Anekdotisch-Epischen zugunsten einer größeren, auch körperlichen Unmittelbarkeit. »Die letzte Phase läßt auch die Figuren fort und umschreibt in Kurve, Schleifspur und Wirbelform nur noch energetische Form, zeigt nur noch spontaner Zeichen für Bewegung.«[73] Stille, meditative, aus Ovalen gebaute Körperanalogien findet Hans Baschang in »lyrischen-bildnerischen Sachverhalten« jenseits einer thematischen Bindung, die in manchen Bildtiteln anklingt. »Die Aktionsform ist gegenwärtig durch meditative Formen ersetzt. Aber jene Bilder hatten vom Prinzip her die gleiche Stimmung des Ungefähr. (...)[74] Walter Stöhrers Farbbänder überspülen die Figur, inspiriert durch literarische Bezüge, stören, öffnen sie und löschen sie aus. »Unter der feinen, gelegentlich durchsichtigen Fläche werden – wie hinter Glas oder unter einer milchigen Flüssigkeit – ferne Geschehnisse, angedeutete bewegliche Figuren sichtbar, erahnbar.«[75] Heinz Schanz sieht Hoffmann als inspirierenden Maler für

In der Wiesbadener Galerie Roepke finden sich Bernd Berner, Piero Dorazio, Gotthard Graubner, Reimer Jochims und Klaus Jürgen-Fischer im Februar 1962 in einer gemeinsamen Ausstellung zusammen, die zugleich Manifest ist: »Komplexe Farbe«, ein Bekenntnis zur chromatischen Erfahrung durch Malerei: »Die bauende, Sichtbarkeit regierende und spiritualisierende Tätigkeit des Malers gelangt nur an das Ziel einer lebenden Ordnung, wenn sie die Farbe nicht wuchern läßt, wie die Natur, sondern sensibel und gewaltlos bemißt.«[108] Diese Ausstellung wird die Keimzelle für eine Künstlergruppe, die nicht nur einen eigenen Beitrag zur Malerei bildet, sondern auch durch die Erfahrungen ihrer Mitglieder mit dem Kunstbetrieb eine professionelle Marketing-Politik betrieb. Diese garantierte den Bestand immerhin bis in die siebziger Jahre und brachte neben zahlreichen Publikationen 20 Ausstellungen und Ausstellungsbeteiligungen.

Die erste Ausstellung von SYN war vom »Kunstwerk« vorbereitet worden. Zeitgleich im April-Juni 1965 erscheint »Neue Abstraktion«, in dem Klaus Jürgen-Fischer die internationalen Dimensionen einer Kunst zwischen Colourfield, Hard Edge und Minimal Art diskutiert[109], die das Bild als Objekt mit geometrisierenden Fragestellungen und farbanalytischen Problemen thematisiert.

Am 29. Mai 1965 lud man in die Galerie Baier in Mainz zu einer »Anti-Eröffnung« mit einem Pseudo-Happening »Ein Popanz der deutschen Kunstkritik« ein. Bernd Berner, Rolf-Gunter Dienst, Klaus Jürgen-Fischer, Eduard Micus und der Engländer Marc Vaux stellten sich als Gruppe SYN der Öffentlichkeit, wobei Gemeinsamkeiten in vergleichbaren künstlerischen Strategien gesehen wurden, die Gruppe aber nicht Ausgangspunkt eines Programms war, dem man sich unterzuordnen hatte. Primat war eine abstrakte Bildsprache. Dabei ist die Gruppe auch für andere Künstler offen. 1967 gesellt sich Erwin Bechthold dazu. Unter dem Titel »synthesen« werden in Ludwigshafen neben den Gründungmitgliedern von SYN 1969/

SYN: Bechtolds, Berners, S. Fischer, Micus, Jürgen-Fischer, Micus, Dienst

1970 u. a. Shusaku Arakawa, Mervyn Baldwin, Erwin Bechthold, Gary B. Kuehn, Wilhelm Loth und Kumi Sugai gezeigt.[110] Aufsehen erregte das Happening, mit der sich die Künstler von der Erweiterung des Kunstbegriffs durch die Aktionskunst distanzierten, sie hatte Jürgen Morschel im »Kunstwerk« vom Januar 1965 am Beispiel von Vostell bereits kritisiert.[111] Auch der Kunstkritik wurde eine deutliche, wenn auch etwas makabre Absage erteilt. Eine Schaufensterpuppe stellte einen distinguierten Herrn mit Brille dar, der von einem Tonband in Floskeln aus Kritiken und Eröffnungsreden die Ausstellung verriß, in dem er u. a. darlegte »daß der Kunstname SYN nichts weiter als gymnasiale Stilisierung eines überaus künstlichen Unternehmens sei«[112], während dessen der Maler Werner Schreib unaufgefordert unter einer Kopfmaske aus Staniolpapier die sensationslüsterne Kunstgemeinde mit der Frage: »Wo ist das Happening?« belästigte. Hernach wurde die Puppe auf die Straße geworfen, von einer Planierraupe überrollt und

Der Kritiker als Popanz, SYN. Mainz 1965

SYN-Aktion. Mainz 1965

am zerschmetterten Bein an einen Baum gehängt. Das Anti-Happening war Antwort auf die schematisierte Kunstkritik, die sich auf poetisch assoziative Nachschöpfungen des Kunstwerks beschränkte, ohne ästhetischen Qualitäten als Formfunktion begrifflich zu definieren.[113] Im März 1965 schreibt Rolf Wedewer dazu: »Die Sachrelation wandelt sich in eine Empfindungsrelation, die die Freiheit des Ichs und der schöpferischen Persönlichkeit beschwört und dabei in die Nähe romantischer Formeln gerät. Der subjektive Faktor des künstlerischen Verhaltens im Sinnhorizont der Formmöglichkeit wird konsequent als Subjektivismus überhaupt mißverstanden. Die Sprache der Wirkungspoetik verfälscht die offene, auf das Mögliche zielende Bildform zu romantischen Psychologismen, wobei der Mensch als Richtpunkt und Orientierungsschema postuliert wird. Dahinter steht eine anthropozentrische Haltung, die die moderne Malerei längst verlassen hat. Kein Wort und keine Formulierung der gängigen Interpretationssprache lassen darauf schließen, daß in der neuen Malerei eine Auseinandersetzung mit der Wirklichkeit sich vollzieht, in die der Mensch eingeschlossen, deren Norm er aber nicht länger ist.«[114]
Wedewer benennt hier zugleich den Rahmen: Die Autonomie der Malerei macht das Bild zum Objekt als ein reales, gegenüberstehendes Bild mit eigenen Gestaltkräften, die sich kompositorischen Fragestellungen widmen und Erfahrungen der Bildbegriffe des Informel, der Monochromie und der seriellen Kunst akkumulieren. Unter dem Titel »SYN : Internationale Beiträge zur neuen Kunst« erscheint gleichzeitig mit der Gründung der Gruppe eine neue Zeitschrift in drei Ausgaben.[115] Die theoretischen Positionen, die Klaus Jürgen-Fischer in den vergangen Jahren entwickelt hat, sind maßgebliche Grundlage des Selbstverständnises dieser Gruppe. Auch seine künstlerische Arbeit bereitet den Ort dieser Gruppe vor. »SYN«, von Jürgen-Fischer herausgegeben, umreißt Dimensionen einer Malerei, die sich dem Tafelbild verpflichtet sieht, keine revolutionäre Tat sein will, sondern im Zusammenspiel unterschiedlicher bildnerischer Mittel eigene Traditionen bilden, Monochromie und die »Neue Abstraktion« fortentwickeln möchte. »SYN = ZUSAMMEN: SYN ERÖFFNET MÖGLICHKEITEN EINER INTEGRALEN KUNST JENSEITS DER FESTLEGUNG EINES FORMALISMUS (KONKRETE KUNST, OPTICAL ART, HARD-EDGE PAINTING) ODER EINES INFORMALISMUS (EXPRESSIONISMUS, TACHISMUS, ACTION-PAINTING) AUF DER GRUNDLAGE REINER BILDNERISCHER PRINZIPIEN.« Bernd Berner bekennt sich zur Befreiung der Farbe durch das Informel und geht analytisch vor: »Farbe und Licht, Fläche und Raum sollten auf ihre Bezüglichkeiten untersucht werden. Ordnung heißt primär eine ökonomische Anwendung dieser malerischen Grundlagen.«[116] Die beherrschte Form gilt als Organisationsstruktur der Farbe, die, flächig aufgetragen bzw. geträufelt, ihre spezifisch optisch-sinnlichen Qualität entfaltet, wobei sie in ihrer Materialität in ein labiles Spannungsgefüge zu den Ebenen des Bildes gestellt ist. In der Synthese Farbe-Fläche-Raum verweben sich die bildlichen Elemente zu einem optisch flukturierenden Gebilde. »Die Verbindung Fläche – Raum konnte in ihrem farblich-strukturellen Aufbau angereichert werden, als Organismen atmen und pulsieren, verharren und Zonen der Ruhe bilden.«[117] Farbe wird in den Bildern Berners körperhaft, dynamisch, aktiv in den geometrischen Bindungen des Rahmens, wobei Emotionales nie getilgt ist, Faktur als optisch haptisches Erlebnis in der Oberfläche erhalten bleibt. Die Analyse der Farbraumformen wird dazu stets intuitiv, nie systematisch entwickelt. Marc Vaux sieht Dualität als maßgebliches Prinzip seiner Malerei, ohne eine vollkommenen Synthese anzustreben.[118] Aus der rein funktionalen Zusammenfügung von Leinwandfeldern gewinnt Eduard Micus das einfaches Gestaltungsprinzip seiner Bilder. »Still und laut – tot und bewegt. Gegensätze steigern sich. Kombinationen, die das Stille stiller machen und das Laute lauter. (...) Coudrage: Zusammenfügen von absoluten Flächen puristischer Ordnung mit bewegten Linien, Schattierungen, Floskeln, Stenogrammen. Coudrage = Synthese.«[119]. Rolf-Gunter Dienst findet in seiner seit 1962 aus der Schreibbewegung abgeleitete Malerei eine Möglichkeit, Farbe zu modulieren, »durch Überlagerungen intensiv verdichtete oder aufgelockerte, in einem Schwebezustand gehaltene Räumlichkeiten im Bild zu schaffen, die geöffnet und geschlossen werden konnten.«[120] Aus divergierenden Bildereignissen wie Bändern, Flächen, Streifen, Begrenzungen, Farbkontrasten und Ornamentalstrukturen entstehen Raum- und Farbfindungen von eigener unkalkulierbarer Dynamik mit Zeichencharakter. »In der Form gleichwertige Partien addieren sich und finden ihre Divergenz in einem gegensätzlichen Farbeinsatz, wobei sich das Bildzentrum oft durch den Aufeinanderprall komplementärer Farbtöne zum Signal verdichtet.«[121] Dies alles fügt sich in beherrschter Malweise zueinander, denn: »Das Bild kann keine Unbestimmtheiten vertragen, solange es sich als Bewußtseinsakt behaupten und sich nicht in nebulosen Darbietung von Zuständen genügen will.« Die skripturalen Elemente der frühen Bilder konzen-

Rolf-Gunter Dienst. Mainz 1965

trieren sich mehr und mehr zu modularen Elementen, die in gleichmäßigem Rhythmus zu nervös und minimal variierenden Farbbänder und Flächen führen, Farbe sowohl als Materie und als lichtmodulierende Struktur zeigen. Diese ausgesprochen kühl kalkulierenden Position relativiert Dienst, im Titel der Werkgruppe »Momentetagebuch«, denn die jeweilige innere Disposition in der Gestaltung des Farbmoduls definiert als unmittelbare wie unbestimmbare Erfahrung, aus der im Bild Bewegung, Spannung, Offenheit erwächst. »In das Bild tritt die aktive Form, die mit Kürzeln besetzt ist und das passive Feld des Fonds, in dem eine plakative Farbe sich ausbreitet. Antipodische Zonen bilden sich, aktive und passive Farbfelder, Negativ- und Positivformen, zur Form und zum Zeichen artikuliertes und Brachliegendes, das im Bild jedoch ebenso seine Funktion hat, wie der Zonenfiligran der Kürzelbänder.«[122] Zwar antwortet Rolf-Gunter Dienst auf die Colourfield und Hardedge Malerei, doch bleibt eine kontrollierte Erfassung des seelisch Unbestimmbaren, sich über seinen Ort in der Kunst Rechenschaft abzulegen.

Die bei allen Künstlern feststellbare bewußt gewählte innere Distanz schließt das formale Ausspielen momentaner Befindlichkeit nicht aus. Das explizite ästhetische Programm der Gruppe macht sie für die Malerei der sechziger Jahre in einem analytischen Sinne signifikant, denn SYN findet neue Dimensionen der Abstraktion. 1967 gibt sich die Gruppe ein Manifest, in dem man ein »entwickeltes kontemplatives Bewußtsein, reine Form und Farbmittel für eine hinweisende, aber nicht festlegbare Bedeutung« einfordert. »SYN entnimmt die Malerei nicht der Theorie, sondern die Theorie der Malerei. Hegels Vollendung des Geistes im Begriff macht einer neuen Ausformung und Geltung des Geistes im Bilde Platz. Die begriffliche Philosophie tritt hinter die überbegriffliche Kunst zurück.«[123]

Die selbstkritische Deutung der eigenen Arbeit hat der Gruppe dann auch den Vorwurf des Unkünstlerisch-Intellektuellen eingetragen.[124]

Der Beitrag Baden-Badens zur Kunst der Gegenwart zeigt sich in den gestalterischen Kräften, die SYN aktiviert hat, einmal mehr. Sicher nicht zufällig ist der letzte große Bericht über einen Kulturraum der Vergangenheit Guido Kaschnitz von Weinbergs Darstellung des Griechenlands des 5. Jahrhunderts mit zwei Essays »Die Transzendenz des Klassischen« und »Der Parthenonfries«.[125] Von da an nimmt die Kunst des 20. Jahrhunderts in aller Ausschließlichkeit vom »Kunstwerk« Besitz. Im Dezember 1964 liest sich dies in einem Auszug aus der »Vorgeschichte der abstrakten Kunst« von Otto Stelzer so: »Bis zum Beweis des Gegenteils stellen wir uns auf den Standpunkt, ›daß kein Künstler unabhängig von Vorläufern und Denkweisen, unabhängig von Traditionen und vorstrukturierten Problemen existiert‹ wie unlängst Ernst Kris in aller Schärfe formulierte. Es gehört zu den Aufgaben der Kunstgeschichte, dies aufzuzeigen.«[126]

Anmerkungen

1 Für sachkundige Auskünfte und vielfache Unterstützung danke ich Bernd Berner, Stuttgart, Rolf-Gunter Dienst, Baden-Baden, Heiner Flaig, Baden-Baden, Karin Grochowiak, Kuppenheim, Hans Hofstätter, Freiburg, Alfonso Hüppi, Baden-Baden, Klaus Jürgen-Fischer, Vaudrément, Dieter Krieg, Quadrath-Ichendorf, Manfred Kröplien, Stuttgart, Dietrich Mahlow, Seeheim, Gert Reising, Karlsruhe, Susanne Reith, Stadtbibliothek Baden-Baden, Fee Schlapper, Baden-Baden, Eva Studinger, Karlsruhe.

2 Otto Stelzer, Originale Kunst ist traditionell, in: Das Kunstwerk 6/XVIII, Dezember 1964, S. 4.

3 Im Kurhaus sind damals u. a. repräsenative Gemälde von Aristide Maillol, Henri Rousseau, Claude Monet, Paul Cézanne, Georges Rouault, Paul Renoir, Paul Gauguin, Henri de Toulouse Lautrec, Vincent van Gogh, Pablo Picasso, Georges Braque, Fernand Léger, Juan Gris, Marc Chagall, Giorgio de Chirico, Henri Matisse gezeigt worden, vgl. auch den Katalog: Moderne französische Malerei – Vom Impressionismus bis zur Gegenwart, Kurhaus Baden-Baden September 1946, Baden-Baden (Woldemar Klein) 1946.

4 Vgl. dazu Leopold Zahn, Französische Malerei – Gestern und heute, in: Das Kunstwerk, Eine Monatsschrift über alle Gebiete der Bildenden Kunst, 1, 1946/47, Heft 3, S. 33–40.

5 Zuvor diente sie in der Zeit der französischen Besatzung der Garnison bis 1949 als Bibliothek und »Centre de documentation«. Das Baden-Badener Theater hielt im Herbst 1950 hier Proben ab, eine Aufführung wurde erwogen. Vgl. dazu und im folgenden Michael Scholz-Hänsel, in: Staatliche Kunsthalle Baden-Baden, Hg., Kunsthalle Baden-Baden 1909–1986, Kunsthalle Baden-Baden 6. bis 29. Juni 1986, Baden-Baden 1986, S. 34ff.

6 Michael Scholz-Hänsel, 1986, ebenda S. 35.

7 Schreiben Oskar Hagemanns vom 9. Mai 1952, in: GLA KA Akte 235/40303, zit. nach Michael Scholz-Hänsel, ebenda S. 36.

8 Heinrich wurde zunächst im Amt wieder bestätigt, die Stelle dennoch ausgeschrieben. »Als dann am 3. Juli 1956 eine Beiratssitzung der Kunsthalle ins Rathaus einberufen wurde, die die eingelaufenen Bewerbungen prüfen sollte, bat man auch den inzwischen über das laufende Verfahren informierten Heinrich dazu. Der durch die Umstände schwer erregte Direktor erlitt noch während der Sitzung einen körperlichen Zusammenbruch, der seinen sofortigen Tod zur Folge hatte.« Michael Scholz-Hänsel, 1986, S. 35.

9 Das Kunstwerk, Heft 2, 1955/66, S. 64.

10 Bis heute haben die Künstlermitglieder das Recht, sich um eine Teilnahme an den Jahresausstellungen der »Gesellschaft« in der Staatlichen Kunsthalle zu bewerben.

11 Badisches Tagblatt, Januar 1957, Nr. 14.

12 Ohne die internationalen Verbindungen des ehemaligen Widerstandskämpfers Willem Sandberg hätte beispielsweise auch Thomas Grochowiak die großartigen Ausstellungen anläßlich der Ruhrfestspiele Recklinghausen nicht verwirklichen können.

13 Vgl. dazu Franz Mon, Dietrich Mahlow, Schrift und Bild, Kunsthalle Baden-Baden 15. Juni bis 4. August 1963, Baden-Baden 1963.

14 Vgl. Interview mit Alfonso Hüppi, in: Staatliche Kunsthalle Baden-Baden, 1986, s. Anm. 5, S. 119.

15 Dietrich Mahlow, 40 Jahre Gesellschaft der Freunde junger Kunst Baden-Baden, 1995, Publ. in Vb.

16 So berichtet Friedrich Matz über Kreta und das frühe Griechenland, André Grabar über byzantinische und russische Kunst, Hans Heinz Ewers über Historismus und Funktionalismus, Klaus Lankheit über Revolution und Restauration im Frankreich des 18./19. Jh. Hofstätter selbst hat über Malerei und Graphik der Gegenwart geschrieben, Heinz Fuchs über die Skulptur, Udo Kultermann über die Architektur des 20. Jh. Die Reihe wurde bis zu Beginn der siebziger Jahre weitergeführt und umfaßte nicht weniger als 52 Bände.

17 U. a. Gotthard Günther, Das Bewußtsein der Maschinen, Eine Metaphysik der Kybernetik, AGIS Verlag Baden-Baden 1957; Louis Couffignal, Kybernetische Grundbegriffe, AGIS Verlag Baden-Baden 1962

18 Vgl. Elisabeth Walther, Bibliographie der veröffentlichten Schriften von Max Bense, AGIS Verlag Baden-Baden 1994

19 Karl G. Fischer, Hg., AGIS, Blätter zur Förderung der Humanität, AGIS Verlag, Krefeld 1953.

20 Max Bense, Hg., Augenblick, Aesthetica, Philosophica, Polemica, AGIS Verlag, Baden-Baden 1955. Diese Zeitschrift hat eine Nachfolge gefunden in »Semiosis«, Internationale Zeitschrift für Semiotik und ihre Anwendungen, die bis heute im AGIS Verlag, Baden-Baden erscheint.

21 G. F. Hartlaub, Felix Weissenfeld, Gestalt und Gestaltung, Das Kunstwerk als Selbstdarstellung des Künstlers, AGIS Verlag, Krefeld 1958.

22 Klaus Jürgen-Fischer, René Hinds, Hg., Vernissage: Kunst · Kritik · Kontakte, Jg. 1–4, Feb. 1960–5/6 III April, 1964.

23 Auf diese bis heute in Baden-Baden zu Unrecht nicht ausreichend gewürdigte Künstlerpersönlichkeit geht wohl der Name der Gruppe zurück, vgl. den Exkurs von Ursula Geiger, Das Quadriga-Poem von René Hinds, in: dies., Die Maler der Quadriga und ihre Stellung im Informel, Arte factum Verlagsgesellschaft mbH, Nürnberg 1990, hg. von Axel-Alexander Ziese und Forschungsinstitut Bildender Künste GbR. Nürnberg.

24 G. F. Hartlaub, Ein konservativer Avantgardist, in: Leopold Zahn zum 70. Geburtstag, Agis Verlag, Baden-Baden 1960, S. 16–19.

25 Leopold Zahn hat Publikationen vorgelegt über »Raffael von Urbino (1923), »Die Handzeichnungen des J. Callot« (1924), »Moderne Pariser Bauten« (1929), »Goya caprichos« (1942), Anselm Feuerbach, Moritz von Schwind, Honoré Daumier, aber auch Monographien zu Friedrich Nietzsche, Christine von Schweden, Königin des Barock und Madame de Staël verfaßt. Neben seinen zahllosen Rezensionen und Aufsätzen entsteht in Baden-Baden u. a. noch eine Geschichte der Kunst.

26 Vgl. dazu, Katrin Lochmaier, Der Kunsthändler Hans Goltz – »ein revolutionärer Konservativer«, in Helmut Friedel, Süddeutsche Freiheit – Kunst der Revolution in München, Lenbachhaus 10. Nov. 1993 bis 9. Jan. 1994, München 1993, S. 61–72.

27 Der Titel ist abgeleitet von einer pseudo-mittelhochdeutschen Inschrift auf dem Tiefenbronner Altar des Lucas Moser von Wil »Schri kunst schri und klag dich ser / din begert iecz niemen mer / so o we 1431«.

28 Anzeige in Das Kunstwerk 1/IX, 1955/56, S. 63.

29 Schri Kunst Schri, ein Almanach alter und neuer Kunst, Woldemar Klein Verlag, Baden-Baden 1952. Literarische Grußbotschaften von Leopold Zahn, Peter Althaus, Erich Kästner, Alfred Döblin und Hermann Hesse sind ergänzt um ästhetische Reflexionen zu Ordnung und Chaos von Kurt Martin, Zitate und Sentenzen von Künstlern der Klassischen Kunst und der Moderne zwischen Impressionismus (Karl Scheffler) und Abstraktion (Willi Baumeister). Marie Luise Kaschnitz nimmt zu Gustave Courbet Stellung, René Huyghe zu Henri Matisse und Paul Westheim zu Oskar Kokoschka, während Jean Paul Sartre sich zu Alexander Calder äußert. Neben den Abbildungen von Werken von Hans Baldung Grien, Raffael, Tizian und Delacroix sind Werke der Zeitgenossen Toni Stadler, Vordemberge-Gildewart, Georg Meistermann, Juan Gris, Mac Zimmermann und Ewald Mataré gestellt.

30 André Malraux, Das imaginäre Museum, Psychologie der Kunst, Woldemar Klein, Baden-Baden 1949.

31 André Malraux, Kunst und Reproduktion, in: Das Kunstwerk, 3. Jahr, Heft 1, 1949, S. 8–12.

32 André Malraux, Das Imaginäre Museum, Woldemar Klein Verlag, Baden-Baden 1949, S. 11.

33 Vgl. Walter Benjamin, Das Kunstwerk im Zeitalter der technischen Reproduzierbarkeit, Suhrkamp, Frankfurt 1955 (4. Aufl. 1970).

34 André Malraux, 1949, s. Anm. 32 S. 16.

35 André Malraux, 1949, ebenda, S. 44.

36 So etwa liest man um 1960 Beiträge von Kurt F. Ertel, Heinz Fuchs, G. F. Hartlaub, Walter Hess, Werner Hofmann, Klaus Jürgen-Fischer, Udo Kultermann, Kurt Leonhard, Dietrich Mahlow, Manfred de la Motte, Lil Picard, Hans Platschek, Pierre Restany, Peter Anselm Riedl, Juliane und Franz Roh, Werner Schmalenbach, Hannelore Schubert, Heinz Spielmann, John Anthony Thwaites, Rolf Wedewer, Egon Vietta, Paul Vogt, Paul Westheim, Leopold Zahn.

37 Margit Staber, Marcel Duchamp, in: Das Kunstwerk, 7/XIV, Januar 1961, S. 3–4.

38 Vgl. Jürgen Morschel, In Ulm, um Ulm und um Ulm herum, Ein Happening in Ulm, in: Das Kunstwerk 7/XVIII Januar 1965, S. 26–39.

39 Dieter Mahlow, Erinnerungen an die Gesellschaft, Manuskript Publ. i. V.

40 Claudia Reising-Pohl, Kalter Krieg – Schauplatz Deutschland, in: Wilfried Rößling, Hg., Vorbilder, Kunst in Karlsruhe 1950–1988, Badischer Kunstverein, 17. Juni bis 31. Juli 1988, Karlsruhe 1988, S. 25–46.

41 »Der Mangel an gültigen gegenständlichen Lösungen war auch in Baden-Baden auffallend, da die Jury nur zu geneigt war, Talente auszuzeichnen, die dem Gegenstand neue Gesichtspunkte abgewinnen. Hier melden sich Künstler zu Wort, die wieder die rein zeichnerischen Umrisse im Stil der neuen Sachlichkeit der zwanziger Jahre betonen, so Konrad Klaphek, der eine Nähmaschine wie ein ›Zeichen‹ behandelt. Aber auch die Maler, die Gegenständliches andeuten, sind schon auf halbem Weg zur Abstraktion, was bei Heimrad Prem, der mit einem Preis bedacht wurde, und dem Preisträger Horst Antes aus der Grieshaber-Klasse sichtbar ist. Das brennende Rot von Antes ist zugleich Aussage über Reales, hier die Schwangerschaft. Johannes Gecelli in Düsseldorf arbeitet mit hauchzarten Andeutungen in seinen schimmernden Graus, sei es einer Figur, sei es von Flaschen, wobei das Vorbild Morandis unverkennbar ist. Das Halbfigurative, für das Hans Platschek in seiner Publikation ›Neue Figuration‹ wirbt, ist noch keine allgemein anerkannte Parole geworden. Bemühungen in dieser Richtung sind allenfalls Tastversuche.« Egon Vietta, Kunstpreis der Jugend in Baden-Baden, Deutsche Kunstausstellung 1959 II, in: Das Kunstwerk 5–6 XIII, November, Dezember 1959, S. 73. Es ist dessen letzte Ausstellungsrezension, denn er stirbt am 29. Nov. 1959 in Baden-Baden.

42 Egon Vietta, 1959, ebenda S. 73.

43 Unter anderen waren hier Umbro Apollonio, Rolf Cavael, Heinz R. Fuchs, HAP Grieshaber, Thomas Grochowiak, Bernhard Heiliger, Hans Kindermann, Alfred Lörcher, Dietrich Mahlow, Willem Sandberg, Werner Schmalenbach, Paul Seylaz, Eduard Trier und Clemens Weiler beteiligt gewesen.

44 Egon Vietta, 1959, s. Anm. 41, S. 73.

45 xxx: Kleiner Tageskalender einer kunstpolitischen Auseinandersetzung, in: Das Kunstwerk, August–September 1959, S. 79.

46 Egon Vietta, FAZ 11. Juli 1959, zit. in: Das Kunstwerk, August-September 1959, S. 79.

47 Claudia Reising-Pohl, 1988, s. Anm. 40, S. 36.

48 Henry Kahnweiler, in: AGIS-Verlag, Hg., Wird die moderne Kunst »gemanagt«?, AGIS-Verlag, Baden-Baden 1959, S. 12; vgl. dazu auch Falko Herlemann, Zwischen unbedingter Tradition und bedingungslosen Fortschritt, zur Auseinandersetzung um die moderne Kunst in der Bundesrepublik Deutschland der 50er Jahre, Peter Lang, Frankfurt 1989, S. 169–191.

49 Egon Vietta, in: AGIS-Verlag, Baden-Baden 1959, ebenda, S. 23.

50 Jürgen Beckelmann, in: AGIS-Verlag, Baden-Baden 1959, ebenda, S. 24.

51 Jürgen Beckelmann, in: AGIS-Verlag, Baden-Baden 1959, ebenda, S. 28.

52 Jürgen Beckelmann, in: AGIS-Verlag, Baden-Baden 1959, ebenda, S. 31.

53 Konrad Farner, in: AGIS-Verlag, Baden-Baden 1959, ebenda, S. 49.

54 Karl G. Fischer, in: AGIS-Verlag, Baden-Baden 1959, ebenda, S. 58.

55 Karl G. Fischer, in: AGIS-Verlag, Baden-Baden 1959, ebenda, S. 61.

56 Klaus Jürgen-Fischer, in: AGIS-Verlag, Baden-Baden 1959, ebenda, S. 63.

57 Klaus Jürgen-Fischer, in: AGIS-Verlag, Baden-Baden 1959, ebenda, S. 67.

58 Theodor W. Adorno, in: AGIS-Verlag, Baden-Baden 1959, ebenda, S. 39.

59 Theodor W. Adorno, in: AGIS-Verlag, Baden-Baden 1959, ebenda, S. 42.

60 HAP Grieshaber, in: AGIS-Verlag, Baden-Baden 1959, ebenda, S. 33.

61 HAP Grieshaber, in: AGIS-Verlag, Baden-Baden 1959, ebenda, S. 36.

62 Ich danke Dieter Krieg, der mich auf dieses bislang unbekannte Künstlerbuch aufmerksam machte.

63 Manfred Kröplien war nach Erscheinen des Heftes mitgeteilt worden, daß eine Fortsetzung des Studiums an der Akademie für Studenten, die sich am Kunstpreis der Jugend in Baden-Baden beteiligen, hier gar einen Sonderpreis erhalten und an einer solchen Publikation mitarbeiten, nicht möglich ist. Erst nach einem Jahr kehrt Kröplin auf Betreiben von Margot Fuerst als Schüler von Manfred Henninger an die Akademie zurück. Heute ist Manfred Kröplien Professor für Graphik-Design und Leiter des Instituts für Buchgestaltung an der Stuttgarter Akademie. Und fast wie zum Trotz, Walter Stöhrer wird 1962 den Kunstpreis der Jugend in Stuttgart für seine kraftvoll skizzierten Figurationen bekommen.

64 Klasse Grieshaber, Karlsruhe, Hg., opferrauch oder flugblatt, ... Staatliche Kunsthalle Baden-Baden, Druck Knodel Stuttgart, 1959

65 Augustinus, Bekenntnisse, zit. nach ebenda.

66 Albrecht Fabri, Brief an HAP Grieshaber vom 4. April 1959, abgedruckt ebenda.

67 Vgl. dazu Gert von der Osten, Hg., ars multiplicata vervielfältigte Kunst seit 1945, Wallraf-Richartz-Museum 13. Jan. bis 15. April 1968, Köln 1968.

68 Albrecht Fabri, Brief an HAP Grieshaber, s. Anm. 66.

69 Albrecht Fabri, Brief an HAP Grieshaber, ebenda.

70 Vgl. dazu z. B. Albrecht Fabri, Interviews mit Sisyphos, Verlag Galerie Der Spiegel, Köln 1952.

71 Kurt Leonhard, H.A.P Grieshaber, Anmerkungen zu seinem Werk, in: Das Kunstwerk, Heft 9/XIV, März 1961, S. 4.

72 Klaus Hoffmann, Neuer Expressionismus in Deutschland, in: Das Kunstwerk, 9/XVIII, März 1965, S. 3.

73 Klaus Hoffmann, Neuer Expressionismus in Deutschland, in: Das Kunstwerk, 9/XVIII, März 1965, S. 3.

74 Klaus Hoffmann, Neuer Expressionismus in Deutschland, in: Das Kunstwerk, 9/XVIII, März 1965, S. 4.

75 Klaus Hoffmann, Neuer Expressionismus in Deutschland, in: Das Kunstwerk, 9/XVIII, März 1965, S. 4.

76 Klaus Hoffmann, Neuer Expressionismus in Deutschland, in: Das Kunstwerk, 9/XVIII, März 1965, S. 15.

77 Dieter Krieg hatte als Schüler eine Wand des großen Saales der Kunsthalle gestaltet und dafür Lobendes von E. Haller, der kompetenten Kritikerin des Badischen Tagblatts geerntet. Später wird er als Aufseher hier arbeiten und für Dietrich Mahlow in der Ausstellung »Bild und Bühne« akribisch tachistisch überformte Gipsobjekte kopieren.

78 Marie Luise Kaschnitz, 3. November, in: Tage, Tage, Jahre, Aufzeichnungen, Mai 1971, Fischer, Frankfurt 1971, S. 107.

79 In: Das Kunstwerk, 1–2/XX, Oktober-November 1966, S.28–32 mit einem Text von Klaus Gallwitz über Dieter Krieg, anläßlich des Kunstpreis der Jugend in Baden-Baden 1966.

80 Zit. nach Juliane Roh, Die Gruppe Spur, in: Klaus Schrenk, Hg., Aufbrüche, Manifeste, Manifestationen: Positionen in der Bildenden Kunst zu Beginn der 60er Jahre, Städtische Kunsthalle, DuMont, Düsseldorf 1984, S. 132.

81 Vernissage 8. Okt. 1960. Wenig später, 7/8 II, Februar 1962, wird über die Beschlagnahme der Zeitschrift SPUR durch den Staatsanwalt wegen Verbreitung unzüchtigen Schrifttums berichtet.

82 Eberhard Roters, zit. nach Lore Ditzen, Stationen der Erinnerung: ein Rückblick in die sechziger Jahre Berlins, in: Klaus Schrenk, Hg., Aufbrüche, ebenda, S. 47.

83 Das Kunstwerk, 4/XIII Oktober 1959.

84 André Malraux, Ansprache anläßlich der Verleihung der internationalen Preise der Biennale von Paris, in: Das Kunstwerk, 7 XIII, Jan. 1960, S. 33.

85 Vgl. Pop Art, in: Das Kunstwerk, 10/XVII, April 1964. Anders als bei früheren Berichten ist hier eine Folge von Originalquellen, Statements und Interviews von Künstlern Kritikern und Kunsthändlern mit zahlreichen Abbildungen zusammengefügt.

86 Abstrakte Kunst: Theorien und Tendenzen, Sonderausgabe, Woldemar Klein Verlag, Baden-Baden 1951 (?) Stets bedacht auf Internationalität, gibt der Band Einblick in die Geschichte seit Wassily Kandinsky, mit einem Rückgriff in die Steinzeit, denn der Ur- und Frühgeschichtler Herbert Kühn stellt Beziehungen zwischen abstrahierender Kunst und vorgeschichtlichen Bildwelten her. Im Interesse stehen nicht nur die deutschen Abstrakten wie E. W. Nay, Ida Kerkovius, Julius Bissier, Willi Baumeister, Hans Uhlmann, Max Ernst, sondern auch die russische und die französische Malerei. Stellvertretend für Österreich wird Fritz Wotruba, für England wird Henry Moore, für Amerika Alexander Calder gewürdigt. Ein Ausblick bindet chinesische Tuschemalerei mit ein. Die weltumspannende Vision wird abgerundet durch einen Bilderatlas zeitgenössischer abstrakter Künstler in aller Welt.

87 »Man radikalisiert den Psychismus innerhalb der gegenstandsfreien Malerei, indem man betont jede Kontrolle des Bewußtseins meidet, um ohne Verzögern aus den Bereichen des Prärationalen, Anonymen und Kollektiven zu schöpfen, einzutauchen in eine transpersonale Einheit von Ich und All. In einem spontanen bildnerischen Akt sucht man jene Spaltung von Subjekt und Objekt zu überspringen, die die Grundlage einer um Form und Objektivierung ringenden Kunst ist.« Klaus Jürgen-Fischer, Was ist Tachismus?, in: Das Kunstwerk, 5/IX 1955/56, S. 18.

88 »In dem Augenblick, in dem der Tachismus, unbekümmert um die Form und die Reinheit der bildnerische Gestalt das Bild auf Bewegung hin oder auf die Wiedergabe seelischer Stimmungen, Erregungen und Affekte oder die Darstellung kosmischer Räumlichkeiten und mikroskopischer Strukturen hin transzendiert, verlegt er das Interesse vom Bildnerischen auf ein Außerbildnerisches, überspringt die Realität des Bildes und stürzt sich in romantische Ideologie.« Klaus Jürgen-Fischer, 1955/56, ebenda S. 21.

89 Klaus Jürgen-Fischer, 1955/56, ebenda S. 21.

90 »Mancher möchte hier von einem Konformismus des Risikos sprechen, das sich ja der öffentlichen Protektion erfreut, womit es nur noch vom Schein des echten Risikos umstrahlt wird. (...) Kunst aus Protest ist also in unserer Situation verbreiteter Prosperität, an der auch die Kunst teilnimmt, eine veraltete, unwahre Parole.« Klaus Jürgen-Fischer, Die II. documenta in Kassel – Fazit eines Unbehagens, in: Das Kunstwerk 2–3 XIII, August/Sept. 1959, S. 30.

91 »Der Konflikt tritt aber dort zum Vorschein, wo das historische Verfahren auf eine Kunst trifft, die aus der reinen Unmittelbarkeit, aus dem reinen künstlerischen Selbst existieren und wirken wollte und die sich gegen alle Prinzipien der Verwaltung, des Systems, der Ordnung, ja im Grunde gegen das Prinzip des Erfolgs sträubt. Der Problematik dieser Ausstellung liegt gewiß ein innerer Zwiespalt der tachistischen Malerei selbst zugrunde. Sie beanspruchte aus der existentiellen Freiheit zu wachsen, außerhalb aller bisherigen Kategorien der Ästhetik, war aber nach ein paar Jahren schon eine handliche Formel, die sich sehr rasch weiterreichen und multiplizieren ließ. (...) Der Tachismus war ein Unternehmen, das ganz aus dem aktuellen Affront entsprang (...) aber im Grunde ungeeignet ist, fern ihrer aktuellen Funktion das Museum zu bewohnen.« Klaus Jürgen-Fischer, 1959, ebenda S. 61.

92 Klaus Jürgen-Fischer, 1959, ebenda, S. 61.

93 Klaus Jürgen-Fischer, Der Fall Jean Fautrier, in: Das Kunstwerk, 7/XIII, Januar 1960, S. 23–24.

94 Kurt Leonhard, Hans Platschek: neue Figuration, in: Das Kunstwerk, 5–6 XIII, November/Dezember 1959, S. 77–78.

95 Klaus Jürgen-Fischer, Neue Figuration als Fragezeichen, in: Das Kunstwerk, 4 XVI, 1962, Oktober, S. 13–14.

96 Rolf Wedewer, Tendenzen des Nach-Tachismus, in: Das Kunstwerk, 10/XIII, April 1960, S. 3.

97 Rolf Wedewer, ebenda S. 4.

98 Vgl. Will Baltzer, Alfons W. Biermann, Hg., Treffpunkt Parnass Wuppertal 1949–1965, Von der Heydt Museum 31. Mai bis 13. Juli 1980, Rheinland Verlag Köln 1980.

99 »Selbstverständlich sind beide Phänomene, das Versperrte und das Leere, nur extreme Möglichkeiten eines und des gleichen Raumgefühls, desen kontinuierliche Zwischenstufen in der Variationsbreite zeitgenössischer Bildkunst aufgehen. Die leere Fläche hat heute etwas von der geistigen Bedeutung wiedergewonnen, die sie im frühen Mittelalter und in Ostasien hatte, und im versperrten Raum leuchten hintergründig die magischen Signale der Tiefe, die jenseits jeder Versperrung ist. Mag am Anfang die Zeitkrankheit des ›reduzierten Menschen‹ stehen – Platzangst, Fluchtwunsch –, die Kunst ist heute, wie zu allen Zeiten nicht nur Diagnose, sondern zugleich Therapie. Reduktion wird ein Weg zur Transzendierung, der leere Raum schafft Weite und Freiheit. Die versperrende Stofflichkeit wird durchlässig gemacht für die Magie des Verborgenen…« Kurt Leonhard, Platzangst, Fluchtwunsch oder neue Wirklichkeit? Zum Raumproblem in der heutigen Malerei, in: das Kunstwerk, 7 XIII, Jan. 1960, S. 34.

100 »Nur eine Kunst, in der gegenüber dem Instinkt die Überlegung herrscht, gegenüber dem Zufall der Einfall und eine methodische Klarheit, weist konstruktiv in die Zukunft. Die Kunst hat, wo sie wesentlich ist, eine ontologische Absicht. Sie ist nicht nur Ausdruck einer individuellen Psychologie, sondern Darstellung einer Seinslage. Die Kunst kann aber nur dann Verhältnisse des Seins zur Darstellung bringen, wenn sie sich aus den Fesseln des Psychologismus befreit.« Klaus Jürgen-Fischer, Ende des Tachismus – Klecks ex!, in: Vernissage 1. Februar 1960, S. 3.

101 Klaus Jürgen-Fischer, 1960 ebenda.

102 Alexander Leisberg, Neue Tendenzen, in: Das Kunstwerk, 9/XIV, März 1961, S. 3.

103 »Selten zuvor bewegte sich die bildende Kunst so nah an der Grenze zum bloß schmückenden, das Auge ermüdenden Muster. (…) In solchem Kunstgewerbe ist das Material in seiner Stofflichkeit belassen und der Mensch, zumal der Künstler nicht länger eine Existenz, die diese Stofflichkeit in der Verwandlung aufzehrt, transzendiert. Bleibt die menschliche Existenz indessen in der neuen Kunst lebendig, hat sie, weil noch stärker von allem figurativen Ballast befreit als die abstrakte Malerei zuvor, die besondere Chance, die spirituelle Radikalität der modernen Kunst neu zu beweisen.« Alexander Leisberg, 1961, ebenda S. 34.

104 Vgl. dazu Vernissage 7/8 II, Februar 1962.

105 Vgl. dazu Vernissage 4/III Okt. 63.

106 Vgl. dazu Vernissage 5/6 / 1961. Die Schau zur 750 Jahrfeier des Deutschherrenordens vereinigte nicht weniger als 550 Gemälde aus fünf Kontinenten mit zweitägiger Diskussion unter Beteiligung der gesamten Kritiker-, Kunsthändler- und Kunsthistorikergemeinde der Informel/Neue Tendenzen-Szene um 1960. Hier sollte gar ein Museum der Kunst der Gegenwart entstehen, ein Gebäude wie eine aus einem Quadrat entwickelte Spirale, das Le Corbusier entworfen hatte, und an dessen Konzeption neben Heinz Ruths Klaus Jürgen-Fischer und sein Vater beteiligt waren.

107 Klaus Jürgen-Fischer, Was ist komplexe Malerei? Baden-Baden, April 1963, vgl. auch Ekkehard Mai, Klaus Jürgen-Fischer, Gemälde Plastiken Zeichnungen, Edition Braus, Heidelberg 1992.

108 Klaus Jürgen-Fischer, Komplexe Fare, Galerie Anna Roepcke 3.–28. Feb. 1962, Wiesbaden 1962 (Faltblatt).

109 Klaus Jürgen-Fischer, Neue Abstraktion, in: Das Kunstwerk, 10–12/XVIII, April–Juni 1965. Zu diesem Zeitpunkt erscheint das »Kunstwerk« auch in englischer Sprache.

110 Vgl. dazu Manfred Fath, Hg., Synthesen, Ludwig Reichert Haus 14. Dez. 1969 bis 31. Jan. 1970, Ludwigshafen 1969.

111 Siehe Anm. Nr. 38; Zufall oder nicht: Das Mainzer Anti-Happening findet eine Woche vor dem legendären 24 Stunden Happening in der Wuppertaler Galerie Parnaß statt, an dem Wolf Vostell, Joseph Beuys, Bazon Brock, Eckart Rahn, Tomas Schmit, Nam June Paik und Charlotte Moorman teilnahmen; vgl. O. F. Gmelin, Beschreibung eines Super-Happenings, in: Das Kunstwerk 2/XIX, August 1965, S. 22.

112 Ruprecht Skasa Weiß, Die Anti-Eröffnung, in: Stuttgarter Zeitung 30. Mai 1965.

113 Bereits 1960 hatte der AGIS-Verlag im Frankfurter Kunstgespräch als Fortsetzung der Veranstaltung in Baden-Baden 1959 die Frage gestellt: »Ist Kunstkritik eine Wissenschaft, Kunst oder Propaganda?«; vgl. dazu Juliane Roh, in: Das Kunstwerk, Nov./Dez. 1960, S. 65.

114 Rolf Wedewer, Wie soll man über Bilder sprechen? Anmerkungen zur Sprache der Kunst, in: Das Kunstwerk, 9/XVIII, März 1965, S. 26.

115 K. Jürgen-Fischer, Hg., SYN Internationale Beiträge zur neuen Kunst, Agis Verlag, Baden-Baden 1965.

116 Bernd Berner, Farbsinnlichkeit und Flächenraum, ebenda S. 65; vgl. auch Susanne Meier-Faust, Bernd Berner, Verlag für moderne Kunst, Nürnberg 1987.

117 Bernd Berner, ebenda S. 65.

118 Vgl. Marc Vaux, Konfrontationen, ebenda S. 59.

119 Eduard Micus, Coudrage, ebenda S. 79.

120 Rolf-Gunter Dienst, Lettern, Kürzel, Bildsignale, in: ebenda 1965, S. 85; zu Rolf-Gunter Dienst vgl. auch: Rolf-Gunter Dienst, Gemälde 1962–1990, Verlag für moderne Kunst, Nürnberg 1990.

121 Rolf-Gunter Dienst, ebenda, S. 85.

122 Rolf-Gunter Dienst, ebenda, S. 85.

123 12 Punkte… SYN, Nassauischer Kunstverein, Städtisches Museum Wiesbaden 18. 6. – 23. 7. 1967, Wiesbaden 1967.

124 Vgl. Dr. Kurt Unold, »Komplexe« junger intellektueller Maler, in: AZ, 13. Januar 1966.

125 Guido Kaschnitz von Weinberg, in: Das Kunstwerk, 1–2/XVI, Juli/August 1962.

126 Otto Stelzer, Originale Kunst ist traditionell, in: Das Kunstwerk 6/XVIII, Dezember 1964, S. 3.

»Der Hans Thoma-Gedenkpreis macht auch dieses Jahr wieder einiges Kopfzerbrechen«[1]
Zur Geschichte eines baden-württembergischen Staatspreises

»Ich habe mich aber schon vor Jahren aus grundsätzlichen Erwägungen heraus entschlossen, keiner Kunst-Jury anzugehören, solange ich meine derzeitige Funktion beim Staat versehe... Ich muß den Staat vor dem Vorwurf bewahren, daß er auf dem Gebiet der Kunst reglementierend eingreift.« Mit diesen programmatischen Worten lehnte der Leiter der Kunstabteilung des Kultusministeriums Baden-Württemberg, Ministerialrat Wolf Donndorf, am 11. April 1963 das Angebot der Künstlergilde Ulm ab, bei der Jury über den Ulmer Jugendkunstpreis den Vorsitz zu übernehmen.[2] Doch gerade Donndorf wußte, daß die Realität anders aussah, und der Staat, den er repräsentierte, auf vielfältige Art und Weise nicht nur regelnd in den Kunstbetrieb eingreifen konnte, sondern dies auch einigen Bereichen permanent tat. So entschied die staatliche Ankaufskommission, in der neben Donndorf die Direktoren der Staatlichen Kunsthallen und Galerien Stuttgart, Karlsruhe, Baden-Baden und Freiburg saßen, über den Ankauf von Kunstwerken und damit letztendlich auch über die Förderung der jeweiligen Kunstrichtungen. Daneben besaß das Kultusministerium mit seinem Vorschlagsrecht an die Kultusministerkonferenz über die Vergabe von Stipendien an der Villa Massimo in Rom und der Cité Internationale des Arts in Paris ein Regelungsinstrument an der Hand, das bestimmte, ob und welche Vertreter einer Kunstrichtung ihre Entwicklung unter materiell abgesicherten Bedingungen, kurzzeitig unbeeinflußt von den Anforderungen des Kunstmarktes, fortsetzen konnten. Die Mitwirkung bei der Vergabe von Kunstpreisen gehörte zweifelsohne in die Reihe der einflußnehmenden Faktoren, da damit nicht nur ein künstlerisches, sondern immer auch ein kunstpolitisches Werturteil verbunden war. Ob Donndorf, als er die Ablehnung nach Ulm formulierte, die zurückliegende Diskussion über den einzigen staatlichen Kunstpreis, den das junge Bundesland Baden-Württemberg jährlich vergab, den »Hans Thoma-Gedenkpreis«, vor Augen hatte, wissen wir nicht. Dabei spiegelt sich in der Geschichte dieses Kunstpreises in geradezu paradigmatischer Weise die Auseinandersetzung zwischen »Moderne« und »Restauration«, zwischen gegenständlicher und gegenstandsloser Kunst wider, eine Kontroverse, die die Kunstpolitik der fünfziger Jahre in hohem Maße beherrschte.

Ihrem 1839 geborenen, berühmten Sohn Hans Thoma war die Gemeinde Bernau in besonderem Maße verbunden. Schon in den ersten Jahren nach Ende des Zweiten Weltkriegs hatte der Bernauer Bürgermeister Dr. Ludwig Baur den Aufbau einer Hans Thoma-Gedenkstube im Rathaus betrieben und zugleich den Zuzug von Künstlern in die Schwarzwaldgemeinde gefördert. Dabei hatte der Bürgermeister neben der identitätsstiftenden Wirkung der Person Hans Thomas für sein Dorf durchaus auch ganz profane Interessen im Sinn, indem er seine Gemeinde zu einem »Wallfahrtsort« und touristischen Anziehungspunkt für alle Kunstinteressierten im deutschen Südwesten umzuwandeln gedachte. Seit Jahren sammelte und erwarb er für die Gemeinde Bernau und ihre geplante Hans Thoma-Gedächtnisstätte im Rathaus Bilder und Devotionalien des Künstlers sowie seiner Schüler. Erster Höhepunkt in den Bemühungen Baurs, der sich der Unterstützung des gesamten Gemeinderats wie der wohlwollenden Förderung der Freiburger Kultusbürokratie sicher sein konnte, stellte die Feier zum 25. Todestag des Künstlers am 18. September 1949 in Bernau dar. An dieser Mischung aus heimatlichem Trachtenfest und Totengedenken nahm neben den Ministern Eduard Lais (Wirtschaft und Arbeit) und Alfons Kirchgäßner (Landwirtschaft) auch der badische Staatspräsident und gleichzeitige Kultusminister Leo Wohleb teil.[3] Offensichtlich ohne vorherige Rücksprache mit der zuständigen Abteilung des badischen Ministeriums des Kultus und Unterrichts kündigte Wohleb bei dieser Gelegenheit die Stiftung eines Staatspreises zu Ehren und unter dem Namen »Hans Thoma-Preis« an, der alljährlich an einen »jungen badischen Künstler« verliehen werden sollte, »der seine Begabung und Fähigkeit bereits unter Beweis gestellt« habe.[4] Der Preis, so Wohleb in vertrauter Runde nach Ende des offiziellen Festaktes, sollte mit einer Fördersumme von DM 2000,– ausgestattet und erstmalig im Jahre 1950 verliehen werden. Aufgabe der Freiburger Ministerialbürokratie war es nun, diese Summe in den Haushalt 1950 einzustellen und eine Satzung für die Preisverleihung zu entwerfen. Der offensichtlichen Spontaneität der Preisstiftung entsprach die geringe Sorgfalt, mit der letztere Aufgabe in die Tat umgesetzt wurde. In sechs dürren Paragraphen präsentierte Ministerialdirektor Paul Fleig erst am 24. Juli des folgenden Jahres die Satzung, die viele Fragen offen ließ und sich in der Folgezeit als vollkommen ungenügend erwies. Weiterhin sollte zwar mit dem Preis »unser großer badischer Maler Hans Thoma geehrt und die Bildende Kunst gefördert werden« (§ 2). In Abänderung zur Ankündigung des badischen Staatspräsidenten allerdings kamen für den Preis nicht mehr nur junge Vertreter in Betracht, sondern jeder badische Künstler »mit anerkannten Fähigkeiten, der schon eine Reihe wertvoller Arbeiten vorweisen kann, künstlerischen Eigenwert besitzt und eine Weiterentwicklung zu hohen Leistungen erwarten läßt« (§ 3). Die Aufteilung des Preises und des Preisgeldes in Höhe von DM 2000,– auf zwei Künstler und die Möglichkeit, die Preisverleihung auszusetzen, »falls sich in einem Jahr kein des Preises würdiger Vertreter der Bildenden Kunst finden läßt«, waren weitere Bestandteile der Satzung (§ 3 und § 4). Die Preisverleihung selbst sollte »alljährlich am 18. September in Bernau in einem landschaftlich eigenständigen, feierlichen Akt, bei dem der Preisträger über sein künstlerisches Arbeiten sprechen soll, verteilt werden« (§ 6).[5]

Die wichtigste Änderung gegenüber der Ankündigung Wohlebs vom Jahre 1949, die Aufhebung der Beschränkung auf einen »jungen« Künstler, war offensichtlich aus der Not des Augenblicks geboren und orientierte sich an der Person des ersten Preisträgers, der im Mai 1950, noch vor Abfassung der Satzung also, bereits feststand. Mit dem 1872 in Stuttgart geborenen Albert Haueisen war eine Künstlerpersönlichkeit ausgewählt worden, die als Grandseigneur der badischen Künstlerszene allgemeine Anerkennung genoß. Als Meisterschüler Thomas hatte Haueisen auch enge Verbindungen zu Bernau selbst aufzuweisen, wo er in den Jahren 1903 bis 1905 im Elternhaus des Bürgermeisters Baur sein Atelier einrichtete und unter dem Einfluß des Meisters fein gezeichnete Grafiken fertigte.[6] Doch Haueisen war nicht bei Thoma stehen geblieben, sondern hatte die zur Tradition erstarrten Grenzen der gegenständlichen Landschaftsmalerei bewußt überschritten. Sein Verzicht auf eine erneute Professur an der Akademie für Bildende Künste in Karlsruhe im Jahre 1933 prädestinierte ihn auch unter politischen Vorzeichen als ersten Preisträger. Auch wenn Haueisen aufgrund seines fortgeschrittenen Alters und seines Gesundheitszustandes an der Preisverleihung am 15. August 1950 – das Heimatfest mit dem in der Satzung vorgeschriebenen »landschaftlich eigenständigen, feierlichen Akt« war vom 18. September auf den unter touristischen Gesichtspunkten sehr viel attraktiveren Feiertag Maria Himmelfahrt verlegt worden – nicht teilnehmen konnte, wurde die Veranstaltung ein Erfolg, und der Hans Thoma-Preis schickte sich an, zu einem Kristallisationspunkt der badischen Kunstszene zu werden, der durchaus geeignet war, »alle lebendigen Kräfte, die sich in diesem Landschaftsraum als solche erweisen« widerzuspiegeln und sie »ohne Bevorzugung oder Zurücksetzung einer künstlerischen Tendenz, ausgehend lediglich vom Gehalt und der künstlerischen Kraft« der Werke zu würdigen.[7]

Dies schien sich durch die Preisverleihung 1951 zu verfestigen, auch gerade weil die Preisträger, was Person, Alter, Reputation und künstlerisches Niveau anbelangte, durchaus als Kontrapunkte zu Haueisen aufgefaßt werden konnten. Der 1908 in Wyhlen geborene, seit 1944 in Basel wohnhafte Maler Josef Hauser und der Student an der Akademie der bildenden Künste Freiburg, Kurt Bildstein, teilten sich 1951 den Preis, der als »finanzielle Hilfe für ihre Weiterbildung« gedacht war.[8] Der Vorschlag für Hauser kam vom 1. Vorsitzenden der »Badischen Secession«, und gleichzeitigem Leiter der Kunsthalle in Baden-Baden, Erwin Heinrich, für Bildstein vom Direktor der Freiburger Akademie, Professor Wilhelm Gerstel.

Im darauffolgenden Jahr hatten sich die Voraussetzungen insofern grundlegend geändert, als mit der Bildung des Südweststaats die Verpflichtungen aus der Stiftung des Hans Thoma-Preises auf das neue Bundesland Baden-Württemberg übergangen war, und nunmehr die Ministerialbürokratie in Stuttgart über die zukünftigen Träger dieses badischen Kunstpreises zu entscheiden hatten. Die Enttäuschung saß tief in Freiburg über den Untergang des selbständigen Landes (Süd)-Baden; der Verlagerung von Kompetenzen nach Stuttgart wurde mit Mißtrauen begegnet. Daß der am 21. Juli 1952 von Bürgermeister Baur als Preisträger offiziell vorgeschlagene Kunstmaler Hans Schroedter kommentarlos die Abwicklungsstelle des Freiburger Kultusministeriums passierte und wenige Tage darauf als bereits entschiedene Tatsache dem baden-württembergischen Kultminister Schenkel präsentiert wurde, bei der es nur noch darum gehe, die Übergabe des Preises durch den Kultminister zu organisieren, entsprach sicherlich nicht dem für die Verleihung des Preises angestrebten Procedere. Diese Vorgehensweise als letzte partikularistische Zukkungen der ehemals autonomen Freiburger Kultusverwaltung zu interpretieren, würde der bei der Fülle der Aufgaben beim Zusammenwachsen des neuen Landes doch eher untergeordneten Bedeutung des Preises nicht entsprechen. Zudem lag nach Ausweis der Quellen nur ein Vorschlag vor, das Thoma-Heimatfest in Bernau stand vor der Tür, eine Entscheidung über den Preisträger hatte innerhalb so kurzer Zeit zu fallen, daß nicht einmal die neue Landesregierung als Rechtsnachfolgerin der badischen Regierung in die Diskussion um den Preisträger mit eingebunden werden konnte. Stellvertretend für sie erklärte sich das Kultministerium in Stuttgart bereit, »in diesem Jahr des staatlichen Übergangs« die Preisvergabe vorzunehmen. Mit diesem deutlichen Signal stellte sich das Kultministerium bewußt in die noch junge Tradition des Preises und versicherte dem einzigen staatlichen Kunstpreis des neuen Landes seine Unterstützung.

Daß es sich damit auf ein unbekanntes und vor allem unwegsames Terrain vorgewagt hatte, mußte das Ministerium in den Folgemonaten erfahren. Mit der Auszeichnung nämlich hatte Stuttgart, sicherlich unbewußt und unwissentlich, Stellung bezogen in einer kunstpolitischen Auseinandersetzung, die in jenen Jahren ihrem ersten Höhepunkt zustrebte.

Ausgelöst durch ein 1951 mit staatlicher Unterstützung in München realisiertes Ausstellungsprojekt, an dem unter Führung des Kunstprofessors Constantin Gerhardinger süddeutsche Künstler teilnahmen, die zu einem erheblichen Teil in der Zeit zwischen 1933 und 1945 auch in Hitlers »Haus der deutschen Kunst« vertreten waren, hatte sich die Diskussion um den Begriff der »kulturellen Restauration« entzündet. Besonders bitter empfanden es die Kritiker, daß das Motto »Zurück zum Naturvorbild« und die mit den Parolen von der »Achtung vor dem Geschöpf«, der »Demut«, der »Ehrfurcht vor dem Schöpfer« und der »sittlichen Hoheit« operierenden Neo-Realisten offensichtlich den Geschmack des breiten Publikums trafen. Verzweifelt suchte man sich diesem konservativen »roll-back« in der Kulturpolitik, dieser drohenden Abstimmung mit den Füßen, bei der »auf ausgetretenen Pfaden wieder ›aus den Kräften des Volkstums, der Rasse und des Heimatbodens‹« gestaltet wurde, entgegenzustemmen. Den Staatsbehörden warf man in diesem Zusammenhang vor, aus einer falsch verstandenen demokratischen Toleranz heraus Tendenzen zu fördern und »einer kulturellen Entwicklung Vorschub zu leisten, über deren mögliche Folgen die deutsche Kulturgeschichte der zwanziger und dreißiger Jahre belehrt«.[9] Neue Nahrung fand dieser Vorwurf durch die Verleihung des Hans Thoma-Preises 1952 an jenen Hans Schroedter, der zwar nicht zu den »Stars vom ›Haus der deutschen Kunst‹« gezählt hatte, Mitte der dreißiger Jahre jedoch in heftigen Worten für die Auflösung der »Badischen Secession« eingetreten war, die er als eine Gruppe charakterisierte, »die in Wirklichkeit nur die Irrtümer und Verbrechen einer überwundenen Zeit zu konservieren sucht«, daher »heute keine Berechtigung mehr« habe und, in Wiederholung eines Zitats des Reichspropagandaministers Dr. Goebbels, es nicht angehe, »daß die Führer von gestern die Führer von heute sein wollen«.[10] Doch es war nicht so sehr die Rolle Schroedters im Dritten Reich, die im Vordergrund der Kritik stand, als vielmehr seine künstlerischen Qualitäten, die nicht den Anforderungen für die Vergabe des Preises entsprachen. Ihm konnten weder anerkannte Fähigkeiten und wertvolle Arbeiten attestiert werden, noch besaß er künstlerischen Eigenwert und eine Weiterentwicklung zu hohen Leistungen war schon ob seines Alters von 80 Jahren ebenfalls nicht mehr zu erwarten. Wie Erwin Heinrich fürchteten viele um das Renommee des Preises und sahen dessen Abgleiten in eine »Schulmeister-Kultur«[11] voraus, wie sie sich in durchaus falsch verstandener Thomascher Traditionspflege in Bernau auszubreiten begann. Vor allem die Hans-Thoma-Gesellschaft mit Sitz in Oberursel (Taunus) beanspruchte unter ihrer langjährigen Vorsitzenden Sofie Bergmann-Küchler die Federführung in allem, was die Pflege und Förderung des künstlerischen Erbes von Hans Thoma anbelangte, inklusive der Beurteilung, welcher der Kandidaten als der »würdigste in künstlerisch-geistiger Beziehung« zu Thoma anzusehen war.[12] Sie war es auch gewesen, die gegen die Verleihung des Preises 1951 protestiert hatte und seitdem in Bernau, gestützt auf die künstlerischen Lokalgrößen Spiegelhalder und Stadelmann sowie auf den Festleiter Otto Berner, aktive Propaganda für das vermeintlich wahre Thomasche Erbe betrieb. Schroedter war der Kandidat der Thoma-Gesellschaft gewesen, weil er »abseits aller modischen Zeitströmungen... sich stets selber treu geblieben« war und dabei eine »Fülle von natur- und volksnahen Schöpfungen«, durchdrungen »von einer sittlichen Hoheit«, geschaffen hatte.[13] Bürgermeister Baur, der sich im Falle Schroedters als Sprachrohr der Hans-Thoma-Gesellschaft hatte benutzen lassen, waren derartige kunstpolitische Fragestellungen fremd. Er verfolgte mit dem Hans Thoma-Preis, dem Hans Thoma-Fest und der damit verbundenen Präsentation von Bildern Absichten, die nicht so sehr auf Hebung des Kunstverständnisses als vielmehr in Richtung auf eine Intensivierung des Fremdenverkehrs zielten. Der »Rummel« um Hans Thoma war in weitem Maße orientiert am Populärgeschmack und als solcher Teil der örtlichen Fremdenverkehrspolitik. Wie wenig sich der Bürgermeister selbst in den handwerklichen Gepflogenheiten der Ausstellungsmacher auskannte, belegt ein Projekt aus dem Sommer 1953, als Baur die Idee einer Emil Rudolf Weiss-Ausstellung im Rathaus von Bernau lancierte. Eine Vorbereitungszeit von drei Wochen, 20. Juni – 15. Juli 1953, schien ihm ausreichend, um eine genügende Anzahl von Bildern nach Bernau zu transportieren und sie zu einer Ausstellung zu komponieren. Erwin Heinrich, der um die Ausleihe von Weiss-Bildern aus der Staatlichen Kunsthalle Baden-Baden angeschrieben wurde, konnte ob dieses dilettantischen Vorgehens nur verwundert den Kopf schütteln und Bürgermeister Baur von »einer derart kurzfristig angesetzten Ausstellung von Werken des Verstorbenen« abraten. Heinrich konnte sich nicht enthalten, in diesem Schreiben die kulturpolitische Entwicklung in Bernau dezent, aber eindeutig zu kritisieren. Ein Grund, weswegen eine Ausstellung des Künstlers in Bernau fehl am Platz war, sei, »dass die hochkünstlerische Arbeit von E. R. Weiss sehr wenig in den Rahmen der seither in Bernau gezeigten Ausstellungen passt«.[14]

Daß mit der Vergabe des Preises an Hans Schroedter der sozialdemokratische Kultminister Schenkel im fernen Stuttgart den »Altbadnern und der Thoma-Gesellschaft mit ihrer ›Teutschen Kunst‹ in die Falle« gegangen war, machte schnell die Runde und warf nicht gerade ein positives Licht auf die Kenntnisse der Stuttgarter Ministerialbürokratie über die Verhältnisse innerhalb der badischen Kunstszene. Daß sich Schenkel zudem in seinen Ausführungen bei der Verleihung des Preises gegen »neue Wege in der Kunst«, insbesondere gegen die »gegenstandslose Kunst« aussprach und vom Künstler »Ehrfurcht vor dem Schöpfer und Achtung vor dem Geschöpf« einforderte, gab denen neue Nahrung, die sich als die wahren Erben der Thomaschen Tradition verstanden[14] und erbittert die modernen Strömungen in der Kunst bekämpften. »Was heißt aber: im Geiste Hans Thomas? Meint man damit etwa diejenigen, die ähnlich wie Thoma malen? Mit anderen Worten: die kleinen Epigonen, die egal in Schwarzwaldmalerei machen? Dann wird sich jedes echte Talent von vornherein für die Verleihung dieses Preises bedanken. Es ist da besser, man geht von Hans Thoma selbst aus, der auch einen harten Kampf bestehen mußte, ehe er sich in Deutschland durchsetzte; denn als er aus Frankreich mit seinen bei Courbet gemachten Erfahrungen zurückkehrte und die mit diesen Erfahrungen gemalten Bilder ausstellte, erhob sich ein Sturm der Entrüstung gegen diese neue Art von Malerei, die der damaligen deutschen Konvention eben nicht entsprach. Man soll nicht das

Bequeme, sondern das Zukunftweisende suchen und fördern, wenn man wirklich im Geiste Hans Thomas handeln will.«[16]
Doch die Diskussion um die Preisverleihung offenbarte auch ein kunstpolitisches Dilemma, in das die Stuttgarter Kultusverwaltung bei unveränderter Übernahme der Vergabemodalitäten leicht geraten konnte. Die Verpflichtung zur Unparteilichkeit und Ausgewogenheit mußte sich für die Kultusbürokratie dann leicht zu einem Bumerang entwickeln, wenn diese Ausgewogenheitsverpflichtung zum Altar wurde, auf dem zur Not auch die künstlerische Qualität geopfert wurde. »Daß eine mit der Verwaltung von Kulturgütern betraute Behörde das Qualitätsprinzip vernachlässigt, weil sie es jedermann rechtmachen will, ist längst kein Einzelfall mehr«, so Hans Maria Wingler in seiner beißenden Kritik an der Thoma-Preisverleihung 1952.[17]
Weg von der kunstpolitischen Opportunität, die durch das zufällige und willkürliche Vorschlagssystem noch gefördert wurde, hin zum Kriterium der künstlerischen Qualität, dieser Forderung konnte sich auch das Stuttgarter Ministerium uneingeschränkt anschließen. Wichtige Voraussetzung für die Durchsetzung dieses Prinzips war, die Kriterien für die Vergabe des Preises nachvollziehbar zu gestalten und an der Entscheidungsfindung de jure interessenunabhängige Institutionen zu beteiligen, um somit partikulare Vereins- und Verbandsinteressen möglichst zurückzudrängen.
Hinter der Beteiligung und Einbindung der beiden neugeschaffenen Regierungspräsidien Karlsruhe und Freiburg in die Auswahl der Kandidaten für den Hans Thoma-Preis stand somit nicht allein die Absicht, die Verantwortung auf eine breitere Basis zu delegieren, als vielmehr der Wunsch und die Notwendigkeit, eine Art Filter zwischenzuschalten, der zukünftig solche, »einer vergangenen Ideologie verhaftete« Preisträger verhindern sollte.[18]
Donndorf begann sofort, dieses neue Konzept in die Tat umzusetzen. Bereits im Mai 1953 erging an die badischen Regierungspräsidien die Aufforderung, Vorschläge für den Hans Thoma-Preisträger 1953 einzusenden. Zugleich wurde von der Abteilung K des Ministeriums der Bildhauer Prof. Karl Albiker aus Ettlingen als aussichtsreichster Kandidat dem Minister vorgeschlagen. Albiker, der zwar keine direkten Kontakte zu Thoma hatte, allerdings mit seiner Kunst »fest in seinem heimatlichen alemannischen Boden« wurzelte, war tatsächlich ein Kandidat, der auf breite Zustimmung stieß.[19]
Der einmal eingeschlagene Weg, den Hans Thoma-Preis »nur an hervorragende Künstlerpersönlichkeiten« zu verleihen[20], die bereit waren, »neue, die Entwicklung weitertragende Wege zu gehen«, mußte in der Folgezeit gegen z.T. massive Einflußnahme vor allem der Hans-Thoma-Gesellschaft verteidigt werden. Sie konnte dabei auf die Schützenhilfe dezidiert nationalistischer Künstlervereinigungen zurückgreifen, die sich im »Bund für freie und angewandte Kunst« mit Sitz in Darmstadt zusammengeschlossen hatten. Anfang 1954 wurde das Kultusministerium mit Anträgen geradezu überhäuft, den Preis in diesem Jahre dem Meersburger Kunstmaler Hans Dieter zu geben. Sowohl die Hans-Thoma-Gesellschaft als auch der Bund für freie und angewandte Kunst sprachen sich nachdrücklich für den »Malerpoeten des Bodensees« aus, auch wenn dieser, nach übereinstimmenden Aussagen der Direktoren der Staatsgalerien, anderer Künstlerverbände und der Experten in den Regierungspräsidien lediglich lokale Bedeutung für das Bodenseegebiet besaß und die künstlerischen Ansprüche für die Verleihung des Preises keineswegs erfüllte.[21]
Dabei ließ sich die Abteilung Kunst des Kultusministeriums auch nicht durch die offensichtliche Strategie der Hans-Thoma-Gesellschaft irritieren, die neben dem eigentlichen Favoriten Hans Dieter noch einen weiteren Namen präsentierte, der keineswegs konsensfähig war. Es handelte sich dabei um den Maler Otto Leiber, dem im Sommer 1954 eine Ausstellung in Bernau gewidmet war, der sich allerdings in der Zeit des Dritten Reiches als »getreuer Gefolgsmann des Führers« zu erkennen gegeben und vehement zur »Reinigung der Kunst von verkappten Bolschewiken« aufgerufen hatte.[22] Bei der erwarteten Ablehnung dieses Kandidaten, so offensichtlich das Kalkül der Hans-Thoma-Gesellschaft, in deren Vorstand neben Sophie Bergmann-Küchler und dem Bernauer Bürgermeister Baur seit 1951 auch der prominente Karlsruher Nationalsozialist und ehemaliger Mitarbeiter im kulturellen Teil der Parteizeitung »Der Führer«, Rektor Fritz Wilkendorf, angehörte, könne das Kultministerium in Stuttgart nicht umhin, Dieter als Kompromißkandidaten zu akzeptieren, zumal ihm politische Verfehlungen in der Vergangenheit nicht vorzuwerfen waren. Um so größer war die Enttäuschung, als der Vorschlag der Gesellschaft von Minister Simpfendörfer in Abstimmung mit Regierungsdirektor Donndorf rundweg abgelehnt wurde und statt dessen der Badenweiler Maler Emil Bizer den Preis 1954 erhielt. Mit »äußerstem Befremden« wurde diese Entscheidung in den Reihen der Gesellschaft aufgenommen und Maßnahmen auf den Affront gegen die ihrer Ansicht nach wirkliche Kunst diskutiert. Doch Donndorf ließ sich auch durch Drohungen mit Pressekampagnen nicht irritieren, zumal er sich der Unterstützung der beiden Regierungspräsidien und der Direktoren der staatlichen Galerien sicher sein konnte. So hatte das Regierungspräsidium Südbaden am 23. Juni 1954 die Hans-Thoma-Gesellschaft wie folgt charakterisiert: »Die Bestrebungen der Gesellschaft gelten einseitig der Pflege der traditionalistischen Kunst. Der modernen Kunst, die bei nicht wenigen ihrer Mitglieder noch immer als ›entartete Kunst‹ gelten dürfte, steht die Gesellschaft ablehnend gegenüber«, woraus konsequenterweise die Forderung nach »größter Zurückhaltung der staatlichen Verwaltung« resultierte, auch weil bei der Gesellschaft »nur noch das Hakenkreuz fehle, um dort das dritte Reich voll aufleben zu lassen«.[23]
Bei dieser Charakterisierung blieben die von der Gesellschaft in den folgenden Jahren vorgeschlagenen »traditionalistischen« Kandidaten durchweg auf der Strecke. Die Angst vor dem

Vorwurf einer mit der künstlerischen Auszeichnung verbundenen politischen Parteinahme für eine bestimmte künstlerische Gruppierung oder die durch den Künstler vertretenen Politik, bestimmte die fünfziger Jahre hindurch das Auswahlverfahren für den Preis. Als 1960 der Maler Rudolf Riester, selbst Preisträger im Jahre 1957, den an der Hamburger Kunstakademie lehrenden, gebürtigen Mannheimer Gustav Seitz als Preisträger vorschlug, war man sich im Ministerium darüber einig, daß damit »wohl eine der bedeutendsten deutschen Künstlerpersönlichkeiten« ausgezeichnet werden würde. Letztendlich führten die gegen Bildhauer Seitz bestehenden »politischen Bedenken« dazu, einen anderen Kandidaten auszuwählen, zumal sich »seine Frau... in der Sowjetzone bis in die jüngste Zeit politisch sehr stark exponiert [hatte, und] er selbst... bis zur Annahme der Lehrtätigkeit in Hamburg auch einer der bevorzugten Künstler der sowjetzonalen Regierung« gewesen war.[24]

So sehr die Preisverleihungspolitik des »juste milieu« politisch nicht opportune Randerscheinungen auszugrenzen in der Lage war, verhinderte sie allerdings lange Zeit eine angemessene Berücksichtigung neuer Tendenzen in der südwestdeutschen Kunstszene. Vor allem der in der Satzung vorgeschriebene »landschaftlich eigenbetonte, feierliche Akt« der Preisverleihung, der, wie Kurt Martin 1956 schrieb, »die Wahl eines ›landschaftlich eigenbetonten Künstlers‹ geradezu forderte«, und der Ort der Preisverleihung waren Begleitumstände, die einer Fortentwicklung der sowieso heterogenen Preisphilosophie nicht gerade förderlich waren. »Es würde uns schwer fallen«, bekannte das Regierungspräsidium Freiburg am 27. Mai 1958, »einen Künstler der völlig gegenstandslosen Richtung für einen Preis in Vorschlag zu bringen, der den Namen von Hans Thoma trägt.« So fand der große alte Mann der südwestdeutschen gegenstandslosen Kunst, Willi Müller-Hufschmid aus Karlsruhe, lange Jahre keine Berücksichtigung, obwohl er immer wieder als geeigneter Kandidat von den Kunsthallenleitern in die Diskussion gebracht worden war; noch waren die in Bernau um Bürgermeister Baur konzentrierten Kräfte zu einflußreich. Gegen sie wagte man im Kultusministerium auch nicht, den Preis grundsätzlich auf eine neue Basis zu stellen. Dies hatte Kurt Martin, der Leiter der Karlsruher Kunsthalle, angeregt, indem er sowohl für einen längeren Vergaberhythmus wie auch für wechselnde Orte plädierte, um den Preis aus seinem »landschaftlich eigenbetonten« Korsett zu befreien. Den ersten gelungenen Versuch in dieser Richtung stellte die Vergabe des seit 1960 auf 5000,– DM angehobenen Hans Thoma-Staatspreises 1964 an Willi Müller-Hufschmid dar, mit der sich die Kunstpreispolitik des Landes den »Abstrakten« und »Gegenstandslosen« öffnete. Wie groß die Reserviertheit hinsichtlich des Preisträgers in Bernau war, belegt der Artikel in der Stuttgarter Zeitung vom 10. August des Jahres, in dem über die Preisverleihung berichtet wurde: »Die Bernauer hatten zu dem festlichen Anlaß ihre bewährten Kulissen hervorgeholt: mächtig geballte Wolken, die vor tiefblauem Himmel über die Kuppen der Weidberge ringsum zogen und ihre Schatten gelegentlich auch auf die Festversammlung vor dem Rathaus warfen, ferne Herden auf den weiten Almenweiden, Fahnen, Girlanden und Trachten... An einem solchen Thoma-Tag wie aus dem Bilderbuch hatte es der Regierungspräsident daher auch ein wenig leichter, die vielen Freunde thoma'scher Landschaftsmalerei mit dem für sie schockierenden Gedanken vertraut zu machen, daß der Thoma-Preis in diesem Jahr zum erstenmal einem ›Abstrakten‹ verliehen wurde. Aber Dichtel berichtete mit treuherziger, spitzbübischer Ueberzeugungskraft davon, wie er auf der Fahrt über die Wacht nach Bernau dem verehrten Altmeister selbst begegnet sei und wie dieser mit Kopfnicken nicht nur der Wahl des Preisträgers, sondern auch der Rechtfertigung zugestimmt habe, wie schwer es sei, heutzutage noch immer die rechten Leute für einen Preis zu finden, der Hans Thomas Namen trage.«[25] Was den Bernauern quasi als Notlösung verkauft werden mußte, stellte in Wirklichkeit die kunstpolitische Anerkennung der »Gegenstandslosen« im Südweststaat dar.

Preisträger des Hans Thoma-Gedenkpreises 1950–1964

1950	Albert Haueisen, Prof. Dr. H. c., Maler, Jockgrim/Pfalz
1951	Josef Hauser, Maler, Basel Kurt Bildstein, Student, Ettenheim
1952	Hans Schroedter, Maler, Hausen vor Wald
1953	Karl Albiker, Prof., Bildhauer, Ettlingen
1954	Emil Bizer, Prof., Maler, Badenweiler
1955	Adolf Strübe, Prof., Maler, Lörrach
1956	Hans Meid, Prof., Maler, Ludwigsburg
1957	Rudolf Riester, Maler, Freiburg
1958	Curth Georg Becker, Maler, Singen
1959	Arthur Fauser, Maler, Frankfurt/Main
1960	Johannes Thiel, Maler, Kirchzarten
1961	Karl Hubbuch, Prof., Maler, Karlsruhe
1962	Wilhelm Schnarrenberger, Prof., Maler, Karlsruhe
1963	Xaver Fuhr, Prof., Maler, Regensburg
1964	Willi Müller-Hufschmid, Karlsruhe

1 Hauptstaatsarchiv Stuttgart (= HStAS) EA 3/203, Bü 592, Schreiben von Kurt Martin an das Kultusministerium v. 14. 4. 1955.

2 HStAS, EA 3/203, Bü 647.

3 Karl Stiefel, Baden 1648–1952, Bd. I, Karlsruhe 1979, S. 395

4 HStAS, EA 3/203, Ablieferungsliste Ministerium für Wissenschaft und Kunst Nr. 991, zukünftig im Staatsarchiv Freiburg.

5 Ebd., Aktennotiz vom 24. Juli 1950.

6 Vgl.: Ausstellungskatalog Prof. Dr. h. c. Albert Haueisen zum 100. Geburtstag. Gemälde und Graphik. Mannheimer Kunstverein e.V., 29. 10. – 26. 12. 72; Ausstellungskatalog Albert Haueisen 1872–1954. Aquarelle und Zeichnungen. Pfalzgalerie Kaiserslautern. 3. 8. – 7. 9. 1986; Antje Michaela Lechleiter, Die Künstlergruppe »Badische Secession«. Geschichte, Leben und Werk ihrer Maler und Bildhauer. Frankfurt 1994, S. 206–215, S. 391.

7 Karl Albiker in seinem Katalog-Geleitwort zur 1950 in Karlsruhe gezeigten Ausstellung »Badische Kunst der Gegenwart«, zit. nach: Andreas Franzke, Die Situation in Baden, in: Kunst der 50er Jahre in Baden-Württemberg, Ausstellungskatalog 1982, S. 12.

8 Begründung Wohlebs in der 125. Sitzung der Landesregierung am 13. 8. 1951, in: HStAS, EA 3/203, Ablieferungsliste Ministerium für Wissenschaft und Kunst Nr. 991, zukünftig im Staatsarchiv Freiburg.

9 Hans Maria Wingler, Kulturelle Restauration. Rezension einer Ausstellung auf der Darmstädter Mathildenhöhe im Jahre 1953, in: Das Kunstwerk 7 (1953), Heft 2, S. 49–50, hier S. 50.

10 Ebd., S. 49.

11 So der in Bernau geborene, in Staufen wohnhaft Keramiker Egon Bregger an Erwin Heinrich v. 21. 9. 1952, in: EA 3/203 Bü 592.

12 Ebd., Schreiben der Hans-Thoma-Gesellschaft vom 29. Mai 1953 an Schenkel.

13 Anonyme Beilage zum Vorschlag des Bürgermeisteramtes Bernau vom 21. 7. 1952, in: HStAS, EA 3/203, Ablieferungsliste Ministerium für Wissenschaft und Kunst Nr. 991, zukünftig im Staatsarchiv Freiburg.

14 EA 3/203 Bü 592, Schreiben v. 4. 7. 1953.

15 Südkurier Singen, Ausgabe v. 12. 8. 1952.

16 Stuttgarter Nachrichten, Ausgabe v. 27. 9. 1952.

17 Wingler (Anm. 9), S. 50.

18 EA 3/203 Bü 592, Schreiben Donndorfs vom 21. 6. 1954.

19 Walter Passarge, der aufgrund seiner klaren Haltung im Dritten Reich geschätzte Direktor der Mannheimer Kunsthalle über Karl Albiker, zit. nach: EA 3/203 Bü 592, Aktennotiz v. 12. 5. 1953.

20 Ebd., Aktennotiz Donndorf v. 29. 4. 1954.

21 Ebd., Schreiben v. 20. 2. 1954; die den Antrag unterzeichnenden Mitglieder der Arbeitsgemeinschaft des Bundes waren: Münchener Künstlergenossenschaft, Hamburgische Künstlerschaft, Sezession Mainz-Wiesbaden, Zunft Kurpfalz, Ludwigshafen, Künstlerbund Taunus, Bad Homburg, Gemeinschaft deutscher Künstler, Karlsruhe, Norddeutscher Künstlerbund, Berlin, Pfälzer Kunstgenossenschaft, Speyer, Künstlerbund Simplicius, Hanau, Hans-Thoma-Gesellschaft, Reutlingen.

22 Ebd., Schreiben des Kulturredakteurs der Badischen Zeitung, Rupert Gießler, an Kultminister Simpfendörfer v. 1. 6. 1954.

23 Ebd., Schreiben von Prof. Dr. Asal an Donndorf v. 24. 6. 1954.

24 Ebd., Schreiben KuMi an Regierungspräsidium Freiburg v. 31. 5. 1960.

25 EA 3/203 Bü 593, Stuttgarter Zeitung v. 10. 8. 1964.

Vom Informel
zur Neuen Figuration

Wilhelm Loth: Torso 4/57. 1957

Heinz Schanz: Kopf. 1958

Otto Herbert Hajek: Raumknoten 109. 1959

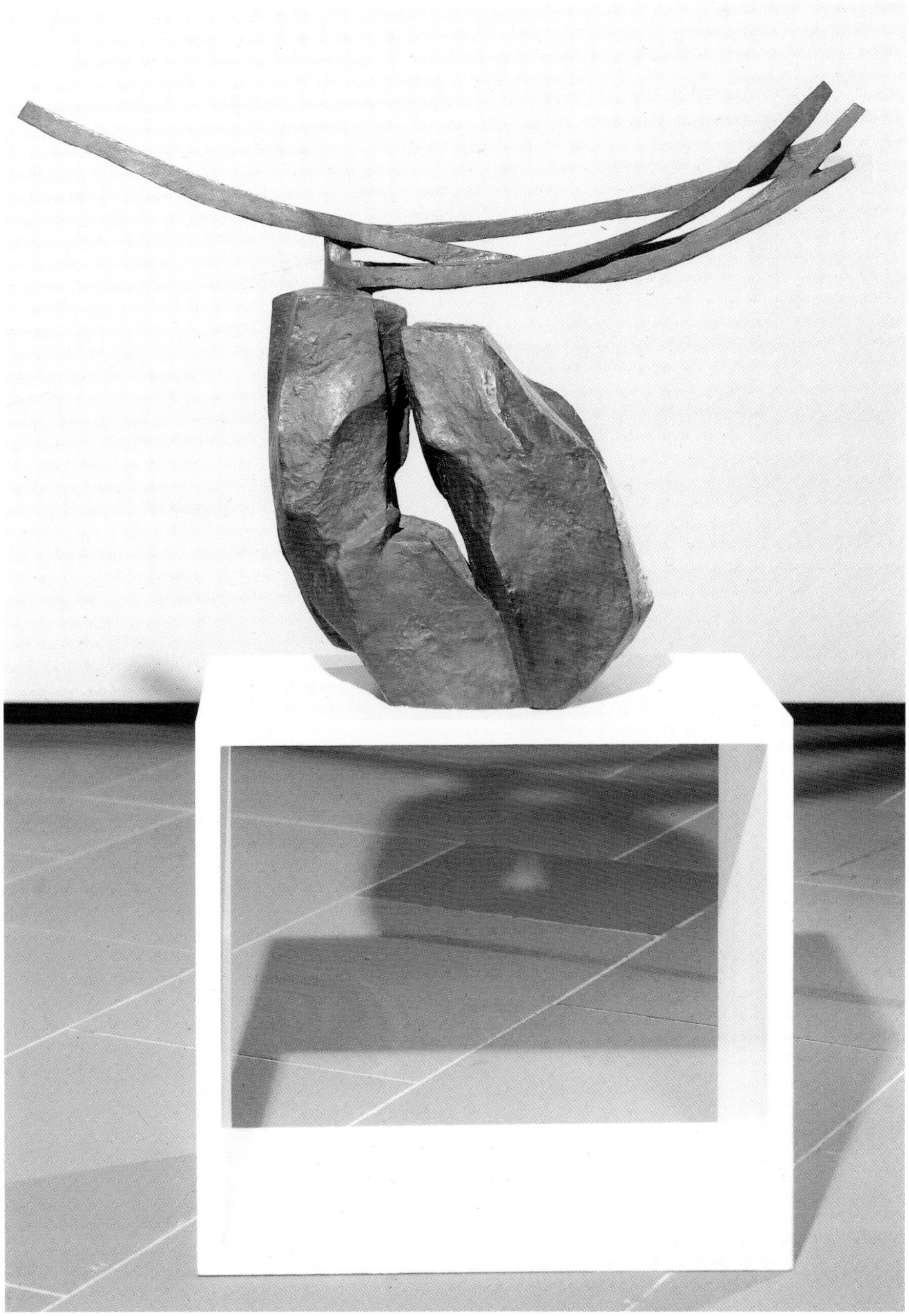

Wilhelm Loth: Figur 4/59. 1959

HAP Grieshaber: Das Milchschaf. 1958

Horst Antes: Bildnisfigur. 1959/60

Heinz Schanz: Ohne Titel. 1959

Walter Stöhrer: Ohne Titel. Um 1958

HAP Grieshaber: Hirte. 1960/61

HAP Grieshaber: Alp. 1960/61

Hans Baschang: Ohne Titel. 1960

Hans Martin Erhardt: Bikini-Girl. 1960

Emil Cimiotti: Baum mit großen Vögeln. 1961

Emil Cimiotti: Der Berg und seine Wolken II. 1960

Wilhelm Loth: Figur 9/62. 1962

Horst Antes: Blaue Figur (Maja). 1962

Heinz Schanz: Ohne Titel. 1962

Horst Antes: Maskierte Figur auf Gelb. 1965

Walter Stöhrer: Ohne Titel (Nr. 1). 1962

Walter Stöhrer: Populus robustus. Hommage à HAP Grieshaber. 1964

Bert Jäger: Ci Gît. 1962

Bert Jäger: Garlaban. 1964

Herbert Kitzel: Luzifer. 1963

Herbert Kitzel: Stürzend. 1965

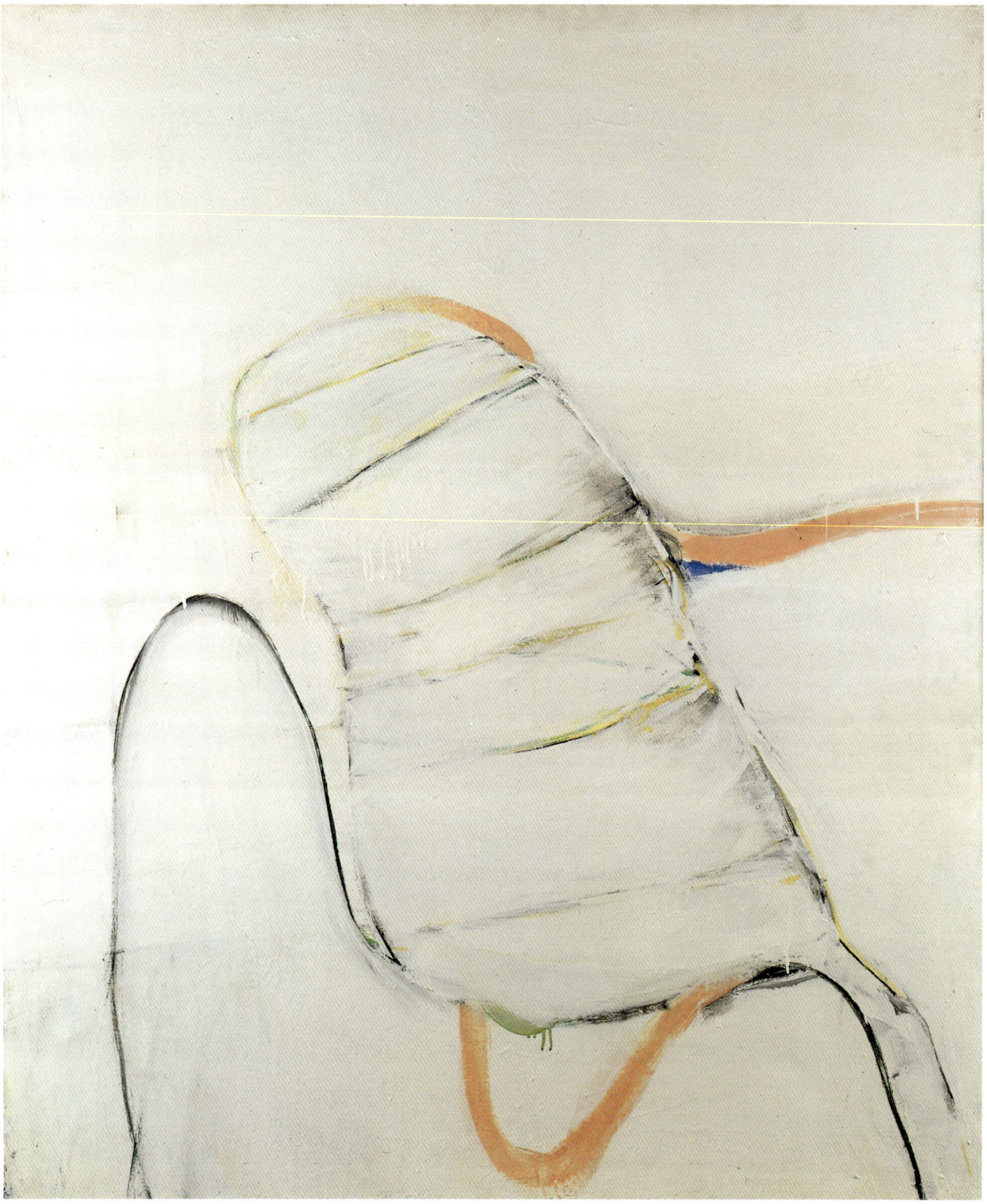

Dieter Krieg: Ohne Titel. 1965

Dieter Krieg: Fuß. 1966

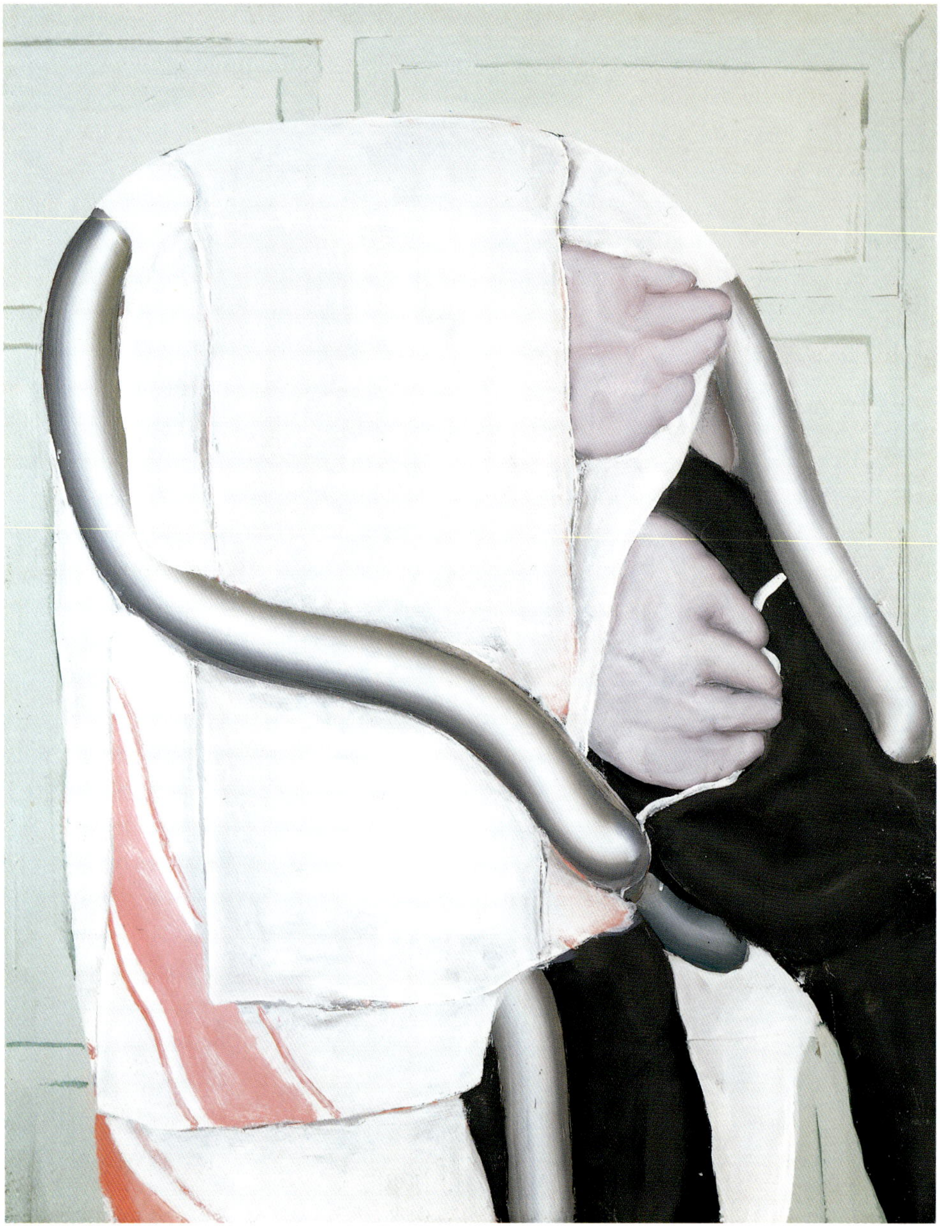

Dieter Krieg: Händchen. 1966

Horst Antes: Familie oder die Lust der Lust. 1967

Walter Stöhrer: Mara. Um 1968

Farbräume, Geometrie und Lineament

Bernd Berner	101, 102, 109
Franz Bernhard	131, 136, 137, 138
Rolf-Gunter Dienst	120, 121, 140
Peter Dreher	118
Otto Herbert Hajek	122, 132
Erich Hauser	127
Peter Herkenrath	113
Klaus Jürgen-Fischer	100
Fritz Klemm	128, 129, 130
Thomas Lenk	124, 125
Wilhelm Loth	141
Georg Meistermann	106, 143
Günter Neusel	123, 126
Georg Karl Pfahler	103, 110, 111, 133
Markus Prachensky	114, 116, 117
Lothar Quinte	107, 108, 112, 119, 134
Felix Schlenker	135
Emil Schumacher	139, 142
K.R.H. Sonderborg	104, 105, 115

Klaus Jürgen-Fischer: Ruba. 1958

Bernd Berner: Flächenraum (Nr. 1023). 1958/59

Bernd Berner: Roter Flächenraum. 1959/60

Bernd Berner: Flächenraum (WV 804). 1960

Georg Karl Pfahler: Formativ. 1961

Georg Karl Pfahler: Formativ 88–55. 1962

Lothar Quinte: Ohne Titel. (Schleierbild). 1962

Peter Herkenrath: Sappho. 1962

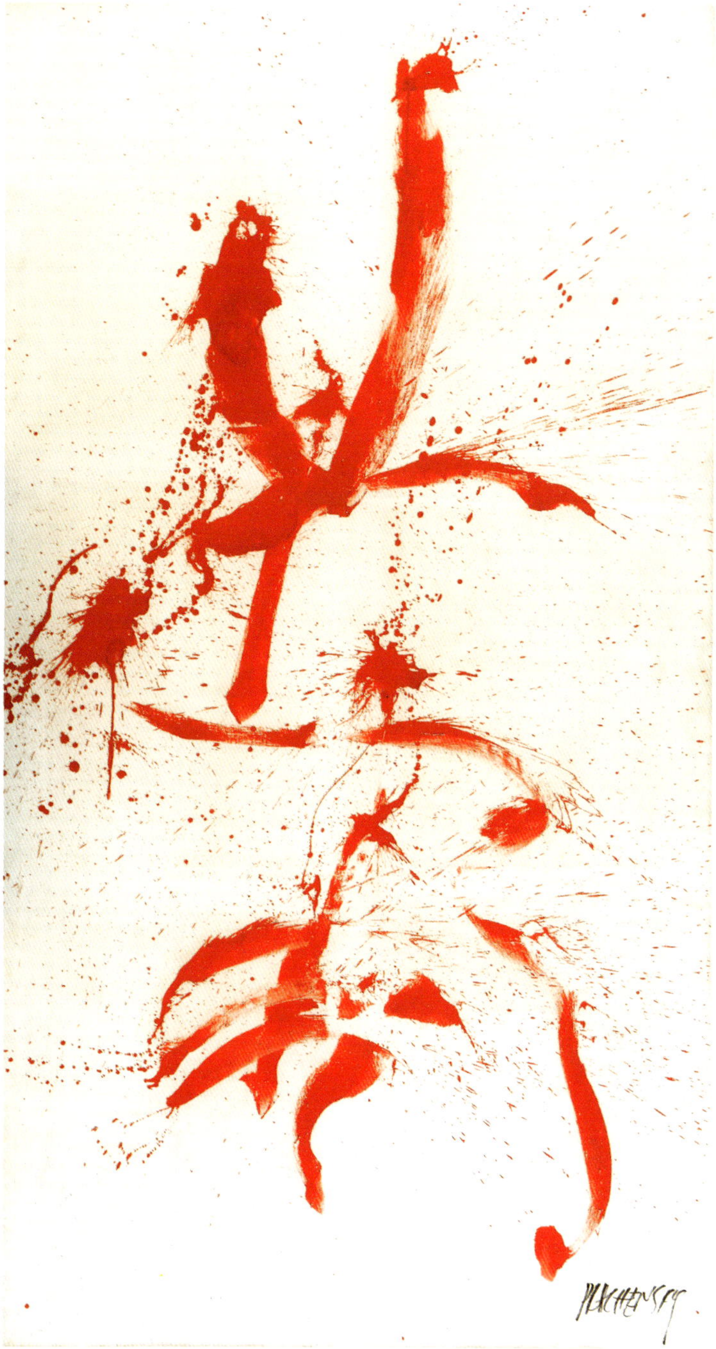

Markus Prachensky: Rouge sur gris. Karlsruhe. 1962

K.R.H. Sonderborg: Ohne Titel. 1962

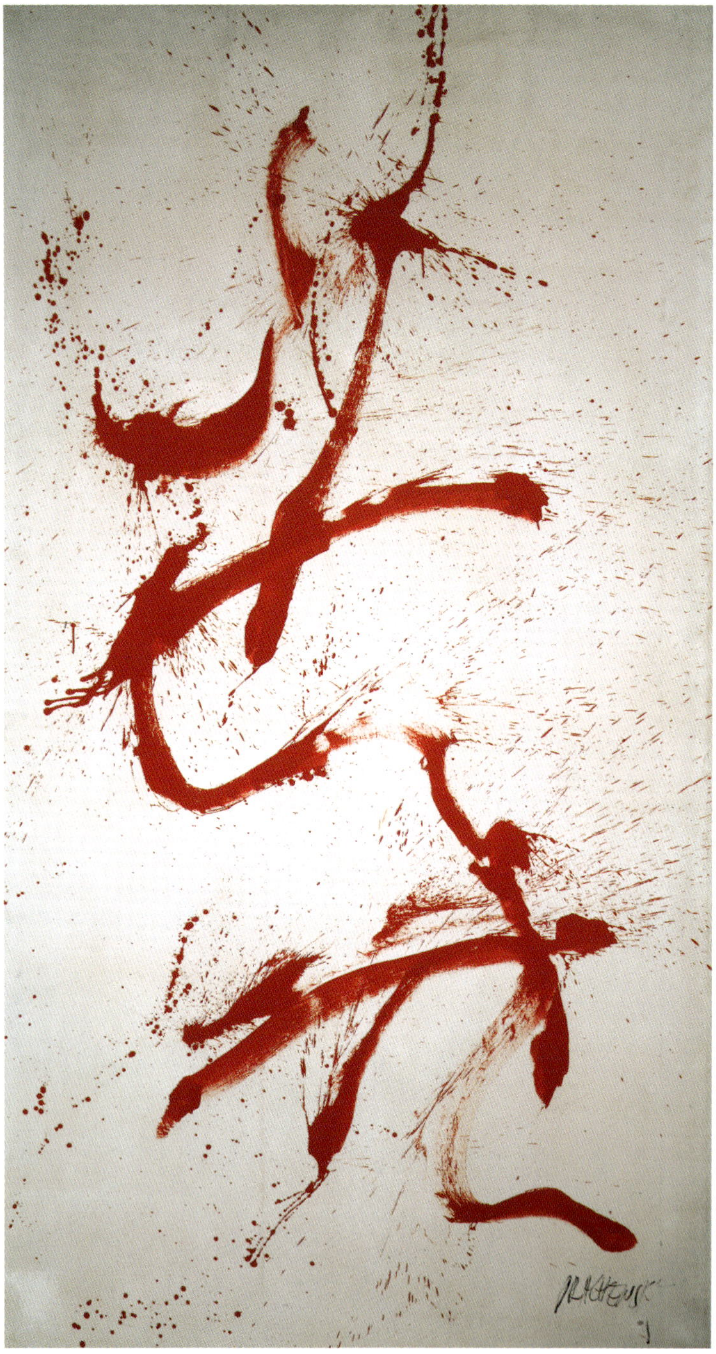

Markus Prachensky: Rouge sur gris – Karlsruhe II. 1962

Markus Prachensky: Rote und grüne Flächen – Solitude I. 1964

Peter Dreher: Stilleben mit Tassen II. 1963

Lothar Quinte: Ohne Titel (Fensterbild). 1963

Rolf-Gunter Dienst: Momentetagebuch 13. 8. – 19. 8. 1963

Rolf-Gunter Dienst: Dr. Benway goes to Tanger. 1963

Otto Herbert Hajek: Farbwege 64/8. 1964

Günter Neusel: Fachwerk 2. 1964

Thomas Lenk: Schichtung. 1964

Thomas Lenk: Schichtung 19. 1965

Günter Neusel: Inek II. 1965

Erich Hauser: Stahl 10/65. 1965

Fritz Klemm: Der Spiegel. Um 1965

Fritz Klemm: Die Wand. Um 1967

Fritz Klemm: Der Wald. Um 1965/67

Franz Bernhard: Relief mit zwei Figuren IV. 1965

Otto Herbert Hajek: Farbwege 67/8. 1967

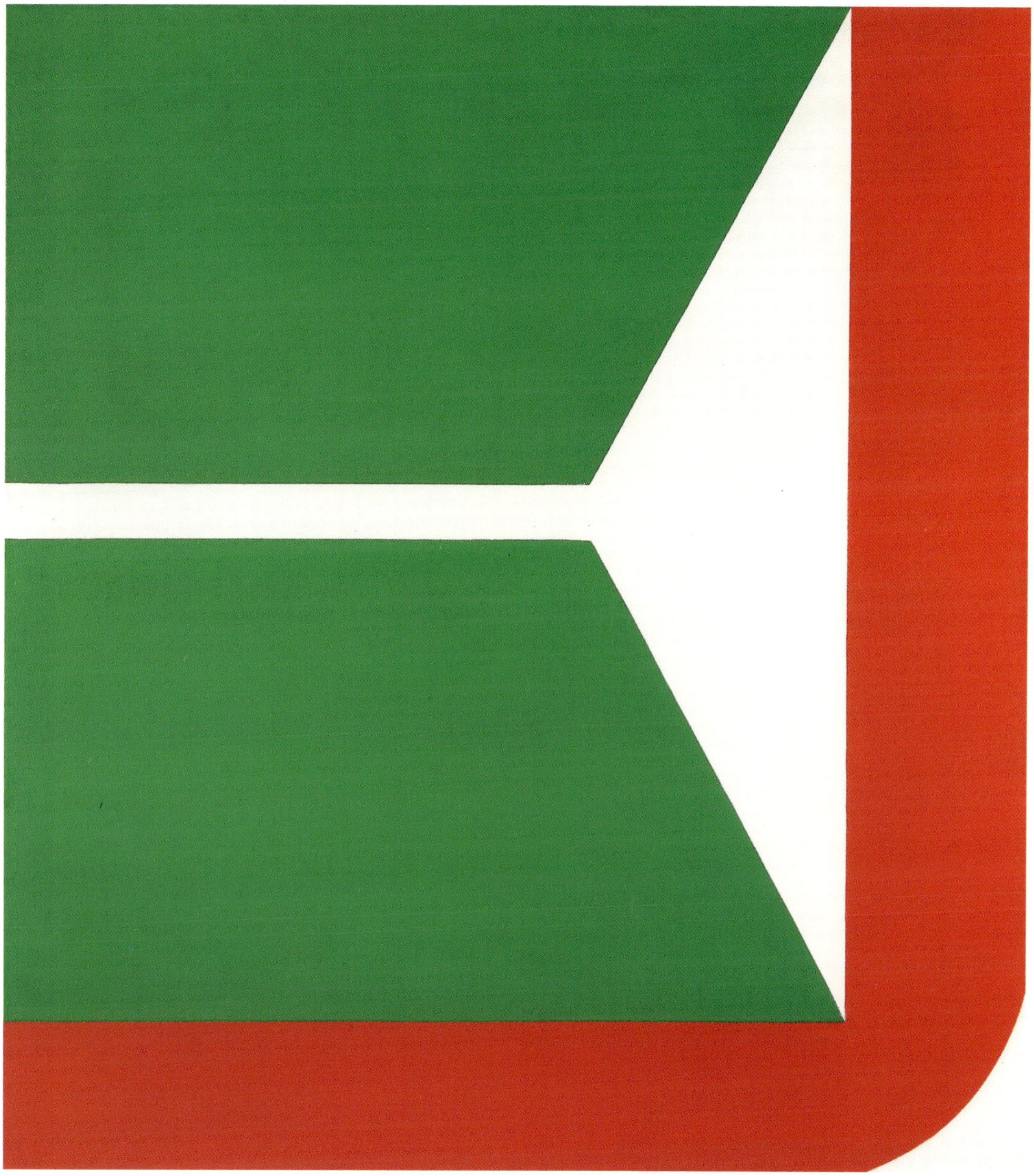

Georg Karl Pfahler: Balla-Balla. 1967

Lothar Quinte: Schlitzbild, vertikal. 1966

Felix Schlenker: T 17, 1968

Franz Bernhard: Kriechende. 1966

Franz Bernhard: Große Liegende II. 1967

Franz Bernhard: Relief HP III. 1968

Emil Schumacher: Bogen auf Rot. 1967

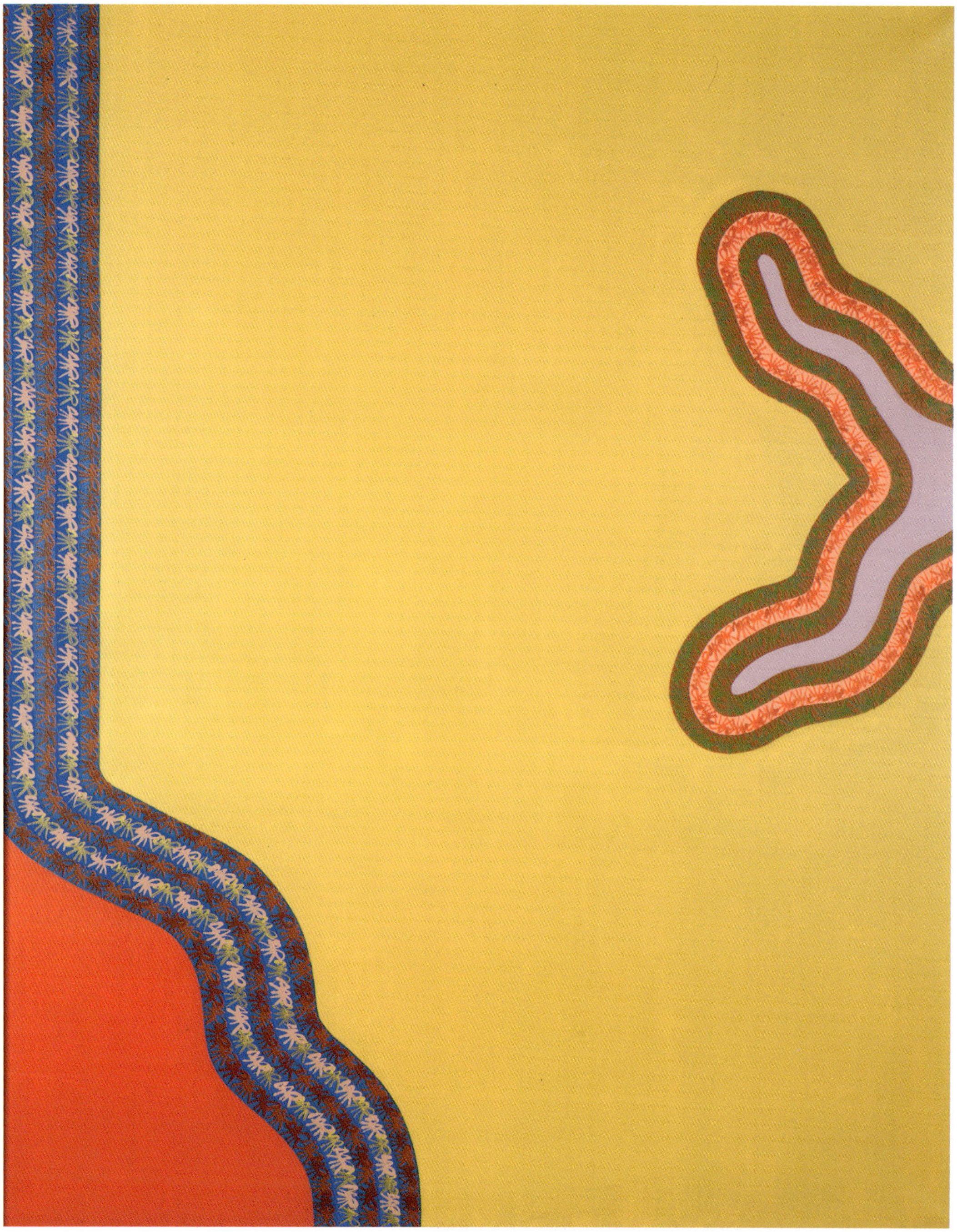

Rolf-Gunter Dienst: Momentetagebuch 20. 7. 69 – Natascha S. nicht in Schmalbach Nr. 9.

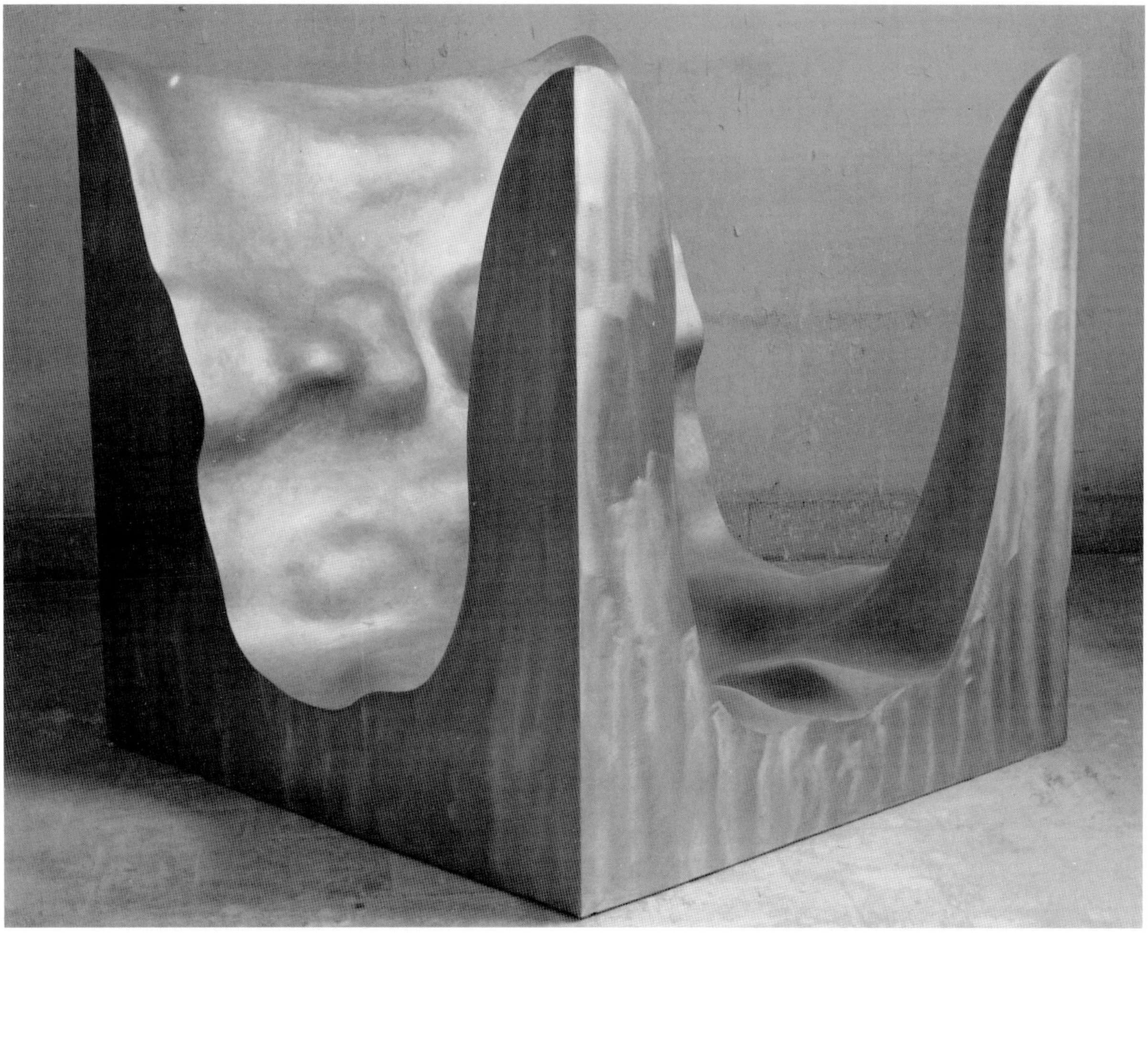

Wilhelm Loth: Plastik 18/69. 1969

Emil Schumacher: Ohne Titel. 1972

Georg Meistermann: Farbige Notizen zur Biographie. 1969–73

Anhang

Alphabetisches Ausstellungsverzeichnis

S. 75
Horst Antes (geb. 1936)
Bildnisfigur. 1959/60
Öl auf Leinwand
124x88 cm
Staatliche Kunsthalle Karlsruhe
(Inv. 2658)

S. 85
Horst Antes
Blaue Figur (Maja). 1962
Aquatec auf Leinwand
120x95 cm
Städelsches Kunstinstitut,
Frankfurt a. M., SG 1246

S. 87
Horst Antes
Maskierte Figur auf Gelb. 1965
Öl auf Leinwand
120x100 cm
Hamburger Kunsthalle (Inv. 5118)

S. 97
Horst Antes
Familie oder die Lust der Lust. 1967
Stahl, bemalt
160x300x150 cm
Ulmer Museum, Inv. Stiftung Fried,
Nr. 69

S. 80
Hans Baschang (geb. 1937)
Ohne Titel. 1960
Eitempera auf Nessel
120x95 cm
Privatbesitz München

S. 101
Bernd Berner (geb. 1930)
Flächenraum (Nr. 1023). 1958/59
Öl auf Leinwand
95x100 cm
Galerie Wilbrand, Köln

S. 102
Bernd Berner
Roter Flächenraum. 1959/60
Öl auf Leinwand
140x150 cm
Privatbesitz Stuttgart

S. 109
Bernd Berner
Flächenraum (WV 804). 1960
Öl auf Leinwand
125x125 cm
Staatliche Kunsthalle Karlsruhe

S. 131
Franz Bernhard (geb. 1934)
Relief mit zwei Figuren IV. 1965
Holz, Zinnblech
60x65x9 cm
Privatbesitz Jockgrim

S. 136
Franz Bernhard
Kriechende. 1966
Holz, Eisen
34x200x60 cm
Privatbesitz Jockgrim

S. 137
Franz Bernhard
Große Liegende II. 1967
Holz, Eisen
200x340x40 cm
Privatbesitz Karlsruhe

S. 138
Franz Bernhard
Relief HP III. 1968
Holz, Papier, Draht
52x47x9 cm
Privatbesitz Jockgrim

S. 83
Emil Cimiotti (geb. 1927)
Der Berg und seine Wolken II. 1960
Bronze
67x84x54 cm
Staatsgalerie Stuttgart
(Inv. PLNA 110)

S. 82
Emil Cimiotti
Baum mit großen Vögeln. 1961
Bronze
45x82,5x44,5 cm
Galerie der Stadt Stuttgart

S. 120
Rolf-Gunter Dienst (geb. 1942)
Momentetagebuch
13. 8. – 19. 8. 1963
Acryl auf Leinwand
120x100 cm
Galerie der Stadt Rastatt

S. 121
Rolf-Gunter Dienst
Dr. Benway goes to Tanger. 1963
Öl auf Leinwand
200x160 cm
Privatbesitz Köln

S. 140
Rolf-Gunter Dienst
Momentetagebuch 20. 7. 69 –
Natascha S. nicht in Schmalbach
Nr. 9
Acryl auf Leinwand
210x170 cm
Privatbesitz Baden-Baden

S. 118
Peter Dreher (geb. 1932)
Stilleben mit Tassen II. 1963
Ei-Öl-Emulsion, Gips, Kohle,
Bleistift auf Nessel
121x140 cm
Staatliche Kunsthalle Karlsruhe
(Lg 1370)

S. 81
Hans Martin Erhardt (geb. 1935)
Bikini-Girl. 1960
Öl auf Leinwand
125x54 cm
manus presse, Stuttgart

S. 74
HAP Grieshaber (geb. 1909)
Das Milchschaf. 1958
Gouache auf Leinwand
89x126 cm
Sammlung Daimler-Benz,
Stuttgart

S. 79
HAP Grieshaber
Alp. 1960/61
Gouache auf Papier
79x96 cm
Privatbesitz Alzey

S. 78
HAP Grieshaber
Hirte. 1960/61
Gouache auf Papier
79x96 cm
Privatbesitz Alzey

S. 72
Otto Herbert Hajek (geb. 1927)
Raumknoten 109. 1959
Bronze, patiniert
64,5x83,3x24,5 cm
Staatliche Kunsthalle Karlsruhe
(Inv. P 153)

S. 122
Otto Herbert Hajek
Farbwege 64/8. 1964
Holz, Farbe
190x62x33 cm
Privatbesitz Stuttgart

S. 132
Otto Herbert Hajek
Farbwege 67/8. 1967
Aluminium, Farbe
135x96x37 cm
Privatbesitz Stuttgart

S. 127
Erich Hauser (geb. 1930)
Stahl 10/65. 1965
100x120x80 cm
Galerie Schlichtenmaier, Grafenau

S. 113
Peter Herkenrath (geb. 1900)
Sappho. 1962
Öl auf Leinwand
120x98 cm
Staatliche Kunsthalle Karlsruhe (Lg 1443)

S. 90
Bert Jäger (geb. 1919)
Ci Gît. 1962
Öl und Acryl auf Leinwand
200x200 cm
Privatbesitz Freiburg im Breisgau

S. 91
Bert Jäger
Garlaban. 1964
Acryl und Papier auf Nessel
150x135 cm
Staatliche Kunsthalle Karlsruhe (Lg 1457)

S. 100
Klaus Jürgen-Fischer (geb. 1930)
Ruba. 1958
Gouache, Feder, schwarze Tusche
auf Leinwand
110x80 cm
Staatliche Kunsthalle Karlsruhe (Lg 987)

S. 92
Herbert Kitzel (geb. 1928)
Luzifer. 1963
Öl und Acryl auf Leinwand
160x177 cm
Staatliche Kunsthalle Karlsruhe
(Inv. 2732)

S. 93
Herbert Kitzel
Stürzend. 1965
Öl auf Leinwand
150x140 cm
Städtische Galerie im Prinz-Max-Palais, Karlsruhe (Inv. 68/141)

S. 128
Fritz Klemm (geb. 1902)
Der Spiegel. Um 1965
Kunstharz und Kreide auf Hartfaserplatte
Staatliche Kunsthalle Karlsruhe (Inv. 2736)

S. 130
Fritz Klemm
Der Wald. Um 1965/67
Kunstharz auf Hartfaser
67x90,5 cm
Staatliche Kunsthalle Karlsruhe (Inv. 2842)

S. 129
Fritz Klemm
Die Wand. Um 1967
Kunstharz auf Hartfaser
111,5x92,5 cm
Staatliche Kunsthalle Karlsruhe (Inv. 2841)

S. 94
Dieter Krieg (geb. 1937)
Ohne Titel. 1965
Latex auf Leinwand
140x116 cm
Ruhr-Universität Bochum, Slg. Schulze-Vellinghausen (Inv. M 122)

S. 95
Dieter Krieg
Fuß. 1966
Latex auf Leinwand
130x114 cm
Ruhr-Universität Bochum, Slg. Schulze-Vellinghausen (Inv. M 28)

S. 96
Dieter Krieg
Händchen. 1966
Latex auf Leinwand
130x100 cm
Privatbesitz

S. 124
Thomas Lenk (geb. 1933)
Schichtung. 1964
Holz, bemalt
150x104x85 cm
Galerie der Stadt Stuttgart (Inv. P 321)

S. 125
Thomas Lenk
Schichtung 19. 1965
Hartfaser, bemalt
48x153x76 cm
Kunsthalle Mannheim

S. 70
Wilhelm Loth (geb. 1920)
Torso 4/57 »Hommage à Käthe Kollwitz«. 1957
Bronze
70,5x34x16 cm
Galerie Schlichtenmaier, Grafenau

S. 73
Wilhelm Loth
Figur 4/59 »Sitzende Frau«. 1959
Bronze, patiniert
80x109,5x40 cm (Sockel: 69x74x47 cm)
Staatliche Kunsthalle Karlsruhe (Lg 1179)

S. 84
Wilhelm Loth
Figur 9/62 »Großer Aphrodite-Torso«. 1962
Bronze, patiniert
66x55x116 cm
Wilhelm-Loth-Stiftung, Karlsruhe

S. 141
Wilhelm Loth
Plastik 18/69 »Große sitzende Figur im Würfel«. 1969
Aluminium
106x107x106 cm
Wilhelm-Loth-Stiftung, Karlsruhe

S. 106
Georg Meistermann (geb. 1911)
Gedämpfter Grund (Komposition). 1960 (WV 454)
Öl auf Leinwand
72,5x87,5 cm
Städtische Galerie im Prinz-Max-Palais, Karlsruhe (Inv. 65/25)

S. 143
Georg Meistermann
Farbige Notizen zur Biographie des Bundeskanzlers Brandt. 1969–73
Öl auf Leinwand
120x70 cm
Friedrich Ebert-Stiftung, Bonn

S. 123
Günter Neusel (geb. 1930)
Fachwerk 2. 1964
Öl auf Leinwand
70x70 cm
Privatbesitz Karlsruhe

S. 126
Günter Neusel
Inek II. 1965
Ahorn
33x33x33 cm
Galerie der Stadt Esslingen (Inv. 36)

S. 103
Georg Karl Pfahler (geb. 1926)
Ohne Titel. 1958/59
Mischtechnik auf Leinwand
110x130 cm
Sammlung Daimler-Benz, Stuttgart

S. 110
Georg Karl Pfahler
Formativ. 1961
Öl auf Leinwand
150x125 cm
Galerie Neuendorf, Frankfurt a. M.

S. 111
Georg Karl Pfahler
Formativ 88–55. 1962
Acryl auf Leinwand
140x160 cm
Galerie der Stadt Stuttgart (Inv. 0-2787)

S. 133
Georg Karl Pfahler
Balla-Balla. 1967
Acryl auf Leinwand
160x140 cm
Galerie Neuendorf, Frankfurt a. M.

S. 114
Markus Prachensky (geb. 1932)
Rouge sur gris – Karlsruhe. 1962
Lack auf Leinwand
260x140 cm
Privatbesitz Mannheim

S. 116
Markus Prachensky
Rouge sur gris – Karlsruhe II. 1962
Lack auf Leinwand
257x138 cm
Sammlung Essl, Klosterneuburg

S. 117
Markus Prachensky
Rote und grüne Flächen – Solitude I. 1964
Öl auf Leinwand
200x100 cm
Sammlung Daimler-Benz, Stuttgart

S. 107
Lothar Quinte (geb. 1923)
Gestik Weiß in Weiß. 1960
Ei-Öl auf Nessel
108x140 cm
Staatliche Kunsthalle Karlsruhe (Lg 1446)

S. 108
Lothar Quinte
I, 1961 (Schleierbild). 1960
Ei-Öl auf Leinwand
185x74 cm
Privatbesitz Walbourg

S. 112
Lothar Quinte
Ohne Titel (Schleierbild). 1962
Ei-Öl auf Leinwand
130,5x97 cm
Staatliche Kunsthalle Karlsruhe (Inv. 1181)

S. 119
Lothar Quinte
Ohne Titel (Fensterbild). 1963
Ei-Öl und Acryl auf Leinwand
180x100 cm
Privatbesitz

S. 134
Lothar Quinte
Schlitzbild, vertikal. 1966
Acryl auf Leinwand
180x130 cm
Privatbesitz

S. 71
Heinz Schanz (geb. 1927)
Kopf. 1958 (WNr. 58/7)
Eitempera auf Leinwand
75x60 cm
Privatbesitz

S. 76
Heinz Schanz
Ohne Titel. 1959 (WNr. 59/10)
Eitempera auf Sackleinen
136x112 cm
Sammlung Deyhle, Stuttgart

S. 86
Heinz Schanz
Ohne Titel. 1962
Tempera und Öl auf Baumwollgewebe
110,5x86 cm
Staatliche Kunsthalle Karlsruhe (Lg 1271)

S. 135
Felix Schlenker (geb. 1920)
T 17, 1968
Acryl auf Hartfaser
151x151 cm
Galerie der Stadt Stuttgart (Inv. 0-2740)

S. 139
Emil Schumacher (geb. 1912)
Bogen auf Rot. 1967
Öl auf Holz
195x205 cm
Stiftung Ludwig Roselius, Bremen

S. 142
Emil Schumacher
Ohne Titel. 1972
Öl auf Leinwand
170,5 x 131,5 cm
Staatliche Kunsthalle Karlsruhe
(Lg 846)

S. 104
K.R.H. Sonderborg (geb. 1923)
Ohne Titel. 1959
Tempera auf Photoleinwand
109 x 70 cm
Sammlung Daimler-Benz, Stuttgart

S. 105
K.R.H. Sonderborg
Ohne Titel. 1959
Öl auf Photopapier auf Leinwand
108,5 x 71 cm
Staatliche Kunsthalle Karlsruhe
(Lg 1283)

S. 115
K.R.H. Sonderborg
Ohne Titel. 1962
Eitempera auf Fotoleinwand
110 x 71 cm
Galerie der Stadt Stuttgart
(Inv. 0-2884)

S. 77
Walter Stöhrer (geb. 1937)
Ohne Titel. Um 1958
Öl auf Leinwand
165 x 147 cm
Privatbesitz, Bremen

S. 88
Walter Stöhrer
Ohne Titel (Nr. 1).1962
Öl auf Leinwand
130 x 150 cm
Privatbesitz Frankfurt a. M.

S. 89
Walter Stöhrer
Populus robustus. Hommage à
HAP Grieshaber. 1964
Acryl auf Nessel
180 x 120 cm
Staatliche Kunsthalle Karlsruhe
(Lg 1291)

S. 98
Walter Stöhrer
Mara. Um 1968
Mischtechnik auf Leinwand
180 x 160 cm
Privatbesitz Langen

Künstlerbiographien

Die Biographien basieren auf den dort genannten Publikationen und dem Badischen Archiv der Staatlichen Kunsthalle Karlsruhe. Sie sind keine vollständigen Verzeichnisse, sondern geben nur die für unsere Ausstellung wichtigen Angaben hinsichtlich der regionalen und internationalen Ereignisse wieder.

Horst Antes

1936 in Heppenheim (Bergstr.) geboren – lebt in Karlsruhe und Berlin
1957–1959 Studium bei HAP Grieshaber, Akademie Karlsruhe
1959 Kunstpreis der Stadt Hannover; Pankover-Preis, Deutscher Kunstpreis der Jugend, 1. Biennale des jeunes artistes, Paris
1960 Stipendium, Kulturkreis der deutschen Industrie
1961 Künstlerpreis, 2. Biennale des jeunes artistes, Paris; Kunstpreis junger westen, Recklinghausen
1962 Villa Romana-Preis, Florenz
1963 Stipendium, Villa Massimo, Rom
1965–1967 Lehrauftrag, Akademie Karlsruhe
1966 Unesco-Preis, Biennale, Venedig
1967 Professur, Akademie Karlsruhe; Garten der Lüste, Karlsruhe
1967–1968 Gastprofessur, Hochschule der Künste, Berlin
1968 Premio Marzotto-Europa, Valdagno
1971 Studienjahr; Staatl. Kunsthalle Baden-Baden (Retrospektive)
1973 Aufgabe der Karlsruher Professur
1984 Professur, Akademie Karlsruhe
1989 Molfenter-Preis, Stuttgart
1991 Kulturpreis des Landes Hessen; Großer Preis, Biennale São Paulo

Einzelausstellungen
1960 Galerie 61, Freiburg
Galerie der Spiegel, Köln
1964 Ulmer Museum
1965 Galerie Stangl, München
1966 Kunsthalle Mannheim
1967 Kunstmuseum Basel; Kunsthalle Baden-Baden
1968 Galerie Stangl, München
1969 Lefebre Gallery, New York
1970 Gimpel & Hanover, Zürich
1971 Staatliche Kunsthalle Baden-Baden (Retrospektive)
1976 Kunsthalle Darmstadt
1978 Kunstverein Karlsruhe
1983 Sprengelmuseum, Hannover
1987 Galerie Der Spiegel, Köln; Galerie Gunzenhauser, München
1988 Galerie Brusberg, Berlin
1989 Galerie Neumann, Düsseldorf
1990 Kunsthalle Kiel
1993 Haus der Kunst, München (Retrospektive); Galerie Thomas, München
1994 Von der Heydt-Museum, Wuppertal (Retrospektive); Galerie Pels-Leusden, Berlin
1995 Galerie Neumann, Düsseldorf; Prinz-Max-Palais, Karlsruhe

Gruppenausstellungen
1963 »Idole und Dämonen«, Wien
1964 documenta III, Kassel
1965 Künstlerbund Baden-Württemberg, Karlsruhe
1968 4. documenta, Kassel
1969 Galerie Beyeler, Basel; Biennale São Paulo
1970 »Jetzt« – Kunsthalle Köln; The Pittsburgh International
1975 Künstlerbund Baden-Württemberg, Karlsruhe; »Der ausgesparte Mensch«, Kunsthalle Mannheim
1976 Deutscher Künstlerbund, Mannheim
1977 Kunsthalle Baden-Baden
1988 »Vorbilder«, Kunstverein Karlsruhe
1992 Die Botschaft der Bilder, Prinz-Max-Palais, Karlsruhe; Ruhrfestspiele, Recklinghausen
1995 Auf Papier. Deutsche Bank, Frankfurt am Main

Lit.: Antes. Bilder 1959–1993. München (Ostfildern-Ruit) 1993

Hans Baschang

15. 4. 1937 in Karlsruhe geboren – lebt in München
1957–1961 Studium bei Herbert Kitzel, Akademie Karlsruhe
1962 Stipendium, Cité des Arts, Paris
1965 Kunstpreisträger, Stadt Karlsruhe
1966 Villa Massimo-Stipendium, Rom; Kunstpreis Böttcherstraße, Bremen
1971 Lehrauftrag, FH Pforzheim, Premio del Fiorini, Florenz
1972–1973 Gastdozent, Akademie Karlsruhe
1974 Dozent, FH Pforzheim
1975 Professur, Akademie München

Einzelausstellungen
1964 Galerie Schiessel, Freiburg i. Br.
1967 Burg Nörvenich
1968 Galerie am Jakobsbrunnen, Stuttgart
1970 Galerie Lienhard, Basel; Galerie Graphikmeyer, Karlsruhe
1972 Galerie studio f, Ulm
1973 Galerie Der Spiegel, Köln
1974 Galerie Fischer, Baden-Baden
1980 Galerie Promenadenplatz, München
1981 Galerie Phoenix, Würzburg
1982 Städt. Museum Leverkusen
1984 Sprengelmuseum Hannover
1986 Spendhaus, Reutlingen
1987 Museum am Ostwall, Dortmund (Retrospektive)
1989 Galerie Fred Jahn, München
1990 Galerie Karlheinz Meyer, Karlsruhe; manus-presse, Stuttgart
1992 Galerie Herzner, München
1995 Galerie Karlheinz Meyer, Karlsruhe; manus-presse, Stuttgart

Gruppenausstellungen
1960 Künstlerbund Baden-Württemberg
1961 Künstlerbund Baden-Württemberg; Kunstpreis junger westen, Recklinghausen
1962 Große Kunstausstellung, München; Kunstpreis der Jugend, Stuttgart
1963 Vier süddeutsche Maler, Worpswede
1964 Deutscher Künstlerbund, München
1965 Kunstpreis junger westen, Recklinghausen
1967 Deutscher Künstlerbund, Karlsruhe
1968 14 x 14, Kunsthalle Baden-Baden
1969 Akt 68, Kunsthalle Recklinghausen
1970 Die grünen Salons, Kunsthalle Baden-Baden
1974 18 deutsche Zeichner, Kunsthalle Baden-Baden
1975 Kunstverein Augsburg
1977 »Villa Romana«, Kunsthalle Baden-Baden
1981 Neue Tendenzen der Zeichnung – dimension '81, München u. a.
1982 Die Handzeichnung der Gegenwart II, Staatsgalerie Stuttgart
1988 Vorbilder, Kunstverein Karlsruhe
1993 Die 60er Jahre. Landeskunstwoche Aalen
1995 Große Kunstausstellung, München

Lit.: Ausst.Kat. Hans Baschang, Dortmund 1989; »Künstler«, Kritisches Lexikon der Gegenwartskunst. Nr. 14, München 1991

Bernd Berner

24. 9. 1930 in Hamburg geboren – lebt in Stuttgart
1948–1951 Ausbildung zum Lithographen
1952 Übersiedlung nach Stuttgart. Kontakt zu Willi Baumeister
1955 1. Parisreise
1964 Skandinavientournee
1965 Gründungsmitglied der Gruppe »SYN«
1965 Londonreise
1967 Villa Romana-Preis, Florenz Tschechoslowakeitournee
1971 Professur, Fachhochschule für Gestaltung, Pforzheim
1973 Cité des Arts-Stipendium, Paris. Letzte »SYN«-Ausstellung in der Kunsthalle Recklinghausen
1985 Atelier in Paris
1993 Ende der Professur in Pforzheim
1994 Bezug eines neuen Ateliers in Stuttgart

Einzelausstellungen

1960 Galerie 59, Aschaffenburg
1962 Galerie Falazik, Bochum
1965 Galerie Beno, Zürich
1969 Galerie Lauter, Mannheim
1974 Goethe-Institut, Paris
1978 Reuchlinhaus, Pforzheim
1979 Galerie St. Johann, Saarbrücken
1982 Kunsthalle Mannheim; Galerie Wilbrand, Köln
1984 Landesmuseum Oldenburg
1987 Galerie Fischer, Baden-Baden
1991 Kunsthalle Mannheim
1992 Galerie Wilbrand, Köln
1995 Galerie Fischer, Baden-Baden

Gruppenausstellungen

1955 Landeskunstausstellung, Stuttgart
1958 Kunstpreis der Jugend, Staatliche Kunsthalle Baden-Baden
1959 Deutscher Künstlerbund, Wiesbaden; »Die neue Generation«, Kunstverein Hannover
1960 Internationale Malerei, Wolframs-Eschenbach
1962 Deutsche Malerei, Situation 62, Kunstverein Oldenburg
1963 Absolute Malerei, Museum Trier; Darmstädter Sezession
1964 Neue Malerei aus Deutschland, Skandinavientournee
1966 »SYN«, Kunstverein Oldenburg
1967 »SYN«, Museum Wiesbaden; Kunst der Bundesrepublik Deutschland, Tschechoslowakeitournee
1975 50 Kunst in Baden-Württemberg. Kunstverein Stuttgart
1977 »Villa Romana«. Staatliche Kunsthalle Baden-Baden
1982 Handzeichnungen der Gegenwart. Staatsgalerie Stuttgart
1987 Mathematik in der Kunst der letzten dreißig Jahre. Wilhelm Hack-Museum, Ludwigshafen
1990 »Blau – Farbe der Ferne«, Kunstverein Heidelberg
1991 Deutscher Künstlerbund
1993 »Positionen der 60er Jahre«, Galerie Schlichtenmaier, Grafenau
1995 Darmstädter Sezession, Darmstadt

Lit.: Ausst.Kat. Städt. Kunsthalle Mannheim, Mannheim 1991; Werkverzeichnis »Frühe Arbeiten 1956–1960«, Stuttgart 1995

Franz Bernhard

17. 1. 1934 in Neuhäuser (CSR) geboren – lebt in Jockgrim (Vorderpfalz)
1946 Übersiedlung nach Siegelsbach (Heilbronn)
1959–1966 Studium bei Wilhelm Loth und Fritz Klemm, Akademie Karlsruhe
1963 Stipendium, Studienstiftung des Deutschen Volkes
1968 Villa Romana-Preis, Florenz
1969 Villa Massimo-Preis, Rom
1970 Gastlehrauftrag, Akademie Karlsruhe; Lehmbruck-Förderpreis, Stadt Duisburg; Mitglied des Deutschen Künstlerbundes und des Künstlerbundes Baden-Württemberg
1971 Stipendium, Kunstpreis Berlin
1972 Umzug von Karlsruhe nach Jockgrim
1975 Pfalzpreis für Plastik
1976 Stipendium, Kulturkreis der deutschen Industrie
1977 Hans Thoma-Preis des Landes Baden-Württemberg
1984 Heitland Foundation-Kunstpreis, Celle
1986 Kunstpreis des Landes Rheinland-Pfalz
1989 Lovis Corinth-Preis, Esslingen

Einzelausstellungen

1967 Galerie am Jakobsbrunnen, Stuttgart
1969 Altes Theater, Ravensburg
1970 Galerie Heberle, Frankfurt a. M.
1971 Galerie Graphikmeyer, Karlsruhe
1972 Goethe-Institut, Paris
1973 Städt. Museum Wiesbaden
1974 Galerie Hetzler, Stuttgart; Galerie Buchholz, München
1975 Galerie Mewes, Hamburg
1976 Galerie Schmela, Düsseldorf
1977 Studio f, Ulm
1978 Galerie Rothe, Heidelberg
1980 Kunstmuseum Düsseldorf (Retrospektive); Kunsthalle Mannheim (Retrospektive)
1981 Wilhelm-Hack-Museum, Ludwigshafen; Galerie Rothe, Heidelberg
1982 Galerie Albrecht, Bozen
1983 Galerie Kaiser, Freiburg
1984 Galerie Rothe, Heidelberg
1985 Kunstverein Stuttgart; W. Lehmbruck-Museum, Duisburg (Retrospektive der Zeichnungen); Galerie Wentzel, Köln
1986 Landesmuseum Mainz
1987 Galerie Rothe, Heidelberg
1988 Bahnhof Rolandseck
1989 Galerie Wentzel, Köln
1992 Galerie Wentzel, Köln
1994 Glaskasten, Marl
1995 Kunstverein Bochum; Suermondt-Ludwig-Museum, Aachen

Gruppenausstellungen

1976 Museum des 20. Jahrhunderts, Wien
1977 Villa Romana, Kunsthalle Baden-Baden
1979 Arche-beelde, s'Hertogenbosch
1980 Graphikbiennale, Mulhouse
1984 Plastik in der BRD, Kunsthalle Mannheim (Tournee im Ausland); Kunstverein Karlsruhe
1986 Galerie Buchholz, München
1987 »Skulptur total«, Museum Leverkusen
1988 Vorbilder, Kunstverein Karlsruhe
1992 DKB, Aachen
1993 De figura – Forum Kunst, Rottweil; Positionen der 60er Jahre, Galerie Schlichtenmaier, Grafenau
1994 Konzeption und Form, Kunsthalle Mannheim

Lit.: Werkverzeichnis der Skulpturen 1964–1989 (Hrsg. Wolfgang Rothe), Münsterschwarzach 1990

Emil Cimiotti

19. 8. 1927 in Göttingen geboren – lebt in Wolfenbüttel
1944–1945 Soldat, Gefangenschaft
1946–1948 Steinmetzlehre
1949–1953 Studium bei Otto Baum, Akademie Stuttgart; Karl Hartung, Hochschule der Künste, Berlin; Ossip Zadkine, Paris
1954 Umzug nach Stuttgart
1956 2. Preis, Kunstpreis der Jugend Baden-Württemberg
1959 Villa Romana-Preis, Rom
1961 Umzug nach Aich
1963 Professur, Kunsthochschule Braunschweig
1969 Biennale d'Arte Premio, Florenz
1981–1983 keine Skulpturen

Einzelausstellungen
1957 Behrgalerie, Stuttgart
1958 Galerie Gunar, Düsseldorf
1960 Kunstverein Köln
1961 Galerie van de Loo, München; Galerie Brusberg, Hannover
1962 Kunstverein Braunschweig; Galerie Brockstedt, Hamburg
1963 Galerie Gunar, Düsseldorf; Galerie Lutz und Meyer, Stuttgart
1965 Galerie S, Berlin; Galerie Gunar, Düsseldorf
1966 Städt. Museum Göttingen
1967 Galerie Schmücking, Braunschweig
1972 Kunstkreis Hameln; Galerie Frenzel, Bonn
1975 Galerie Brusberg, Hannover
1976 Galerie van de Loo, München
1977 Kunsthalle Mannheim
1978 Galerie Brusberg, Hannover
1984 Galerie Brusberg, Hannover
1987 Kunstverein Braunschweig (Retrospektive)
1992 Kunsthalle Recklinghausen; Museum Osnabrück
1994 Galerie Schlichtenmaier, Grafenau

Gruppenausstellungen
1955 Kunstpreis der Jugend, Kunsthalle Baden-Baden; Kunstausstellung Baden-Württemberg, Kunstverein Stuttgart
1957 Kunsthalle Recklinghausen
1958 Biennale, Venedig; The Pittsburgh International
1959 Preis der Freunde Junger Kunst, Baden-Baden; documenta, Kassel; Deutsche Künstler der Gegenwart, Kunsthalle Basel
1960 Biennale, Venedig
1961 Biennale Junger Kunst, Paris
1962 Deutsche Plasik der Gegenwart, Kunsthalle Kiel
1966 Junge Generation, Akademie Berlin
1970 Handzeichnungen der Gegenwart, Staatsgalerie Stuttgart
1974 Kunst in der Bundesrepublik Deutschland, Kunstmuseum Bonn
1977 »Der Kopf«, Wilhelm-Lehmbruck-Museum, Duisburg
1978 Kunsthalle Baden-Baden
1985 Kunst in der Bundesrepublik Deutschland 1945–1985, Nationalgalerie, Berlin
1993 Die 60er Jahre in der Kunst des deutschen Südwestens, Aalen; Positionen der 60er Jahre, Galerie Schlichtenmaier, Grafenau
1995 Europäische Plastik des Informel 1945–1965, Wilhelm-Lehmbruck-Museum, Duisburg

Lit.: Werkverzeichnis der Plastiken, Hannover 1978; Ausst.Kat. Braunschweig, Braunschweig 1981

Rolf-Gunter Dienst

18. 11. 1942 in Kiel geboren – lebt in Baden-Baden und Kauffenheim (Als.)
1960–1965 Mitherausgeber der literarischen »Revue Rhinozeros«
1965 Redakteur der Zeitschrift »Das Kunstwerk«
1966–1968 als Maler und Kritiker in New York.
1967 International Artists Seminar, F.D. University, Madison, USA
1968 Villa Romana-Preis, Florenz
1969 Stipendium, Kulturkreis der Deutschen Industrie. Lehrauftrag, Hochschule Braunschweig
1970 Gastdozentur, Städelakademie, Frankfurt
1971–1972 Cité des Arts, Stipendium, Paris
1975 Vortragsreise, USA
1976 Gastdozentur, School of Art, Churchill, Australien
1977 Gastdozentur, School of Art, Sydney, Australien
1979 Villa Massimo-Preis, Rom
1981 Stipendium, Kunstfonds, Bonn
1986 Aufenthalt auf den Osterinseln
1989–1990 Gastprofessur, Akademie Stuttgart
1990 Japanaufenthalt
1992 Professur, Akademie Nürnberg

Einzelausstellungen
1963 Galerie Die Insel, Hamburg
1964 Freie Galerie, Berlin
1965 Landesmuseum Schleswig
1968 Studio DuMont, Köln
1969 Kunsthalle Baden-Baden
1970 Altes Theater, Ravensburg
1971–1972 Galerie Appel und Fertsch, Frankfurt
1972 Museum Wiesbaden
1974 Kunstmuseum Bochum
1975 Galerie van de Loo, München
1977 Kunsthalle Baden-Baden
1978 Museum Leverkusen
1980 Kunstverein Kassel
1981 Galleria L'Attico, Rom
1984 Galerie Defet, Nürnberg
1986 Saarland Museum, Saarbrücken
1988 Kunsthalle Kiel
1989–1990 Quadrat, Bottrop
1990 Kunstverein Stuttgart
1992 Museum am Ostwall, Dortmund
1993 Museum Leipzig (Retrospektive)
1994 Galerie Appel und Fertsch, Frankfurt

Gruppenausstellungen
1964 »Möglichkeiten«, Haus am Waldsee, Berlin
1965 German Painters ICA, London; SYN, Galerie Bayer, Mainz
1966–1968 Junge Generation, Akademie Berlin
1968 Ornamentale Tendenzen, Haus am Waldsee, Berlin
1969 40 Deutsche unter 40, Norwegentournee
1970 Prisma, Landesmuseum, Bonn
1971–1972 Haus der Kunst, München
1972 DKB, Bonn; 14x14, Kunsthalle Baden-Baden
1975 Contemporary German Art, University Art Gallery, Melbourne
1977 Villa Romana, Kunsthalle Baden-Baden
1982 Die Handzeichnung der Gegenwart II, Staatsgalerie Stuttgart
1983 Villa Massimo 1978–1982, Kunstverein Karlsruhe
1984 Kunstlandschaft Bundesrepublik, Kunstverein Oldenburg
1987 The Open Image, San Francisco Art Institute
1990 Blau – Farbe der Ferne, Kunstverein Heidelberg
1993 Die 60er Jahre in der Kunst des deutschen Südwestens, Aalen

Lit.: Gemälde 1962–1990. Eine Anthologie. Nürnberg 1990

Peter Dreher

24. 8. 1932 in Mannheim geboren – lebt in Freiburg
1950–1956 Studium bei K. Hubbuch, W. Schnarrenberger, E. Heckel, Akademie Karlsruhe
1958 Kunstpreis der Jugend
1965 Villa Massimo-Preis, Rom. Leiter der Malklasse, Außenstelle Freiburg der Akademie Karlsruhe
1968 Professur, Akademie Karlsruhe
1976 Reinhold Schneider-Preis, Stadt Freiburg
1979 Hans Thoma-Preis des Landes Baden-Württemberg

Einzelausstellungen

1954 Kunsthalle Mannheim
1969 Galerie Kröner, Oberrimsingen
1973 Galerie 3, Waldshut
1974 Museum Folkwang, Essen
1975 Kunstverein Freiburg; Städt. Galerie Überlingen
1976 Galerie Schneider, Karlsruhe
1977 Städt. Galerie Tuttlingen; Kunsthalle Baden-Baden
1978 Galerie Art in Progress, Düsseldorf
1979 Museum Leverkusen; Altes Theater, Ravensburg
1980 Städtische Galerie Konstanz
1982 Von der Heydt-Museum, Wuppertal
1984 Städt. Galerie Villingen-Schwenningen
1986 Galerie Oevermann, Frankfurt a. M.
1987 Galleria Fossati, Kilchberg, CH
1990 Museum für Neue Kunst, Freiburg (Retrospektive); Kunsthalle Mannheim (Retrospektive); Galerie Hans Meyer, Düsseldorf
1991 Kunstverein Konstanz
1992 Galerie Wehr, Stuttgart
1993 Kunstverein Karlsruhe
1994 Kunstverein Säckingen
1995 Galerie Wehr, Stuttgart; Galerie Thieme, Darmstadt

Gruppenausstellungen

seit 1956 Künstlerbund Baden-Württemberg
1961 Darmstädter Sezession
1964 Musée du Travail, Montpellier
1966 Deutscher Holzschnitt, Kunsthalle Baden-Baden
seit 1970 Deutscher Künstlerbund
1985 Kunsthalle Recklinghausen
1986 Himmelschreiber, Kunstverein Kassel
1988 Vorbilder, Kunstverein Karlsruhe
1993 Kunst der 90er Jahre, Kunstverein Karlsruhe
1994 Galerie Thieme, Darmstadt

Lit.: Ausst.Kat. Freiburg/Mannheim 1990; Ausst.Kat. Karlsruhe 1993

Hans Martin Erhardt

28. 10. 1935 in Emmendingen geboren – lebt in Karlsruhe
1954–1961 Studium bei Wilhelm Schnarrenberger und HAP Grieshaber, Akademie Karlsruhe
1960 freischaffender Künstler
1961 Stipendium, Studienstiftung des Deutschen Volkes
1965 Kulturpreis der Stadt Karlsruhe
1968 Stipendium der Cité International, Paris
1970 Lehrauftrag, Akademie Stuttgart
1973 Hans Thoma-Preis des Landes Baden-Württemberg
1980 Professur, Universität Karlsruhe (Malerei und Graphik)

Einzelausstellungen

1958 Galerie Gallwitz
1963 Badischer Kunstverein Karlsruhe
1965 Galerie Valentien, Stuttgart
1966 Reuchlinhaus, Pforzheim
1967 Galerie Klang, Köln
1968 Staatliche Kunsthalle Baden-Baden
1969 manus-presse, Stuttgart; Galerie Rothe, Heidelberg
1970 Galerie Graphikmeyer, Karlsruhe
1974 Kunstverein Freiburg; Galerie Regio, Freiburg
1975 manus-presse, Stuttgart
1976 Städt. Galerie Nordhorn
1977 Galerie Hilbur, Karlsruhe
1979 Galerie Die Treppe, Lahr; manus-presse, Stuttgart
1980 Reuchlinhaus, Pforzheim
1981 Galerie Hilbur, Karlsruhe
1983 manus-presse, Stuttgart
1985 Galerie art contact, Karlsruhe
1986 manus-presse, Stuttgart
1987 Galerie Hilbur, Karlsruhe; Kunstverein Rastatt; Hans-Thoma-Gesellschaft, Reutlingen
1988 Galerie Rothe, Heidelberg
1990 Graphisches Kabinett, Frankfurt

Gruppenausstellungen

1965 Badischer Kunstverein Karlsruhe
1973 Staatliche Kunsthalle Baden-Baden
1975 Staatliche Kunsthalle Baden-Baden; KBBW, Karlsruhe
1976 Seit 1976 KBBW; Galerie Fischer, Baden-Baden
1979 Chicago – Karlsruhe, Ettlingen
1984 Galerie Hilbur, Karlsruhe
1988 Vorbilder, Badischer Kunstverein Karlsruhe
1991 Die Zeichnung nach der Landschaft, Hans-Thoma-Gesellschaft, Reutlingen
1992 Hans-Thoma-Museum, Bernau
1993 Kunstverein Bretten; Grieshaber Bernstein Karlsruhe, Landkreis Esslingen; die 60er Jahre in der Kunst des deutschen Südwestens, Aalen
1994 Grieshaber Bernstein Karlsruhe, die Fähre, Saulgau; KBBW, Karlsruhe
1995 Von hier aus. Galerie art-contact, Karlsruhe

Lit.: Manus Presse, Stuttgart 1978

Helmut Andreas Paul Grieshaber

15. 2. 1909 in Rot a. d. Rot geboren – gestorben am 12. 5. 1981 auf der Achalm/Reutlingen
1926–1928 Schriftsetzerlehre, Nagold und Reutlingen; Studium des Buchdrucks bei Ernst Schneider, Akademie Stuttgart
1928–1931 Studienreisen nach London und Paris
1931–1933 freier Künstler, Reisen nach Ägypten, Arabien, Griechenland
1933–1940 Mal- und Ausstellungsverbot
1940–1946 Soldat, Kriegsgefangenschaft
1947 Achalm
1950 Mitbegründer des DKB
1951 1. Preis, Kunstpreis Junger Westen, Recklinghausen
1951–1953 Lehrer der Bernsteinschule, Sulz/Neckar.
1955–1960 Professur, Akademie Karlsruhe. Mitbegründer des Künstlerbundes Baden-Württemberg
1957 Oberschwäbischer Kunstpreis
1962 Corneliuspreis, Stadt Düsseldorf; Kunstpreis der Stadt Darmstadt
1968 Kunstpreis des DGB, Recklinghausen
1970 Kunstpreise in Banská Bystrica (CSSR); Buenos Aires
1971 Dürer-Preis, Nürnberg
1972 Ehrensenator, Universität Tübingen
1976 Stiftung des Jerg Ratgeb-Preises
1978 Gutenberg-Preis der Stadt Leipzig
1980 Konstanzer Kunstpreis

Einzelausstellungen
1932 Alexandria, Ägypten
1938 Galerie Valentien, Stuttgart
1954 Kunstverein Stuttgart
1957 Die Fähre, Saulgau
1958 Stedelijk Museum, Amsterdam
1959 Kunstverein Freiburg
1960 Palazzo Grassi, Venedig
1961 Museum Gelsenkirchen
1962 Museum Schaffhausen
1964 Kestnergesellschaft, Hannover; Kunstverein Karlsruhe (Retrospektive)
1965 Kunstmuseum Luzern
1967 Auckland City Art Gallery
1968 Bodensee-Museum, Konstanz
1969 Kunstverein Braunschweig; Kunstverein Stuttgart
1971 Kunstverein Karlsruhe; Germanisches Nationalmuseum Nürnberg
1972 Künstlerhaus Wien
1974 Museum Schaffhausen
1976 Tel Aviv Museum
1978 Kunsthalle Rostock
1980 Kunstverein Salzburg
1989 Spendhaus Reutlingen
1993 Kunsthalle Rostock
1994 Galerie Schlichtenmaier, Grafenau; Spendhaus Reutlingen

Gruppenausstellungen
1964 Kunstverein Stuttgart, Kestner-Gesellschaft, Hannover
1959 documenta, Kassel; Vitalitá nell 'Arte, Venedig; Grieshaber und sein Kreis, Kunsthalle Recklinghausen; Spendhaus Reutlingen
1960 Deutsche Kunst, Rio de Janeiro, Ljubljana
1962 Biennale, Venedig
1963 16 deutsche Maler, Corcoran Gallery, Washington
1964 documenta, Kassel; 1. Internationale der Zeichnung, Darmstadt
1968 Ars multiplicata, Köln; Kunst der BRD, CSSR-Tournee
1973 Biennale der Ostseeländer, Rostock
1975 Galerie Schmücking, Freiburg
1987 Bildzyklen 1933–1945; Staatsgalerie Stuttgart
1994 Galerie Brusberg, Berlin; Spendhaus, Reutlingen

Lit.: Ausst.Kat. Stuttgart 1984

Otto Herbert Hajek

27. 6. 1927 in Kaltenbach, Böhmen, geboren – lebt in Stuttgart
1947–1954 Studium, Staatliche Akademie Stuttgart
1968 Goethe-Institut, New York
1972–1979 Vorsitzender des Deutschen Künstlerbundes
1975 Vortragsreise, Südamerika, Australien
1980 Professor, Akademie Karlsruhe; Mitbegründer der Initiative »Nord-Süd-Dialog«
1983 Studienreise, Klasse Hajek, nach Indien
1984 Studienreise, Klasse Hajek, in die Tschechoslowakei
1985 Teilnahme, ISZE-Kulturforum, Budapest
1986 Vortragsreise nach Südostasien, Iberische Halbinsel, Türkei

Einzelausstellungen
1951 Junges Theater, Stuttgart
1955 Neue Galerie, Linz
1957 Galerie Schüler, Berlin
1959 Galerie St. Stephan, Wien
1960 Museum Haus Lange, Krefeld, Kunsthalle Mannheim
1961 Galerie Handschin, Basel
1963 Kunsthalle Bremen; Galerie Rottloff, Karlsruhe
1964 Gemeentemuseum, Den Haag
1965 Museum Folkwang, Essen
1966 (op)-art galerie, Esslingen; Galerie Spàla, Prag
1968 Goethe-Institut, New York
1971 Kunsthalle Bielefeld
1975 Gallery Hobarth, Sydney
1976 Ostdeutsche Galerie, Regensburg
1977 The Gallery, Adelaide (Retrospektive)
1980 Museum Helsinki
1981 Museo Nazionale, Castel Sant' Angelo, Rom (Retrospektive)
1987 Retrospektive, Florenz; Germanisches Nationalmuseum Nürnberg (Retrospektive)
1988 Waldstejnpalais, Prag (Retrospektive)
1989 Zentrale Kunsthalle, Moskau (Retrospektive);
1994 Staatsgalerie Eger (Retrospektive)

Gruppenausstellungen
1953 Smithsonian Institute, Washington
1954 Lateran Museum, Rom
ab 1956 Deutscher Künstlerbund
1957 Biennale Antwerpen
1958 Biennale Venedig
1959 documenta, Kassel
1964 documenta, Kassel
1973 Biennale, Antwerpen
1979 Metallbildhauer, Tokyo
1989 Museum für Moderne Kunst, Nagoya

Kunst im öffentlichen Raum
1953–1955 St. Aurelius, Hirsau
1960–1963 Kreuzweg Maria Regina Martyrum, Berlin
1962–1964 Frankfurter Frühling
1965 Studentenhaus, Mensa, Uni Saarbrücken
1970 Universität Stuttgart
1977 Universität Heidelberg
1979 Mineralbad Leuze, Stuttgart
1992 Platzraumgestaltung, Ankara

Lit.: Ausst.Kat. Rom 1981; Ausst.Kat. Germanisches Nationalmuseum, Nürnberg 1987; Ausst.Kat. Moskau 1989

Erich Hauser

15. 12. 1930 in Rietheim/Kreis Tuttlingen geboren – lebt in Rottweil
1945–1948 Lehre als Stahlgraveur
1953 Belobigung, Kunstpreis der Jugend, Baden-Baden
1958 Förderpreis, Kunstpreis der Jugend, Stuttgart
1963 Kunstpreis »Junger Westen«, Recklinghausen; Ehrenpreis, 3. Biennale de Paris
1964–1965 Gastdozent, Hochschule Hamburg
1965 Kunstpreis der Stadt Wolfsburg
1966 Burdapreis für Plastik
1969 Großer Preis, Biennale, São Paulo; Mitglied der Akademie Berlin
1984–1985 Gastprofesser, Hochschule Berlin
1995 Oberschwäbischer Kunstpreis

Einzelausstellungen
1961 Studio f, Ulm
1962 Kunstverein Freiburg i. Br.
1963 Galerie Müller, Stuttgart
1966 Kunsthalle Mannheim
1967 Galerie Defet, Nürnberg
1968 Galerie der Stadt Stuttgart
1971 Gimpel Fils Gallery, London
1972 Studio f, Ulm; Aargauer Kunsthaus
1973 Kunsthalle zu Kiel
1974 Kunstverein Braunschweig
1978 Forum Kunst, Rottweil
1981 Germanisches Nationalmuseum Nürnberg
1992 Kunstverein Konstanz; Galerie Schlichtenmaier, Grafenau

Gruppenausstellungen
1954 Kunstpreis der Jugend
1958 Kunstpreis der Jugend
1959 Kunstpreis der Jugend, Kunsthalle Baden-Baden
1960 Deutscher Kunstpreis der Jugend, Kunsthalle Mannheim
1962 Kunstverein Stuttgart
1963 »Kunstpreis Junger Westen 63«, Recklinghausen; »3eme Biennale de Paris«
1964 documenta 3, Kassel; Salon Comparaisons, Musée d'Art Moderne, Paris; »Duitse Kunst van heden«, Museum Boymans-van Beuningen, Rotterdam
1965 Kunstverein Hannover
1966 Junge Generation, Akademie, Berlin; »Plastik Südwest«, Kunsthalle Baden-Baden
1967 »2. Internationale der Zeichnung«, Darmstadt
1968 documenta 4, Kassel
1969 »40 Deutsche unter 40 in Skandinavien«; »X. Biennale«, São Paulo
1970 »Jetzt«, Kunsthalle Köln
1973 »12. Biennale Middelheimpark«, Antwerpen
1977 documenta 6, Kassel
1979 3. Biennale Sydney
1980 1. Triennale, Fellbach
1981 »Phoenix«, Alte Oper Frankfurt
1985 »1945–1985 Kunst in der Bundesrepublik Deutschland«, Nationalgalerie Berlin
1986 »Symmetrie«, Darmstadt
1987 »Mathematik in der Kunst«, Wilhelm-Hack-Museum, Ludwigshafen

Lit.: Ostfildern-Ruit 1995

Peter Herkenrath

8. 4. 1900 in Köln geboren – gestorben am 13. 11. 1992 in Mainz
1917–1920 Kriegsdienst und Gefangenschaft
1920–1923 Autodidaktische Ausbildung in Malerei
1923 Eintritt in die väterliche Textilfirma
1945 Mitbegründer der Rheinischen Künstlergemeinschaft Köln
1952–1955 Vorsitzender der Neuen Rheinischen Sezession
ab 1955 Deutscher Künstlerbund
1958 Karl-Ernst-Osthaus-Preis der Stadt Hagen; Preis des Deutschen Künstlerbundes
1958–1959 Stipendiat der Villa Romana Florenz
1958–1983 Westdeutscher Künstlerbund
1961 Stipendiat der Deutschen Akademie Villa Massimo, Rom
1962–1970 Leiter einer Malklasse, Akademie Karlsruhe
ab 1963 Künstlerbund Baden-Württemberg
1965 Kunstpreis, Stadt Köln; Wohnsitz in Cipressa
1966 Professor
1980 Ehrenmitglied, Accademia d'Italia, San Gimignano

Einzelausstellungen
1933 Kölnischer Kunstverein
1947 Galerie Günther, Mannheim
1950 Kölnischer Kunstverein
1952 Galerie der Spiegel, Köln; Suermondt-Museum, Aachen
1955 Schloß Morsbroich, Leverkusen
1958 Städtisches Museum, Gelsenkirchen
1959 Kölnischer Kunstverein
1962 Städtisches Museum Trier
1965 Kölnischer Kunstverein
1971 Galerie der Landesgirokasse Stuttgart; Kölnischer Kunstverein
1972 Galerie Klang, Köln
1974 Galerie Anna Friebe, Köln
1978 Galerie der Landesgirokasse Stuttgart
1979 Galerie Rothe, Heidelberg
1980 Museum Ludwig, Köln
1981 Galerie Völmel, Düsseldorf
1985 Galerie Orangerie, Köln; Galerie Völmel, Düsseldorf
1990 Galerie Völmel, Düsseldorf
1993 Galerie Orangerie Reinz, Köln

Gruppenausstellungen
1931 Kölnischer Kunstverein
1941 Kölnischer Kunstverein
1942 Kulturwerk Köln-Aachen
1943 Kölnischer Kunstverein (vorzeitig aus der Ausstellung entfernt)
1945–1951 Rheinische Künstlergemeinschaft, Köln
1948 Kölnischer Kunstverein
1949 Staatenhaus der Messe, Köln
1950 Darmstädter Sezession
1950–1969 Neue Rheinische Sezession
1950–1986 Neue Gruppe München
1954 Schloß Morsbroich, Leverkusen
1956 Stedelijk Museum Amsterdam
1957 Staatliches Museum für Moderne Kunst, Tokio
1959 documenta, Kassel
1961 Wanderausstellung Deutscher Museen und Kunstvereine
1963 German Art of Today, Afrikatournee
1967 Palazzo Strozzi, Florenz; Kunst der Bundesrepublik Deutschland, Prag, Ljubljana, Zagreb, Belgrad

Lit.: Toni Feldenkirch (Hg.), Über Peter Herkenrath, Ausst.Kat. Kölnischer Kunstverein 1971; Ausst.Kat. Museum Ludwig, Köln 1980, Günter Aust, Peter Herkenrath, Köln 1987

Bert Jäger

11. 1. 1919 in Karlsruhe geboren – lebt in Freiburg i. Br.
1934–1939 Studium an der Karlsruher Akademie bei Hermann Goebel, Siegfried Czerny und Georg Siebert
1937 Besuch der Ausstellung »Entartete Kunst« in München
1939–1944 Soldat
1942 Studium in Wien bei Herbert Boeckl
1944–1949 Gefangenschaft
1949 nach Freiburg entlassen. Mitglied der »Jungen Gruppe Baden«. Zahlreiche Reisen, vor allem nach Paris
1954 Mitglied der Verbindung »Freie Gruppe Oberrhein«
1960 Mitbegründer der »Galerie 61«, Freiburg
1963 Bis dahin zahlreiche Aufträge für »Kunst am Bau«
1970 Aufgabe der Malerei
1987 Wiederbeginn der Malerei
1995 Maria Ensle-Preis, Kunststiftung Baden-Württemberg

Einzelausstellungen

1962 Galleria XXII Marzo, Mailand; Galerie Lutz & Meyer, Stuttgart
1963 Galerie Knöll, Basel; Kunstverein Freiburg
1968 Galerie Gräber, Freiburg
1970 Galerie Gräber, Freiburg
1986 Augustinermuseum Freiburg (Fotografieen); Museum für Neue Kunst, Freiburg
1987 Fähre, Saulgau
1988 Galerie Rolf Ohse, Bremen
1989 Galerie pro arte, Freiburg
1990 Galerie Pierre Rippstein, Basel
1991 Galerie Linda Treiber, Ettenheimmünster
1994 Morat-Institut, Freiburg; Kunstverein Kirchzarten (Retrospektive)

Gruppenausstellungen

1954 Ausstellung u. a. mit Gunter Fruhtrunk, Walter Schelenz im Kunstverein Freiburg; Ausstellung »Junge Badische Kunst«, Kunsthalle Baden-Baden
1955 Künstlerbund Baden-Württemberg, Stuttgart; II. Triennale, Mailand
1958 Badische Künstler, Kunsthalle Baden-Baden
1962 Premio Marzotto, Valdagno, Eindhoven, London; Künstlerbund Baden-Württemberg
1963 Künstlerbund Baden-Württemberg
1965 »Bild und Bühne«, Kunsthalle Baden-Baden; Künstlerbund Baden-Württemberg
1967 Künstlerbund Baden-Württemberg, Baden-Baden
1968 Künstlerbund Baden-Württemberg, Stuttgart
1988 »Vorbilder«, Badischer Kunstverein Karlsruhe
1992 Museum für Neue Kunst, Freiburg

Lit.: Ausst.Kat. Bert Jäger. Retrospektive 1944–1994, Freiburg 1994, Staatliche Kunsthalle Karlsruhe: Neuerwerbungen für die Gemäldegalerie 1984–1994. Karlsruhe 1995, S. 60–61, Abb. S. 222

Klaus Jürgen-Fischer

23. 10. 1930 in Hüls/Krefeld geboren – lebt in Vaudrémond/Lothringen
1949 Studium bei Paul Binder und Otto Coester, Akademie Düsseldorf
1950 Studium bei Willi Baumeister, Akademie Stuttgart
1954 Redakteur der Zeitschrift »Das Kunstwerk«. Lebt in Baden-Baden
1956 Graphikpreis, Kunstpreis der Jugend, Baden-Baden
1958 Biennale des Jeunes, Paris
1961 Manifest »Komplexe Farbe«
1964 Londonreise mit Pfahler, Quinte, Galerist Müller, Stuttgart
1965 Mitbegründer der Gruppe SYN
1965–1971 Dozent, Universität Mainz
1966 Aufenthalt in New York
1970 Gastdozent, Städelsche Akademie, Frankfurt
1971 Abbruch der Dozentur
1974 Übersiedlung nach Schloß Munzingen bei Freiburg
1977–1978 Gastdozentur, Akademie Karlsruhe
1978–1980 Komm. Leitung, Institut für Bildende Kunst, Universität Karlsruhe
1983–1995 Professur, Universität Mainz. 2. Wohnsitz: Schloß Vaudrémont

Einzelausstellungen

1950 Kunstkabinett Uhrig, Krefeld
1955 Kaiser-Wilhelm-Museum, Krefeld; Zimmergalerie Franck, Frankfurt
1959 Neue Galerie Parnass, Wuppertal; Drian Gallery, London
1960 Galleria Il Grifo, Turin
1961 Galerie Brusberg, Hannover
1962 Galleria XXII Marzo Venedig
1963 Galerie Rottloff, Karlsruhe; Galerie Baier, Mainz
1965 Galerie Falazik, Bochum
1969 Kunstverein Freiburg
1970 Forum Kunst, Rottweil
1975 Galerie van de Loo, München
1977 Kunsthalle Mannheim
1989 Landesmuseum Mainz
1990 Augustinermuseum, Freiburg

Gruppenausstellungen

1953 Junge deutsche Maler, Akron Museum, Akron/Ohio
1955 Kunstpreis der Jugend, Kunsthalle Baden-Baden
1956 Maler und Bildhauer, Kunstverein Stuttgart
1957 Gruppe 11, New Vision Centre Gallery, London; Deutscher Künstlerbund, Berlin; Kunstpreis der Jugend, Kunsthalle Baden-Baden
1958 Das rote Bild. Atelier Piene, Düsseldorf; Ars Viva, Kunstverein Oldenburg; Deutscher Künstlerbund, Essen
1959 Deutscher Kunstpreis der Jugend, Kunsthalle Baden-Baden; Biennale des Jeunes, Paris
1960 Monochrome Malerei, Museum Leverkusen
1961 Internationale Malerei 1960–61, Wolframs-Eschenbach; Avantgarde 61, Museum Trier
1962 Deutscher Kunstpreis der Jugend, Stuttgart; Situation 62, Kunstverein Oldenburg
1963 Absolute Farbe, Museum Trier
1964 Deutsche Malerei heute, Landesmuseum Münster
1965 Six German Painters, ICA, London
1967 2. Internationale der Zeichnung, Darmstadt
1968 SYN, Kunstverein Kiel
1970 Synthesen, Kunstsammlungen Ludwigshafen
1989 Hommage à Baumeister, Galerie Schlichtenmaier, Grafenau
1993 Positionen der 60er Jahre, Galerie Schlichtenmaier, Grafenau

Lit.: Gemälde, Plastiken, Zeichnungen. Heidelberg 1992

Herbert Kitzel

5. 5. 1928 in Halle/Saale geboren – gestorben am 25. 8. 1978 in Karlsruhe
1945–1950 Studium bei Herbert Post, Kunstschule Burg Giebichenstein/Halle
1950–1957 freiberuflich als Maler in Halle
1955 Mitglied des Deutschen Künstlerbundes; Preis, Bundesverband der Deutschen Industrie
1957 Leiter einer Malklasse, Akademie Karlsruhe
1958 Übersiedlung nach Karlsruhe
1961 Caprireise
1962 Professur, Akademie Karlsruhe; Caprireise
1964 Kunstpreis der Stadt Darmstadt
1965 Vorstandsmitglied, Künstlerbund Baden-Württemberg. Ibizareise
1966 1. Alteaaufenthalt (Costa Dorada, Spanien)
1969–1970 Rückzug vom Kunstbetrieb
1971 Studienreise mit Studenten nach Amsterdam
1973 Sommer in Altea
1976 Studienreise nach Amsterdam
1977 Sommer in Spanien

Einzelausstellungen

1956 Galerie Henning, Halle
1959 Akademie Karlsruhe
1963 Von der Heydt-Museum, Wuppertal
1965 Kunstverein Mannheim
1966 Kunstverein Celle; Altes Theater, Ravensburg
1967 Galerie Galetzki, Stuttgart; Städt. Museum Heilbronn
1968 Galerie Langer, Braunschweig
1973 Galerie der Spiegel, Köln; Galerie Rothe, Heidelberg
1974 Kunsthalle Baden-Baden (Retrospektive)
1976 Galerie Girokasse, Stuttgart
1979 Galerie Haus 11, Karlsruhe
1982 Kunstverein Karlsruhe (Retrospektive)
1983 Karl Ernst Osthaus-Museum, Hagen (Retrospektive)
1983 Kunstverein Singen (Retrospektive)
1985 Altes Theater, Ravensburg
1986 Galerie Ohse, Bremen
1987 Galerie Döbele, Stuttgart
1988 Wilhelmshöhe, Ettlingen; Galerie Baumgarten, Freiburg
1989 Galerie Pels-Leusden, Berlin
1991 Galerie Terbrüggen, Heidelberg
1993 Staatl. Galerie Moritzburg, Halle (Retrospektive)
1994 Prinz-Max-Palais, Karlsruhe (Retrospektive)

Gruppenausstellungen

seit 1952 Deutscher Künstlerbund
seit 1956 Große Kunstausstellung, München; Biennale des Jeunes Artistes, Paris
1957 Staatliche Galerie Moritzburg, Halle
seit 1960 Künstlerbund Baden-Württemberg
seit 1960 Kunstverein Hannover
1960 Art allemand de Baden-Württemberg, Nancy
1961 Junger Westen, Kunsthalle Recklinghausen
1962 Sammlung Pachen, Galerie der Stadt Mainz
1964 Deutsche Malerei heute, Kopenhagen, Helsinki
1965 Signale. Kunsthalle Recklinghausen; 5 Maler aus Karlsruhe, Museum Wiesbaden
1973 Das kleine Format, Kunsthalle Baden-Baden
1975 Sammlung Lütze II, Rathaus Singen
1980 Kunstpreis Darmstadt: 25 Jahre
1981 Kunst für den Bund. Kunstmuseum Bonn
1984 Die Fähre, Saulgau
1988 Vorbilder, Kunstverein Karlsruhe
1992 Sammlung Deschler, Museum Ulm
1993 Galerie Holzwarth, Stuttgart; Schlichtenmaier, Grafenau

Lit.: Werkverzeichnis und Retrospektive. Karlsruhe 1982 (2 Bde.); Die Zeit in Halle. Halle 1993

Fritz Klemm

14. 8. 1902 in Mannheim geboren – gestorben am 17. 8. 1990 in Karlsruhe
1919–1922 Lehrerseminar Karlsruhe
1922–1925 Landeskunstschule Karlsruhe
1925–1948 Lehrtätigkeit an verschiedenen Schulen
1948 Werklehrer, Akademie Karlsruhe
ab 1956 Künstlerbund Baden-Württemberg
1961–1970 Professur
1977–1987 Vorstandsmitglied Künstlerbund Baden-Württemberg
1984 Max-Lütze-Medaille
1985 Ehrenstipendiat, Villa Massimo, Rom
1987 Hans Thoma-Preis, Museum Bernau

Einzelausstellungen

1973 Galerie Heberle, Frankfurt; Ulmer Museum; Galerie Schneider, Karlsruhe; Galerie Die 2, Stuttgart
1974 Galerie Mewes, Hamburg; Galerie Orny, München
1975 Tekeningen, 's-Hertogenbosch; Galerie Edition Schneider, Karlsruhe
1976 Ulmer Museum (Retrospektive)
1978 Mannheimer Kunstverein
1983 Galerie Waßermann, München
1985 Kunstverein Karlsruhe (Retrospektive)
1992 Staatliche Kunsthalle Karlsruhe (Retrospektive)

Gruppenausstellungen

1951 Freie Künstlervereinigung Darmstadt
1952 Kunstverein Karlsruhe
1953 Bildende Hände, Staatliche Kunsthalle Baden-Baden
1954 100 Jahre Akademie, Kunsthalle Karlsruhe
1966 Deutscher Künstlerbund, Essen
1967 Deutscher Künstlerbund, Karlsruhe
1972 Galerie Edition Schneider, Karlsruhe
1979 Werkübersichten, Kunstverein Stuttgart
1981 Prinzip Collage, Südamerika
1986 Von Zwei Quadraten, Wilhelm Hack Museum, Ludwigshafen
1988 Signaturen, Gent
1990 Goethe Institut, London

Lit.: Fritz Klemm, Retrospektive, Ulmer Museum, Ulm 1976; Fritz Klemm, Zeichnungen, Aquarelle, Gouachen, Collagen 1948–1985, Bad. Kunstverein, Karlsruhe 1985;
Fritz Klemm, Retrospektive 1992, Staatliche Kunsthalle Karlsruhe, Karlsruhe 1992

Dieter Krieg

21. 5. 1937 in Lindau/Bodensee geboren – lebt in Quadrath-Ichendorf
1958–1962 Studium bei HAP Grieshaber und Herbert Kitzel an der Kunstakademie Karlsruhe
1966 Deutscher Kunstpreis der Jugend, Malerei, Baden-Baden
1968 Biennale-Preis Danuvius 68, Bratislava
1969 Kunstpreis der Böttcherstraße, Bremen
1970 Kunstpreis der Stadt Darmstadt
1971/72 Gastlehrauftrag an der Kunstakademie Karlsruhe
1975/76 Gastdozentur, Städelschule, Frankfurt am Main
1978 Professur, Kunstakademie Düsseldorf
1985 Karl-Ströher-Preis, Frankfurt
1989 Internationaler Kunstpreis des Landes Vorarlberg
1993 Hans Thoma-Preis des Landes Baden-Württemberg

Einzelausstellungen
1966 Kunstverein Karlsruhe
1967 Der Spiegel, Köln
1968 Der Spiegel, Köln
1970 Der Spiegel, Köln
1971 Galerie Stangl, München
1972 Kunsthalle Darmstadt
1973 Städt. Galerie Nordhorn
1976 Der Spiegel, Köln
1983 Von der Heydt-Museum, Wuppertal: Kunstverein Karlsruhe
1985 Galerie Herzer, München
1986 Galerie Wentzel, Köln
1987 Städt. Galerie Nordhorn, Suermondt-Museum, Aachen
1988 manus-presse, Stuttgart
1989 Galerie Der Spiegel, Köln
1991 Kunstmuseum Düsseldorf
1992 Galerie art-contact, Karlsruhe, Galerie Gmyrek, Düsseldorf
1993 Spendhaus, Reutlingen; manus-presse, Stuttgart; Forum Kunst, Rottweil
1994 Wilhelmshöhe, Ettlingen
1995 Galerie Herzer, München

Gruppenausstellungen
1967 Wege, Museum am Ostwall, Dortmund; Biennale de Paris
1968 Menschenbilder, Kunsthalle Darmstadt
1969 4x14, Kunsthalle Baden-Baden
1970 »Jetzt«-Künste in Deutschland, Kunsthalle Köln
1971 Biennale, São Paulo
1975 Triennale, Indien; Contemporary German Art, Melbourne
1977 documenta 6, Kassel
1978 Biennale, Venedig
1979 Schlaglichter, Landesmuseum, Bonn
1983 8 in Köln, Kunstverein Köln
1985 German Art 1945–1985, Tai pei Art Museum
1988 Vorbilder, Kunstverein Karlsruhe; Refigured Painting 1960–1988, Guggenheim Museum New York
1989 Neue Figuration, Kunstmuseum Düsseldorf; Schirn, Frankfurt

Lit.: Arbeiten 1965–1993, 2 Bde. Stuttgart 1993

Thomas Lenk

15. 6. 1933 in Berlin geboren – lebt in Tierberg (Hohenlohe)
1950 Kunstakademie Stuttgart, danach Lehre als Steinmetz
1967 Übersiedlung nach Stuttgart. Reisen nach New York und London; International Purchase Award Preis, Pittsburgh
1968 Reisen nach Italien und in den Ostblock
1969 Socha Piestanskych Parkov-Preis, Bratislava
1974 Übersiedlung nach Schloß Tierberg; Preis der Graphik-Biennale Fredrikstad (Nor)
1976 Kairoreise
1978 Gastprofessur, Heluwan-Universität, Kairo
1981 Reisen nach Österreich und die Tschechoslowakei
1982 Katalonienreise
1989 Ernennung zum Professor

Einzelausstellungen
1958 Galerie Boukes, Wiesbaden
1962 Galerie Müller, Stuttgart
1963 Galerie Parnaß, Wuppertal
1964 studio f, Ulm
1965 Galerie Müller, Stuttgart
1966 Galerie Handschin, Basel
1967 Fischbach Gallery, New York
1968 Kunstverein, Münster
1970 Biennale Venedig
1971 Kunstmuseum Düsseldorf
1974 Kunstverein, Stuttgart
1976 Kölnischer Kunstverein
1977 Staatsgalerie Stuttgart
1978 Gallery Fikrum wa Fann, Alexandria
1980 Kunsthalle Düsseldorf
1984 Kunstverein Heilbronn
1985 Kunsthalle Mannheim
1986 Galerie Rottloff, Karlsruhe
1992 Galerie Neuendorf, Frankfurt
1994 Galerie Schlichtenmaier, Grafenau

Gruppenausstellungen
1961 »30 junge Deutsche«, Museum Leverkusen
1963 »V. Biennale d'Arte, Padua
1963–1969 Ausstellungen des deutschen Künstlerbundes
1965 »Farbobjekte und Signale«, Haus am Waldsee, Berlin
1966 »New shapes of color«, Stedelijk Museum, Amsterdam
1967 »Formen der Farbe«, Kunstverein Stuttgart; Kunsthalle Bern; »Sculpture from twenty nations«, Guggenheim-Museum, New York
1968 Biennale Venedig; »Documenta IV«, Kassel
1969 »40 Deutsche unter 40«, Skandinavientournee; Wiener Secession, Wien
1970 »Weltausstellung Osaka«
1971 »Deutsche Kunst«, Museum of Modern Art, Tokyo
1972 »IV. Internationale Grafik-Biennale« Krakau; »IXe Biennale Internationale d'Art«, Menton
1973 »12. Biennale Middelheim«, Antwerpen
1974 »25 Jahre Kunst in der Bundesrepublik Deutschland«, Kunstmuseum Bonn
1975 »X. Biennale Internationale del Bronzetto«, Padova
1976 »Licht und Geometrie«, Bab-el-Louk, Kairo; 3. Norwegische Grafik-Biennale, Fredrikstad
1977 »12. Grafik-Biennale«, Ljubljana
1978 »Juni 78«, Moderna Galerija, Ljubljana
1980 »Koffer für Rottweil«, Forum Kunst Rottweil; »1. Triennale Fellbach«
1981 »Avantgarden retrospektiv«, Kunstverein Münster
1983 »Kunst – Landschaft – Architektur«, Nationalgalerie Berlin
1985 Musik und Kunst im 20. Jahrhundert, Staatsgalerie Stuttgart
1986 Symmetrie, Mathildenhöhe, Darmstadt
1991 Landesmuseum Cottbus
1995 Anhaltinische Galerie, Dessau

Lit.: Werkverzeichnis der Serigraphien, Karlsruhe 1985; Köln 1986

Wilhelm Loth

24. 9. 1920 in Darmstadt geboren – gestorben am 17. 2. 1993 in Darmstadt
1935 Lehre als Vermesser
1940 Arbeitsdienst, Kriegsdienst in Rußland
1944–1946 Kriegsgefangenschaft in England
1947 Studium in Darmstadt bei Fritz Schwarzbeck
1948 Hauptassistent, TH Darmstadt
seit 1951 Reisen nach Paris, Italien, Holland, Belgien, Dänemark, Schweden und England
1953–1955 Vorsitzender der Darmstädter Sezession
1954 Josef-Hoffmann-Ehrung, Wiener Sezession
1954–1956 Lehrstuhl, TH Darmstadt
1955 Kunstpreis der Stadt Darmstadt
1958–1986 Leiter Bildhauerklasse, Akademie Karlsruhe
1959 Stipendiat der Villa Massimo, Rom
1960 Professur
1965 Großer Kunstpreis, Stadt Köln
1967 Stipendiat in der Cité International des Arts, Paris
1979/80 Studiensemester in Venice, Kalifornien, Beginn der Malerei
1982 Ehrengast, Villa Massimo, Rom
1988 Reise nach Tokio
1989 Erster Vorsitzender des Deutschen Künstlerbundes

Einzelausstellungen
1948 Galerie Robert d'Hooghe, Darmstadt
1951 Frankfurter Kunstkabinett
1955 Galleria d'Arte Totti, Mailand
1956 Mathildenhöhe Darmstadt
1960 Galerie Günther Franke, München
1962 Städtische Kunsthalle Mannheim
1965 Kölner Kunstverein
1966 Kunstverein Braunschweig
1968 Kunstverein, Karlsruhe
1970 Kunsthalle Recklinghausen
1971 Kunsthalle Darmstadt
1973 Galerie d'Eendt, Amsterdam
1974 Dommuseum, Lübeck
1976 Städtische Kunsthalle Mannheim
1980 Vanguard-Gallery, Los Angeles
1981 Ostasiatische Gesellschaft, Tokyo
1983 Haus der Kunst, München
1990 Spendhaus Reutlingen (Retrospektive)
1991 Kunstverein Jena; Kunsthalle Karlsruhe (Retrospektive)
1992 Galerie Schlichtenmaier, Grafenau
1995 Mathildenhöhe Darmstadt

Gruppenausstellungen
1950 Das Menschenbild in unserer Zeit, Darmstadt
1953 Les Surindépendants, Paris
1954–1956 Deutscher Künstlerbund, Frankfurt
1957 4. Biennale Middelheim, Antwerpen
1958–1986 Aufbruch zur modernen Kunst, München
1959 2. Biennale, Carrara; Deutsche Künstler, Basel; 5. Biennale, Middelheim, Antwerpen
1961 2. Internationale Skulpturenausstellung, Paris
1963 Forum 63, Gent; 7. Biennale Middelheim, Antwerpen
1964 Deutsche Kunst Heute, Rotterdam; documenta 3, Kassel; 1. Internationale Zeichnung, Darmstadt
1965 4. Biennale für Skulptur, Carrara
1968 Salon de Mai, Paris
1971 15. Deutsche Künstler, Mailand; Image of Man, Hakone Museum, Tokio
1975 Biennale del Bozetto, Padua
1978 Europäische Triennale für Skulptur, Paris
1979/80 Deutsche und japanische Metallbildhauer, Tokio
1985 Kunst von 1945 bis 1985 in der BRD, Berlin
1987 Rätsel Wirklichkeit, Darmstadt
1988 Vorbilder, Badischer Kunstverein, Karlsruhe

Lit.: Spendhaus Reutlingen, 1990; Staatliche Kunsthalle Karlsruhe, 1991; Darmstadt, 1995

Georg Meistermann

16. 6. 1911 in Solingen geboren – gestorben am 12. 6. 1990 in Köln
1928–1933 Studium bei Heinrich Nauen und Ewald Mataré, Akademie Düsseldorf
1932 1. Ausstellung in Wuppertal
1933 Studienverbot, bis 1940 freischaffender Künstler
1937, 1938 Parisreisen
1940–1943 gibt Zeichenunterricht an Solinger Gymnasium
1941 Wehrmacht, verweigert Eid, wird für verrückt erklärt. Bekanntschaft mit dem Münchener Kunsthändler Günther Franke
1945 Kulturamtsleiter Solingen, Berater für den Collecting Point, Marburg
1948 Freundschaft mit Heinrich Böll
1949 Übersiedlung nach Köln. Karl Osthaus-Preis, Hagen
1950 Gründungsmitglied des Deutschen Künstlerbundes
1951 Kulturpreis der Stadt Wuppertal
1952 Stefan Lochner-Preis, Köln
1953 Lehrer, Städelschule, Frankfurt a. M.
1955 Professor für freie und monumentale Malerei, Akademie Düsseldorf
Großer Kunstpreis des Landes Nordrhein-Westfalen
1956 Glaswand, Universität Freiburg i. Br.
1957 Glaswand (294 qm), Bottrop
1958 Preis für Glasmalerei, Biennale, Salzburg
1960–1976 Professor, zeitweilig Rektor, Akademie Karlsruhe
1963 Altarfresko, »Maria Regina Martyrum«, Berlin
1966 Purrmann-Preis, Speyer
1967–1972 Präsident des Deutschen Künstlerbundes
1985 Entfernung des Brandt-Porträts aus der Bundeskanzlergalerie, Bonn

Einzelausstellungen
1946 Wuppertal
1949 Kölner Kunstverein
1961 Retrospektive, Köln
1971 Retrospektive, Landesmuseum Bonn
1981 Retrospektive, Germ. Nationalmuseum Nürnberg

Gruppenausstellungen
1937 Moderne deutsche Kunst seit 1933, Kunsthalle Bern
1948 Ausstellung »Junger Westen«, Recklinghausen; Kunstschaffen in Deutschland, Zürich; 3ième Salon Realitès Nouvelles, Paris
1950 Das Menschenbild in unserer Zeit, Darmstadt
1953 Biennale, São Paulo; 1. documenta, Kassel
1959 2. documenta, Kassel

Lit.: Georg Meistermann. Monographie und Werkverzeichnis. Herausgegeben von Karl Ruhrberg und Werner Schäfke. Werkverzeichnis von Inge Herold. Köln 1991

Günter Neusel

22. 12. 1930 in Kassel geboren – lebt in Karlsruhe und Kassel
1949 Studium, Werkakademie Kassel
1950–1952 Studium bei L. Mataré, Akademie Düsseldorf
1952–1954 Studium an der Hochschule, Berlin
1956 lebt in Stuttgart; ars-viva-Stipendium
1971 Lehrauftrag Akademie Karlsruhe
1972 Stipendium, Cité des arts, Paris
1973 Professur

Einzelausstellungen

1965 Galerie am Berg, Stuttgart
1966 Galerie U. Wendtorf, Oldenburg
1968 Studiengalerie der Universität Stuttgart; Galerie »patio«, Frankfurt a. M.; Galerie »daedalus«, Berlin; Galerie »58«, Rapperswil/Schweiz
1969 Instituto aleman, Madrid/Spanien; Galerie Heide Hildebrand, Klagenfurt; Galleria Barozzi, Venedig
1970 Galerie Appel & Fertsch, Frankfurt a. M.
1971 Galerie Berner, Stuttgart; »whitegallery«, Lausanne
1973 Studio Kausch, Kassel; Galleria Villa Massimo, Rom
1974 Galerie Behr, Stuttgart
1977 Galerie Südwest, Karlsruhe
1978 Galerie »Edition e«, Feldkirchen
1979 Galerie Seestraße, Rapperswil
1981 Kunstverein Karlsruhe; Kasseler Kunstverein
1985 Galerie Hotz, Karlsruhe
1992 Kunstverein Karlsruhe

Gruppenausstellungen

1962 Deutsche Plastik nach 1945, Stockholm
1964 Deutsche Plastik seit 1900, Paris, Musée Rodin
1965 Kunstpreis »junger westen«, Recklinghausen
1966 Plastik »Südwest«, Kunsthalle Baden-Baden
1967 Ausstellung »Ordo« studio di informazione aestethica, Turin
1968 »Systematische Programme«, Galerie Teufel, Koblenz; »Public Eye«, Kunsthaus Hamburg
1969 Biennale Nürnberg, Belgrad
1970 »jetzt«, Künste in Deutschland heute, Kunsthalle Köln; »Nebenprodukte«, Galerie nächst St. Stephan, Wien
1974 Galerie Sanguine, Collioure; Plastik der Gegenwart, Kunstverein Augsburg
1975 Kunst in Württemberg, Kunstverein Stuttgart
1977 Gesellschaft der Freunde junger Kunst, Kunsthalle Baden-Baden
1978 Galerie 58, Rapperswil
1979 Galerie Südwest, Karlsruhe; Badische Galerien, Kunstverein Karlsruhe
1980 Relief konkret in Deutschland heute, Saarland-Museum, Saarbrücken
1983 Deutsche Bildhauer der Gegenwart, Augsburg
1984 Plastik der 60er und 70er Jahre im Südwesten, Villa Merkel, Esslingen
1988 Vorbilder, Kunstverein Karlsruhe
1991 Konstruktive Tendenzen, Kunstverein Kirchzarten

Lit.: Ausst.Kat. Karlsruhe 1991

Georg Karl Pfahler

8. 10. 1926 in Emetzheim, Bayern, geboren – lebt in Fellbach bei Stuttgart
1950–1954 Studium, Kunstakademie Stuttgart
1957 Kunstpreis der Jugend, Baden-Württemberg
1972 Preis National-Galerie Wroclawie
1981 Gastprofessur Helwan Universität, Kairo
1984–1993 Professur Akademie Nürnberg
1984 Goldmedaille, Norwegische Grafikbiennale. Frederikstad
1987 Dozent der internationalen Sommerakademie, Salzburg
1992 Molfenter-Preis, Stadt Stuttgart

Einzelausstellungen

1957 Galerie Contemporains, Brüssel
1960 Galerie Müller, Stuttgart
1961 studio f, Ulm; Galerie Boukes, Wiesbaden
1962 Galerie Springer, Berlin
1964 Galerie Rottloff, Karlsruhe; Galleria del Cavallino, Venedig
1965 Kunstverein Münster
1966 Fischbach Gallery, New York
1967 Galerie Renée Ziegler, Zürich; Galleria del Naviglio, Mailand
1968 Landesmuseum Darmstadt
1969 Kestner-Gesellschaft, Hannover
1970 Galerie Müller, Köln
1971 Museum Folkwang, Essen
1974 Kunsthalle Mannheim
1975 Staatsgalerie Stuttgart
1976 Kunsthalle Tübingen (Retrospektive)
1981 Biennale São Paulo
1985 Kunsthalle Mannheim
1990 Staatsgalerie Stuttgart (Retrospektive)
1991 Museum Cottbus; Mittelböhmische Galerie Prag
1992 Galerie der Stadt Stuttgart; Galerie Neuendorf, Frankfurt a. M.
1995 Kunsthalle Nürnberg

Gruppenausstellungen

1957 Galerie 17, München
1962 30 deutsche Maler – Situation 1962, Kunstverein Oldenburg
1963 Schrift und Bild. Stedelijk-Museum, Amsterdam / Kunsthalle Baden-Baden
1965 Signale, Kunsthalle Basel
1966 Musische Geometrie, Kunstverein Hannover
1967 Formen der Farbe, Stedelijk-Museum. Amsterdam / Kunstverein Stuttgart / Kunsthalle Bern; Sculpture from 20 nations, Guggenheim. New York
1968 Biennale Venedig
1970 Nationalmuseum, Warschau
1971 Museum Folkwang, Essen
1976 Acht deutsche Künstler, Museum Kairo
1981 Avantgarden-Retrospektiv 1831–1981, Kunstverein Münster
1985 Kunst in der Bundesrepublik Deutschland 1945–1985, Nationalgalerie Berlin
1986 Abstrakt – Konkret, Wilhelm Hack-Museum, Ludwigshafen
1990 Kunstmienen, Kunstmuseum Düsseldorf
1995 Kunst in Deutschland, Bundeskunsthalle Bonn

Lit.: Stuttgart 1990; Frankfurt a. M. 1992

Markus Prachensky

21. 3. 1932 in Innsbruck geboren – lebt in Wien
1952 Studium der Architektur in Wien
1953 Studium der Malerei
1956 Abschluß des Architekturstudiums mit Diplom; Gründung der Gruppe »Galerie St. Stephan«
1957 Mitglied der Wiener Secession; Parisaufenthalt; Hamburgaufenthalt
1958 Aufenthalt in Paris
1959 Wiesbadenaufenthalt
1960 Aschaffenburgaufenthalt
1962 Karlsruheaufenthalt; Atelier in Stuttgart
1963 Berlinaufenthalt
1964 Atelier in Berlin
1966 lebt in Stuttgart und Berlin; Wienaufenthalt
1967 New Yorkaufenthalt; Atelier in Los Angeles
1969 Mexikoreise
1970 über London nach Hannover, dort Atelier
1971 Rückkehr nach Wien
1975–1979 Apulienreisen
1983 Professur, Akademie Wien
1986–1989 Umbrienreisen
1989–1991 Sardinienreisen

Einzelausstellungen

1957 Wiener Secession; Galerie 5, Reutlingen
1958 Galerie St. Stephan, Wien
1960 Galerie St. Stephan, Wien; Galerie 59, Aschaffenburg
1961 Galerie Rottloff, Karlsruhe
1962 Galerie St. Stephan, Wien; studio f, Ulm
1963 Galerie Rottloff, Karlsruhe
1964 Galerie St. Stephan, Wien
1965 Galerie Schüler, Berlin
1966 Akademie, Berlin
1968 Los Angeles County Museum
1970 Kunstverein Hannover (Retrospektive)
1971 Galerie St. Stephan, Wien; Galerie Defet, Nürnberg
1972 Ulmer Museum (Retrospektive)
1975 Galerie Ulysses, Wien
1976 Galerie Wentzel, Hamburg
1979 Akademie, Wien (Retrospektive)
1980 Galerie Ulysses, Wien
1982 Galerie Löhrl, Möchengladbach
1986 Galerie Fischer, Baden-Baden
1989 Galerie Heimeshoff, Essen
1990 Galerie Ulysses, New York
1993 Galerie Thoman, Innsbruck (Retrospektive)
1995 Kunstverein Augsburg

Gruppenausstellungen

1955 Galerie St. Stephan, Wien
1957 Premio Lissone; Völkerkundemuseum Hamburg
1958 Galerie Der Spiegel, Köln, Galerie 33, Bern
1959 documenta, Kassel; Jeunes peintres d'aujourd 'hui, Paris
1960 Antagonismes, Louvre, Paris
1961 Neue österreichische Kunst, Aschaffenburg, Bochum; Internationale Malerei, Wolframs-Eschenbach
1963 Deutscher Künstlerbund, Stuttgart
1965 Österreichische Kunst, Zagreb
1966 Salon International, Lausanne
1967 Weltausstellung Montreal
1969 Creative Austria, 20th Century, Philadelphia Art Museum
1974 Deutsche Kunst im 20. Jahrhundert, Wolfsburg
1982 Wiener Secession, Darmstadt
1983 Deutscher Künstlerbund, Berlin
1987 Europalia, Brüssel
1993 Steierischer Herbst, Graz
1994 Aufbrüche österr. Malerei und Plastik der 50er Jahre, Wien
1995 Die Kraft der Bilder, Slg. Essl, Parlament, Wien

Lit.: Ausst.Kat. Innsbruck 1993

Lothar Quinte

13. 4. 1923 in Neisse/Oberschlesien geboren – lebt in Wintzenbach (Elsaß)
1937–1941 Malerlehre in Leipzig
1941–1945 Kriegsdienst
1946–1951 Kunstschule, Kloster Bernstein, Ldkrs. Horb
1952 Atelier in Reutlingen
1953 II. Preis, Kunstpreis der Jugend
1954 Kunstpreis der Jugend, Baden-Baden
1956 Kunstpreis Junger Westen
1957 Atelier in Lauterbourg/Elsaß
1959–1960 Gastdozent, Werkkunstschule Krefeld
1960 Wohnsitz in Karlsruhe
1964 Fenster, Dom Lübeck
1965 Burda-Preis, München
1966 Wandbild im Staatstheater Bonn
1967 Umzug nach Wintzenbach/Elsaß
1975/76 Weltreise
1986–1994 jährliches Winteratelier in Colva/Goa, Indien
1993 Kulturpreis Schlesien des Landes Niedersachsen
1995 Ernennung zum Professor

Einzelausstellungen

1954 Galerie Hanna Bekker vom Rath, Frankfurt a. M.
1958 Galerie 33 Bern; Galerie Nächst St. Stephan Wien
1959 Kaiser-Wilhelm Museum, Krefeld
1960 Märkisches Museum, Witten; Galerie 59, Aschaffenburg; Galerie Boukes, Wiesbaden
1961 Punt 31, Dordrecht
1962 Galerie Rottloff, Karlsruhe; studio f, Ulm
1963 Galerie Müller, Stuttgart
1965 Galerie Müller, Stuttgart
1966 Galerie Bischofsberger, Zürich
1968 Kunstverein Oldenburg
1969 Galerie Müller, Stuttgart
1984 Augustinermuseum, Freiburg; Museen der Stadt Aschaffenburg
1987 Kunstverein Heilbronn
1991 Galerie Haus Geiselhart, Reutlingen; Galerie Thieme, Darmstadt
1992 Galerie Riecker, Heilbronn
1993 Kunsthalle Karlsruhe
1995 Galerie Jahnhorst und Preuss, Berlin; Galerie Stadthalle, Kehl

Gruppenausstellungen

1949 Schüler des Bernstein, Horb
1952 Spendhaus Reutlingen
1954 Kunsthalle Recklinghausen
1955 Kunstpreis der Jugend, Baden-Baden
1956 Kunstverein Konstanz
1957 Fähre Saulgau; Musée des Arts Décoratifs, Paris
1962 Große Kunstausstellung München
1963 Deutscher Künstlerbund, Stuttgart
1964 Werkkunstschule Krefeld; Salon Comparains, Paris; Carnegie International, Pittsburgh/USA
1965 Institut for Contempory Arts, London; NT 3 international, Zagreb
1966 Museum of Modern Art, New York
1967 Carnegie International, Pittsburgh/USA
1969 13 Deutsche Maler, Tokio
1974 International Point-Exhibition of Japan and Germany, Tokio
1981 Pawilon Wystawowy Krakau
1995 Nationalgalerie Warschau

Lit.: Ausst.Kat. Freiburg 1984; Ausst. Kat. Kunsthalle Karlsruhe, Ostfildern-Ruit 1993

Heinz Schanz

21. 3. 1927 in Genkingen geboren – lebt in Karlsruhe
1942 Zimmermannslehre
1943–1944 Tätigkeit als Zimmermann
1944–1945 Militärdienst
1946–1948 Praktikum im Architekturbüro Bodo Rasch, Stuttgart
1949–1950 Praktikum, Landschaftsgärtner in Memmingen
1952–1953 Studium bei HAP Grieshaber, Bernsteinschule, Horb/Neckar
1956–1960 Studium bei HAP Grieshaber, Akademie Karlsruhe
ab 1960 freischaffender Künstler, Karlsruhe
1962 Kulturpreis, Stadt Karlsruhe
1977 Villa-Romana-Preis, Florenz
1978 Villa Massimo-Preis, Rom
1981 Stipendiat, Ekely/Oslo; Förderpreis, Künstlerbund Baden-Württemberg
1987 Kunstpreis, Kreissparkasse Esslingen-Nürtingen
1990 Kunstpreis, Stadt Stuttgart
1993 Oberschwäbischer Kunstpreis

Einzelausstellungen

1961 Badischer Kunstverein, Karlsruhe; Kunstverein Mannheim; Galerie Lutz und Meyer, Stuttgart
1962 Galerie Baier, Mainz
1963 Kleine Galerie, Schwenningen; Galerie von Loehr, Frankfurt/Main
1964 Reuchlinhaus, Pforzheim
1966 Kunstverein Mannheim
1975 Schloßhofgalerie, Kißlegg/Allgäu
1976 Galerie Südwest, Karlsruhe
1978 Galerie von Laar, München
1981 Galerie Rottloff, Karlsruhe
1983 Spendhaus Reutlingen
1984 »manus presse« Stuttgart
1985 Galerie Art-contact, Karlsruhe; Galerie Losch, Schallstadt
1986 Galerie R. Ohse, Bremen; Wilhelmshöhe, Ettlingen
1987 Reuchlinhaus, Pforzheim
1989 Galerie Bernd Slutzky, Frankfurt
1990 Galerie der Stadt Stuttgart
1991 Galerie Holzwarth, Stuttgart; Otto-Galerie, München
1992 Kunstverein Friedrichshafen
1993 Galerie Rolf Ohse, Bremen; Galerie Schlichtenmaier, Grafenau

Gruppenausstellungen

1954 Reutlinger Künstler, Spendhaus, Reutlingen
1956 Photohaus Näher, Reutlingen
1957 Galerie Gallwitz, Karlsruhe
1958 Galerie 5, Reutlingen
1959 Grieshaber und sein Kreis, Recklinghausen; Kunstpreis der Jugend, Kunsthalle Baden-Baden
1960 Künstlerbund Baden-Württemberg (ab 1960)
1961 Deutscher Künstlerbund, München
1963 Galerie Friedrich und Dahlem, München
1965 Extra, Museum Wiesbaden
1973 14x14, Kunsthalle Baden-Baden
1982 Malerei der 60er Jahre, Kreissparkasse Esslingen
1988 Vorbilder, Kunstverein Karlsruhe
1989 Landeskunstwochen Donaueschingen
1993 Grieshaber, Bernstein, Karlsruhe, Landratsamt Esslingen
1993–1995 Sammlung Deyhle, Wanderausstellung

Lit.: Ausst.Kat. Reutlingen 1983, Grafenau 1993

Felix Schlenker

12. 7. 1920 in Schwenningen/Neckar geboren – lebt in Schwenningen
1945–1978 Lehrer
1967 Mitglied des Deutschen Künstlerbundes
1970 Mitbegründer von »Forum Kunst Rottweil«
1990 Bürgermedaille Stadt Villingen-Schwenningen; Professor
1991 Ehrengast der Villa Massimo, Rom
1992 Stiftung der »Sammlung Felix Schlenker«, Stadt Villingen-Schwenningen

Einzelausstellungen

1960 Malura München
1964 Galerie Schiessel, Freiburg
1965 Club bel etage Zürich, Galerie am Jakobsbrunnen, Bad Cannstatt
1967 »Fähre« Saulgau
1969 Galerie Apfelbaum Karlsruhe
1970 Galerie Cornels Baden-Baden
1973 Konvikt Rottweil: »Kreuzweg 73«
1975 Städtische Museen Freiburg
1977 »galerie drei« Waldshut
1978 Städtische Galerie Villingen-Schwenningen
1979 Galerie Papala, Karlsruhe
1980 Galerie Kaiser, Freiburg
Galerie Domberger, Reutlingen
1981 Kunstverein Marburg
1983 Galerie im Bürgerhaus, Haigerloch
1984 Galerie Wack, Kaiserslautern
Galerie Treiber, Ettenheimmünster; studio a, Ottendorf/Niederelbe
1988 Galerie St. Johann, Saarbrücken
Augustinermuseum Freiburg
1989 Städtische Galerie, Villingen-Schwenningen
1990 Forum Kunst, Rottweil
1995 Galerie Treiber, Ettenheimmünster

Gruppenausstellungen

1964–1977 Deutscher Künstlerbund
1960–1977 Künstlerbund Baden-Württemberg
1967–1973 Große Kunstausstellung München
1963–1977 Gesellschaft der Freunde junger Kunst, Baden-Baden
1966 Forum Stadtpark Graz
1968 Galerie Reckermann, Köln
1969 »Objekte, Bildreliefs«, Staatsgalerie Stuttgart
1973 Deutsche Gesellschaft für Christliche Kunst, München; Konvikt Rottweil Kreuzweg 1973
1977 Kunstraum Rottweil, Stuttgart; Neue Gruppe Saar, Saarbrücken; Pont-à-Mousson, Remscheid
1979 Ankäufe des Landes Baden-Württemberg, Freiburg; Neue Darmstädter Sezession
bis 80 Arbeitskreis 68, Wasserburg am Inn
1980 Galerie Wack, Kaiserslautern
1982 Avantgarde um 1960, Wasserburg am Inn
1983 Galerie »drei«, Waldshut
1985 Neue Darmstädter Sezession
1986 Kunstverein Stuttgart
1988 Landeskunstwochen, Villingen-Schwenningen
1991 Darmstädter Sezession
1995 Kreissparkasse Esslingen

Lit.: 1957–1988 Ausst.Kat. Villingen-Schwenningen 1988

Emil Schumacher

29. 8. 1912 in Hagen geboren – lebt in Hagen
1932–1935 Studium, Kunstgewerbeschule in Dortmund
1935–1939 Freier Maler; Studienreisen nach Holland und Belgien
1939–1945 Technischer Zeichner
1947 Gründung der Künstlervereinigung junger westen, Recklinghausen
1948 Kunstpreis junger westen, Stadt Recklinghausen
1951 Reise nach Paris
1955 Kunstpreis, Stadt Iserlohn
1956 Konrad-von-Soest-Preis, Stadt Münster
1958 Karl-Ernst-Osthaus-Preis, Stadt Hagen; Guggenheim Award (National Section) New York; Reisen nach Spanien, Italien und Tunesien
1958–1960 Professur, Hochschule Hamburg
1959 Preis 5th International Art Exhibition Tokyo; Menzione d'Onore, 11. Premio Lissone
1962 Reise nach Libyen und Tunesien; Premio Cardazzo, Biennale Venedig; First Prize International Arts Exhibition, Saigon
1963 Reisen nach Südamerika; Sommeraufenthalt in Anguillara; Großer Kunstpreis, Land Nordrhein-Westfalen
1965 Jugoslawienreise; 2. Preis der VIe Exposition Internationale, Ljubljana
1966 Reise durch Norwegen
1966–1977 Professur, Akademie Karlsruhe
1967–1968 Gastprofessor (Visiting Artist), Minneapolis School of Art; USA-Reise
1968 Mitglied der Akademie, Berlin
1969 Winteraufenthalt, Insel Djerba, Tunesien
seit 1971 Regelmäßige Frühjahrs- und Sommeraufenthalte auf Ibiza
1974 Ibiza '74, Preis der Stadt Ibiza
1978 August-Macke-Preis, Stadt Meschede
1982 Rubenspreis, Stadt Siegen; Ehrenring, Stadt Hagen
1983 Marokko-Reise
1985 Ehrengast, Villa Massimo, Rom
1987 Jörg-Ratgeb-Preis, Stadt Reutlingen
1990 Herbert Boeckl-Preis, Wien
1991 Harry Graf Keßler-Preis, Deutscher Künstlerbund
1992 Ehrendoktorwürde der Universität Dortmund

Einzelausstellungen

1947 Studio für neue Kunst, Wuppertal
1956 Galerie Parnass, Wuppertal
1957 Galerie 22, Düsseldorf
1958 Karl Ernst Osthaus-Museum, Hagen
1959 Gallery Kootz, New York; Galleria La Medusa (Kat.), Rom; Galerie Schüler, Berlin; Galerie Müller, Stuttgart
1960 Galerie van de Loo, München
1961 Kestner-Gesellschaft, Hannover
1962 Kunstverein, Münster; Kunstverein Hamburg; Galleria la Medusa, Rom; Galleria Blu, Mailand
1963 Galleria L'Indiano, Florenz; Galerie nächst St. Stephan, Wien
1964 Galleria L'Indiano, Florenz
1965 Galerie van de Loo, München
1968 Lefebre Gallery, New York
1969 Galerie de Montréal, Montréal
1971 Kunstverein, Düsseldorf
1972 Kunstverein, Karlsruhe; Haus am Waldsee, Berlin
1973 Galerie Rothe, Heidelberg
1975 Karl Ernst Osthaus Museum, Hagen
1976 Neue Galerie, Linz
1977 Karl Ernst Osthaus Museum, Hagen
1978 Modern Art Gallery, Wien; Kunstverein Braunschweig
1980 Galerie Schlegl, Zürich
1981 Overbeck-Gesellschaft, Lübeck
1982 Sprengel Museum, Hannover
1983 Kunsthalle Darmstadt; Wilhelm-Hack-Museum, Ludwigshafen; Landesmuseum, Münster
1984 Kunsthalle Bremen, Bremen
1985 Kunstverein, Karlsruhe; Kunstverein, Augsburg
1986 Gallery Herstand, New York; Galerie Strelow, Düsseldorf
1987 Städt. Galerie, Lüdenscheid; Karl Ernst Osthaus Museum, Hagen
1988 Nationalgalerie, Berlin
1989 Kunstsammlung Nordrhein-Westfalen, Düsseldorf
1990 Josef Albers-Museum, Bottrop
1991 Andre Emmerich Gallery, New York; Galerie Strelow, Düsseldorf
1992 Saarland Museum, Saarbrücken
1993 Galerie Strelow, Düsseldorf
1994 Prinz-Max-Palais, Karlsruhe; Galerie Strelow, Düsseldorf
1995 Wilhelmshöhe, Karlsruhe; Galerie Strelow, Düsseldorf

Gruppenausstellungen

1948 Junge Kunst, Hagen
1950 Deutsche und französische Kunst der Gegenwart, Recklinghausen
1952 Mensch und Form unserer Zeit, Recklinghausen
1954 Stedelijk Museum, Amsterdam
1955 Neues Museum, Wiesbaden; IX. Premio Lissone, Lissone
1956 Städt. Museum, Leverkusen
1957 Premio Lissone
1958 Biennale, Venedig; Museum of Art, Pittsburgh; Guggenheim Museum, New York
1959 documenta 2, Kassel
1960 National Museum, Tokio; Galerie Xxème Siècle, Paris
1961 Palazzo Grassi, Venedig
1962 Biennale, Venedig
1964 documenta 3, Kassel
1965 Moderne Galerie, Ljubljana; Art Gallery, Auckland
1967 Museum of Art, Pittsburgh; Expo 67, Montreal
1968 Art Museum, Adelaide
1970 Museum of Art, Pittsburgh; Expo Museum of Fine Arts, Osaka
1971 II. Triennale, New Delhi
1973 Biennale, Sydney
1974 Kunsthalle, Düsseldorf
1975 Boston Art Museum, Boston
1976 Kunsthalle, Bremen
1977 documenta 6, Kassel; Europalia, Brüssel
1980 Landesmuseum (Retrospektive), Münster; Kunsthaus Zürich
1981 Westkunst, Köln
1985 Landesmuseum, Bonn; Nationalgalerie, Berlin
1986 Kunsthalle, Baden-Baden; Altes Museum, Berlin (Ost); Albertinum, Dresden
1988 Stationen der Moderne, Berlin; Vorbilder, Kunstverein Karlsruhe
1993 junger westen, Kunsthalle Recklinghausen
1995 Kunstverein Eislingen; Galerie Zimmer, Düsseldorf

Lit.: Ausst.Kat. Karlsruhe 1994

K.R.H. Sonderborg

5. 4. 1923 in Sonderborg, Dänemark geboren – lebt in Stuttgart, Paris, Berlin und Chicago
1938–1940 kaufmännische Lehre, Hamburg
1941–1942 Gestapohaft in Hamburg
1947–1949 Studium der Malerei und Graphik, Landeskunstschule, Hamburg
1951 Italienreise, Stromboli
1953 Mitglied der Gruppe ZEN 49
1955 Lichtwark-Preis, Stadt Hamburg Karl-Ernst-Osthaus-Preis, Stadt Hagen
1958 Umzug nach Paris
1959 Londonaufenthalt
1960 Biennale-Preis, Tokyo
1960–1961 Aufenthalt in New York
1963 Biennale-Preis, São Paulo
1963–1964 Aufenthalt Ascona, Tessin
1964–1965 Aufenthalt in New York
1965 Professur, Akademie Stuttgart
1968 Biennale-Preis von Mentone
1969–1970 Gastprofessur, Minneapolis College of Art
1983 Mitglied, Akademie Berlin
1985 Villa Massimo, Rom
1986 Gastprofessur, Art Institute, Chicago
1987 Hans-Molfenter-Preis, Stadt Stuttgart
seit 1987 Ateliers in Chicago und Berlin
1989 Hans-Thoma-Preis des Landes Baden-Württemberg
seit 1990 Atelier, Schloß Solitude, Stuttgart

Einzelausstellungen

1956 Kestner-Gesellschaft, Hannover
1957 Galerie van de Loo, Essen; Galerie Springer, Berlin; Galerie René Drouin, Paris
1960 Galerie Flinker, Paris
1961 Lefèbre Gallery, New York
1962 Galerie Handschin, Basel; Galerie Müller, Stuttgart; Galerie Schmela, Düsseldorf
1963 7. Biennale São Paulo
1964 Biennale Venedig
1965 Galerie Karl Flinker, Paris; Lefèbre Gallery, New York
1966 Galerie Stangl, München; Tokyo Gallery, Tokyo
1968 Galerie Daniel Gervis, Paris
1969 Galerie Daniel Gervis, Paris
1972 Kunstforening Oslo, Kopenhagen
1977 Galerie Beyeler, Basel; Ulmer Museum; Galerie Politiken, Kopenhagen
1978 Nordjyllands Kunstmuseum, Aalborg; Kunstverein Sonderborg
1983 Galerie Hubert Winter, Wien
1985 Kunstverein Augsburg; Staatsgalerie Stuttgart
1986 Bischoff Gallery, Chicago
1987 Saarland-Museum, Saarbrücken
1988 Tokyo Gallery, Tokyo; Galerie der Stadt Stuttgart
1991 Galerie Georg Nothelfer, Berlin
1992 Märkisches Museum, Witten
1993 Kunstverein Stuttgart, (Retrospektive); Kunsthalle Baden-Baden

Gruppenausstellungen

1949 Kunstverein Hamburg
1951 Kunstverein Hamburg
1953 Galerie Böhler, München: ZEN 49; Art Institute, Chicago; Deutscher Künstlerbund, Hamburg
1954 Duitse kunst na 1945; Stedelijk Museum Amsterdam; Stedelijk Museum Eindhoven
1955 Wallraf-Richartz-Museum, Köln; Kunstverein Hamburg; Westdeutsche Kunst 1945–55; Galleria Nazionale d'Art Moderna, Rom; Palais des Beaux Arts, Brüssel; Musée d'Art Moderne, Paris; Akademie Karlsruhe: 17 deutsche Maler 1955
1956 Junger Westen 56, Kunsthalle Recklinghausen;
1957 Frühjahrsausstellung, Kunstverein Hannover; Lebendige Farbe – couleur vivante, Museum Wiesbaden; Triennale Mailand
1958 29. Biennale Venedig; Quadriennale Rom; Biennale Tokyo
1959 Die neue Generation, Musée d'Art Moderne, Paris; Salon de Mai, Musée d'Art Moderne, Paris; Salon des Réalités Nouvelles; 5. Biennale São Paulo; documanta 2, Kassel; Deutsche Künstler der Gegenwart, Kunsthalle Basel; Deutsche Kunst 1959, Staatliche Kunsthalle Baden-Baden
1960 Museo de Arte Moderna. Rio de Janeiro: Arte alemao desde 1945
1961 Salon Comparaisons, Musée d'Art Moderne, Paris
1962 Gegenwart bis 1962, Haus am Waldsee, Berlin; Skripturale Malerei, Haus am Waldsee, Berlin; Galerie DuMont, Köln
1963 Salon de Mai, Musée d'Art Moderne, Paris; Stedelijk Museum Amsterdam; Schrift en beeld, Kunsthalle Baden-Baden
1964 32. Biennale, Venedig; 1. Internationale der Zeichnung, Darmstadt
1965 Salon de Mai, Musée d'Art Moderne Paris; Painting without Brush, Institute of Contemporary Art, Boston
1966 Pejlinger '66, Louisiana Museum, Humlebaek
1967 Kunst des 20. Jahrhunderts, Kunsthalle Düsseldorf
1968 Neue Malerie in Deutschland, Staatsgalerie Stuttgart; Arte Contemporanea, Galleria Nationale d'Arte Moderna, Rom; 7. Biennale de Peinture 1968, Ville de Menton
1970 Guggenheim Museum: International Exhibition, New York; Modern Art Gallery, Minneapolis; 36. Biennale Venedig
1972 Guggenheim Museum: Postwar Era, New York
1974 10. Biennale de Menton; 25 Jahre Kunst in der Bundesrepublik Deutschland, Kunstmuseum Bonn
1975 Kunsthalle Düsseldorf; Surrealität, Bildrealität 1924–74, Kunsthalle Baden-Baden
1977 Lefèbre Gallery, New York
1979 8. Biennale der Ostseeländer, Kunsthalle Rostock
1981 Westkunst, Köln; Kunst für den Bund; Kunstmuseum Bonn
1982 Die Handzeichnung der Gegenwart II, Staatsgalerie Stuttgart; G. K. Pfahler, K.R.H. Sonderborg – frühe Bilder, Max Ulrich Hetzler GmbH, Stuttgart
1983 Grauzonen, Kunst und Zeitbilder, Farbwelten 1945–55, Akademie Berlin
1985 Vom Klang der Bilder, Staatsgalerie Stuttgart; 1945–85. Kunst in der Bundesrepublik Deutschland, Nationalgalerie Berlin
1986 ZEN 49, Kunsthalle Baden-Baden
1987 Painting Since World War 2. Guggenheim Museum, New York
1989 Stationen der Moderne, Berlinische Galerie, Berlin
1991 Galerie Georg Nothelfer, Berlin

Lit.: Ausst.Kat. Stuttgart (Ostfildern-Ruit) 1993

Walter Stöhrer

15. 1. 1937 in Stuttgart geboren – lebt in Scholderup/Schleswig Holstein und Berlin
1937–1945 mit der Familie im Nordschwarzwald
1945 Übersiedlung nach Karlsruhe
1953–1955 Lehrer als Werbegraphiker
1956–1960 Studium an der Akademie der Bildenden Künste Karlsruhe
1962 Deutscher Kunstpreis der Jugend, Stuttgart; Übersiedlung nach Berlin
1964 Kritikerpreis der Stadt Berlin
1971 Will Grohmann-Preis der Akademie der Künste, Berlin
1973 Stipendiat in der Cité International des Arts, Paris
1976 Berliner Kunstpreis der Akademie der Künste, Berlin
1977 Villa Romana-Preis, Florenz
1978 Kunstpreis der Böttcherstraße, Bremen
1981–1982 Gastprofessur an der HdK Berlin
1982 Kunstpreis der Stadt Nordhorn
1984 Mitglied der Akademie der Künste, Berlin
1986 Professur, HdK Berlin
1995 Hans Molfenter-Preis der Stadt Stuttgart

Einzelausstellungen
1961 Galerie H. A. Baier, Mainz
1962 Galerie Schüler, Berlin; Galerie H. A. Baier, Mainz
1963 Galerie Lutz und Meyer, Stuttgart
1964 Galerie Schüler, Berlin
1965 Galerie nächst St. Stephan, Wien
1980 Kunstverein Stuttgart
1983 Museum Ulm
1984 Kunstmuseum Düsseldorf; Saarland-Museum, Saarbrücken
1985 Galerie Lefèbre, New York
1987 Berlinische Galerie, Berlin (Retrospektive)
1990 Kunsthalle Kiel
1993 Kunsthalle Bremen
1994 Galerie Haftmann, Zürich
1995 Staatliche Kunsthalle Karlsruhe (Retrospektive) Galerie der Stadt Stuttgart

Gruppenausstellungen
1959 Museum der Stadt Ulm; 1. Biennale der Jugend, Paris
1960 Künstlerbund Baden-Württemberg, Baden-Baden
1961 Künstlerbund Baden-Württemberg
1962 Künstlerbund Baden-Württemberg, Baden-Baden
1963 Kunstpreis der Jugend, Baden-Baden
1964 Kunstpreis der Jugend, Mannheim; 4. Biennale Tokio; Salon Comparaison, Paris
1966 »Junge Berliner Künstler«, Basel, Genf, Mailand, Paris
1967 Deutscher Künstlerbund; Große Kunstausstellung München
1969 Neue Darmstädter Sezession
1970–1994 Deutscher Künstlerbund; Große Kunstausstellung München
1975 Neue Darmstädter Sezession
1977 »21 Deutsche Künstler«, Humlebaek, Dänemark
1978 Grafik Biennale, Florenz
1980 »Realism and Expressionism in Berlin Art«, University of California, Los Angeles
1981 Neue Darmstädter Sezession
1984 Nationalpinakothek, Athen
1985/86 German Art 1945–85, Taipeh Fine Arts Museum Taiwan
1987 Berlin Art 1961–1987, Museum of Modern Art, New York

Lit.: Günter Bose, Werkverzeichnis der Druckgraphik. Bd. 1 Radierungen 1960–1966, Berlin; »Walter Stöhrer, Werke auf Papier 1959–1995«, Staatliche Kunsthalle Karlsruhe (Ostfildern-Ruit) 1995

Allgemeine Literatur

Marianne Adelmann (Hrsg.), Europäische Plastik der Gegenwart, Die Sammlung Parthenon, Stuttgart 1966

G. C. Argan N. Ponente, Italia, in : L'arte dopo il 1945, hrsg. v. Will Grohmann, Milano 1959

F. Arcangeli, Dal romanticismo all'informale, Torino 1977

H. H. Arnason, Geschichte der modernen Kunst, Malerei – Skulptur – Architektur, Bremen 1971

Renato Barilli, L'Informale, in: Ausst.Kat. XIV Mostra nationale Premio del Fiorino, Firenze 1963

Renato Barilli, L'informale, All'Insegna del Pesce d'Oro, Milano 1964

Renato Barilli, Informale ogetto comportamento, Milano 1972, 2 Bde.

Renato Barilli Franco Solmi (Hrsg.), Ausst.Kat. Mailand: L'informale in Italia, Milano 1983

Fritz Barran, Kunst am Bau – heute. Wandbild, Relief und Plastik in der Baukunst der Gegenwart, Stuttgart 1964

Ausst.Kat. Basel: Skulptur im 20. Jahrhundert, Merian Park 1984, Basel 1984

Willi Baumeister, Das Unbekannte in der Kunst, Stuttgart 1947, Köln 1960 u. 1988

F. Bayl, Bilder unserer Tage, Köln 1960

Katja Blomberg-Schneider, Zwischen Figuration und Abstraktion. Tendenzen deutscher Plastik der Nachkriegszeit – eine morphologische Untersuchung der Œuvres von H. Uhlmann, K. Hartung, W. Loth, F. Koenig, B. u. M. Matschinsky-Denninghoff, O. H. Hajek, E. Cimiotti und N. Kricke zwischen 1945 und 1965 (Diss.), Heidelberg 1991

Ausst.Kat. Bologna: Il tempo dell'informale 1955–1961, Bologna 1975

Gianmario Borio, Musikalische Avantgarde um 1960: Entwurf der Theorie der informellen Musik (Diss.), Berlin 1993

C. Brandi, Significa dell'informale, in: Arte e cultura contemporanee, Firenze 1964

Alberto Burri u. a., Manifesto del gruppo Origine, Roma 1951

Maurizio Calvesi, Ausst.Kat. Rom: Sette giovani pittori e uno scultore, Roma 1959

Hilde Cammel (Hrsg.), Alles van waarde is weerlos – Keramiek van Cobra leden, s'Hertogenbusch 1993

J. E. Cirlot, Informalismo, Barcelona 1959

J. Claus, Theorien zeitgenössischer Malerei, Hamburg 1963

Enrico Crispolti, Ausst.Kat. Rom: Alberto Burri, Ennio Morlotti, Emilio Vedova, Roma 1957

Enrico Crispolti u. a., Ausst.Kat. Rom: Possibilità di relazione, Roma 1960

Enrico Crispolti u. a., Ausst.Kat.: Arezzo – Rom, Sei pittori italiani dagli anni Quaranta ad oggi: Burri, Cagli, Fontana, Guttuso, Moreni, Morlotti, Arezzo – Roma 1967

Enrico Crispolti, Ricerche dopo l'informale, Roma 1968

Enrico Crispolti, Pittura d'avanguardia nel dopoguerra in Europa, Milano 1970

Enrico Crispolti, Ausst.Kat. Ferrara: Possiblità di relazione, Ferrara 1970

Enrico Crispolti, L'informale, Assisi – Roma 1971, 4 Bde.

Enrico Crispolti, Ausst.Kat. München: Europäische Avantgarde nach 1945, Galerie Schuler, München 1974

Martin Damus, Kunst in der BRD 1945–1990, Funktionen der Kunst in einer demokratischen verfaßten Gesellschaft, Reinbek bei Hamburg 1995

Rolf-Gunter Dienst, Deutsche Kunst: Eine neue Generation, Köln 1970

Ausst.Kat. Dortmund: Informel. Goetz, Schultze, Hoehme, Museum am Ostwall, Dortmund 1980

Jean Dubuffet, L'art brut préféreaux arts culturels, Paris 1949

K. F. Ertel, Moderne deutsche Plastik, Bayreuth 1966

Hans Gerhard Evers (Hrsg.), Darmstädter Gespräch. Das Menschenbild in unserer Zeit, Darmstadt 1950

Lucio Fontana, Manifesto tecnico, Congresso internazionale delle proportioni, IX Triennale, Milano 1954

Heinz Fuchs, Plastik der Gegenwart, Baden-Baden 1970

Ursula Geiger, Die Maler der Quadriga und ihre Stellung im Informel: Otto Greis, K.-O. Götz, Bernard Schultze, Heinz Kreuz (Diss.), Nürnberg 1987

Katalog Genf: Catalogue Sculpteurs, Editions Claude Givaudin, Genève, 1966

A. Germain, Regards sur l'Allemagne – Deutsche Kunst und Künstler im 20. Jahrhundert, Paris 1970

Karl Gustav Gerold, Deutsche Malerei unserer Zeit, München – Wien – Basel, 1956

Ulrich Gertz, Plastik der Gegenwart (Die Kunst unserer Zeit 8), Berlin 1955

Ulrich Gertz, Plasik der Gegenwart (Die Kunst unserer Zeit 17), Berlin 1964

Carola Giedion-Welcker, Plastik XX. Jh., Volumen und Raumgestaltung, Stuttgart 1955

Siegfried Gohr, Bestandskatalog Museum Ludwig Köln, München 1986

Will Grohmann, Ausst.Kat. Berlin: Junge Generation, Maler und Bildhauer in Deutschland, Akademie der Künste, Berlin 1966

Will Grohmann, Kunst unserer Zeit, Köln 1966

Ludwig Grote, Deutsche Kunst im 20. Jahrhundert, München 1953

B. von Gruenigel, Vom Impressionismus zum Tachismus. Malerei, Lithographie, Photographie, angew. Graphik, Basel – Stuttgart 1964

Waldemar Grzimek, Deutsche Bildhauer des 20. Jahrhunderts, Leben, Schulen, Wirkungen, München 1968

Ernst-Gerhard Güse, Ausst.Kat. Münster Reliefs-Formprobleme zwischen Malerei und Skulptur im 20. Jahrhundert, Westfälisches Landesmuseum für Kunst und Kulturgeschichte, Landschaftsverband Westfalen – Lippe, Münster 1980

A. M. Hammacher, The evolution of modern sculpture, New York 1969, Die Entwicklung der modernen Skulptur, Berlin 1973

Carl Georg Heise, Plastik im Freien, Hamburg 1953

Falko Herlemann, Zwischen unbedingter Tradition und bedingungslosem Fortschritt: zur Auseinandersetzung um die moderne Kunst in der Bundesrepublik Deutschland der 50er Jahre (Diss.), Frankfurt/M. 1989

Werner Hofmann, Die Plastik des 20. Jahrhunderts, Frankfurt/M. 1958

Dieter Honisch (Hrsg.), Ausst.Kat. Berlin: 1945–1985 Kunst in der Bundesrepublik Deutschland, Berlin 1985

Ausst.Kat. Kassel: documenta, Kunst des 20. Jahrhunderts, München 1955

Ausst.Kat. Kassel: documenta III, Bd. 1, Köln 1964, Bde. 2, 3 Kassel 1964

Knaurs Lexikon der modernen Plastik, München – Zürich 1960

Georg W. Költsch (Hrsg.), Skulptur, Plastik und Zeichnungen von Bildhauern des 19. und 20. Jahrhunderts aus der Sammlung der modernen Galerie des Saarland-Museums, Saarbrücken 1989

Udo Kultermann, Englische Plastik der Gegenwart, in: Das Kunstwerk 7/XII, Januar 1959, S. 3

Udo Kultermann, Junge deutsche Bildhauer, Mainz 1963

Udo Kultermann, Neue Dimensionen der Plastik, Tübingen 1967

Dominique Le Buhan, Corps – figures, Le figuration humaine dans la sculpture du XXe siècle, Paris 1989

Christa Lichtenstern, Metamorphose in der Kunst des 19. und 20. Jahrhunderts, 2 Bde., Weinheim 1992

Ausst.Kat. London: 20th Century British Sculpture, Whitechapel Art Gallery, London 1981

Edward Lucie-Smith, Sculpture since 1945, London 1987

Paul Maenth, Die 50er Jahre. Formen eines Jahrzehnts, Stuttgart 1978

G. Mathieu, Au-delà du tachisme, Paris 1960

Dona Meilach / Donald Seiden, Direct Metal Sculpture, New York 1966

Jürgen Morschel, Deutsche Kunst der 60er Jahre. Plastik, Objekte, Aktionen. Teil II, München 1972

Manfred de la Motte, Bemerkungen zur deutschen Kunst, Düsseldorf 1960

Manfred de la Motte (Hrsg.), Dokumente zum deutschen Informel, Bonn 1976

Gilles Néret, Avantgarde: Malerei und Plastik 1945–1975, München 1988

Nouveau dictionnaire de la sculpture moderne, Paris 1970

Helmuth Odenhausen, Wandplastiken aus Stahl, Düsseldorf 1961

Gert von der Osten, Plastik des 20. Jahrhunderts in Deutschland, Österreich und der Schweiz, Die Blauen Bücher, Königstein/T. 1962

Katalog Otterlo: Sculptuur – Beelhouwerken von het Rijksmuseum Kröller-Müller, collectie-catalogus, Otterlo 1981

Ausst.Kat. Paris: Les Années 50, Musée National d'Art Moderne, Éditions du Centre Pompidou, Paris 1988

Hans Platte, Plastik. Zur Kunst des 20. Jahrhunderts, München 1957

Herbert Read, The philosophy of modern art, New York 1955

Herbert Read, Geschichte der modernen Plastik, München – Zürich 1966

A. C. Ritchie (Hrsg.), Ausst.Kat. New York: The New Decade. 22 European Painters and Sculptors, Metropolitan Museum of Modern Art, New York 1955

Franz Roh, Deutsche Plastik von 1900 bis heute, München 1963

Juliane Roh, Deutsche Bildhauer der Gegenwart, in : Frühe und späte Abstrakte, München 1957

Juliane Roh, Zum Mengenproblem der modernen Plastik, in: Quadrum, Brüssel 1959, S. 53 ff.

Juliane Roh, Deutsche Plastik der Gegegenwart, München 1965

Ausst.Kat. Saarbrücken: Informel, Moderne Galerie des Saarland Museums, Saarbrücken 1982

Roberto Salvini, Moderne italienische Skulptur, Mailand 1961

Henry Schaefer-Simmern, Sculpture in Europe today, Los Angeles 1955

Gabriele Schultheiß, Ausst.Kat. Frankfurt: Zwischen Krieg und Frieden, Gegenständliche und realistische Tendenzen in der Kunst nach 1945, Kunstverein Frankfurt, Berlin 1980

Sammlung Allianz. Stuttgart 1993

Von Arp zu Warhol. Sammlung Daimler-Benz. Stuttgart 1992

Enrico Crispolti. Das Informel (und die informelle Skulptur) in Europa in: Ausst.Kat. Europäische Plastik des Informel 1945–1965. Duisburg 1995, S. 11–28

Rolf-Gunter Dienst. Gemälde 1962–1990. Eine Anthologie. Nürnberg 1990

Einhundertfünfzig Gemälde. Ausgewählte Werke der Staatlichen Kunsthalle Karlsruhe. Band 1, Karlsruhe 1988

Robert Fleck. Avantgarde in Wien. Die Geschichte der Galerie nächst St. Stephan Wien 1954–1982. Kunst und Kunstbetrieb in Österreich. Wien 1982

Andreas Gabelman: Erich Apenzeller (1919–1991). Ein Schüler der Karlsruher Akademie in der Nachkriegszeit. Werke 1946–1965. MA-Arbeit. Karlsruhe 1994

Siegmar Holsten: Die Sammlung der Moderne. Staatliche Kunsthalle Karlsruhe. Heidelberg 1993

Landeskunstwoche 1993. Aalen

Jochen Ludwig. Museum für Neue Kunst Freiburg. Freiburg 1991

Karin von Maur, Gudrun Inboden. Malerei und Plastik des 20. Jahrhunderts. Staatsgalerie Stuttgart. Stuttgart 1982

Georg Meistermann. Monographie und Werkverzeichnis. Hrg. Karl Ruhrberg und Werner Schäfke. Werkverzeichnis von Inge Herold. Köln 1991

Klaus Henning Rosen. Georg Meistermann malt Willy Brandt. Bad Honnef 1993

Wolfgang Rothe (Hrg.): Franz Bernhard. Werkverzeichnis der Skulpturen 1964 bis 1989. Heidelberg und Frankfurt a. M. 1990

Olivia Schott: Wilhelm Loth. Die konsequente Figürlichkeit. Phil. Diss. Bochum 1995

Emil Schumacher. Retrospektive. Locarno 1994

Eva Studinger. Fritz Klemm – Leben und Werk. Phil. Diss. Heidelberg 1995

Ausst.Kat. Bernd Berner. Heidelberg 1991
Ausst.Kat. Sammlung Kurt und Vera Deschler. Die ersten zwanzig Jahre. Ulm und Stuttgart 1992

Ausst.Kat. Das deutsche Informel und die Gruppe 11. Kreissparkasse Esslingen a. N. 1994. Esslingen 1994

Ausst.Kat. Sammlung Deyle. Schleswig 1993

Ausst.Kat. Duitse kunst van heden. Museum Boymans-van Beuningen. Rotterdam 24. 9.–1. 11. 1964 (u. a. Cimiotti, Antes, Grieshaber, Hajek, Hauser

Ausst.Kat. Europäische Plastik des Informel 1945–1965. Duisburg 1995

Ausst.Kat. Raimund Girke. Ostfildern-Ruit 1995

Ausst.Kat. HAP Grieshaber. Gouachen – Entwürfe – Holzschnitte. Grevenbroich 1993

Ausst.Kat. Grieshaber. Sein Freundeskreis und seine Schüler. Kunsthalle Recklinghausen, Spendhaus Reutlingen. Recklinghausen 1959

Ausst.Kat. HAP Grieshaber. Galerie Schlichtenmaier. 1994

Ausst.Kat. Fritz Klemm. Retrospektive 1992. Karlsruhe (Ostfildern) 1992

Ausst.Kat. Malerei der 60er Jahre im Südwesten. Esslingen 1982

Ausst.Kat. Neue Figuration. Deutsche Malerei 1960–88 (Kunstmuseum Düsseldorf, Schirn Kunsthalle, Frankfurt) München 1989

Ausst.Kat. Plastik Südwest. Staatliche Kunsthalle Baden-Baden. 30. 4.–10. 7. 1966 (Bernhard, Cimiotti, Hauser, Jürgen-Fischer, Lenk, Loth, Neusel, Pfahler)

Ausst.Kat. Markus Prachensky. Galerie Thoman. Insbruck 1993

Ausst.Kat. Heinz Schanz. Galerie Schlichtenmaier. Schloß Dätzingen, 1993

Ausst.Kat. Felix Schlenker. Villingen-Schwenningen 1978

Impressum

Herausgeber:
Staatliche Kunsthalle Karlsruhe

Redaktion:
Gert Reising

Fotos:
Dirk Altenkirch, Karlsruhe
Nikolaus Beismann, Stuttgart
Armin Buhl, Ulm
Joachim Fliegner, Bremen
Ellen Frank, Karlsruhe
Andreas Freytag, Stuttgart
Ina Häusser, Mannheim
Robert Häusser, Mannheim
Matthias Hoffmann, Rastatt
Alfonso Hüppi, Düsseldorf
Hans Kinkel, Stuttgart
Heike Kohler, Karlsruhe
Dieter Krieg, Köln
Carl Näher, Reutlingen
Hans Namuth, New York
Christian Peschke, Frankfurt
Philipp Schönborn, München
Kuno Schlichtenmaier, Grafenau
Herbert Schwöbel, Düsseldorf
Uwe Seyl, Stuttgart
Adelheid Stillmark, Karlsruhe
Elke Walford, Hamburg
Inge Werth, Frankfurt

Umschlag:
Detail aus S. 91
Bert Jäger: Garlaban. 1964

Gestaltung:
Signe Brunner

Gesamtherstellung:
Dr. Cantz'sche Druckerei, Ostfildern-Ruit

© 1995 Staatliche Kunsthalle Karlsruhe
Cantz Verlag

© 1995 der abgebildeten Werke von
Josef Albers, Horst Antes, Willi Baumeister,
Franz Bernhard, Jean Dubuffet,
HAP Grieshaber, Käthe Kollwitz, Uwe Lausen,
Richard Lindner, Günter Neusel,
Georg Karl Pfahler, Jackson Pollock,
Felix Schlenker, Emil Schumacher,
Pierre Soulages, Walter Stöhrer,
Lambert Maria Wintersberger
bei VG Bild-Kunst, Bonn 1995,
sowie bei den Künstlern und ihren Rechtsnachfolgern

Verlagsausgabe:
ISBN 3-89322-819-5

Erschienen im
Cantz Verlag
Senefelderstraße 9
73760 Ostfildern-Ruit
Telefon 07 11/4 49 93-0
Telefax 07 11/4 41 45 79

Printed in Germany